Learning the Hard Way

The Rutgers Series in Childhood Studies

The Rutgers Series in Childhood Studies is dedicated to increasing our understanding of children and childhoods, past and present, throughout the world. Children's voices and experiences are central. Authors come from a variety of fields, including anthropology, criminal justice, history, literature, psychology, religion, and sociology. The books in this series are intended for students, scholars, practitioners, and those who formulate policies that affect children's everyday lives and futures.

Edited by Myra Bluebond-Langner, Board of Governors Professor of Anthropology, Rutgers University, and True Colours Chair in Palliative Care for Children and Young People, University College London, Institute of Child Health

Advisory Board
Perri Klass, New York University
Jill Korbin, Case Western Reserve University
Bambi Schiefflin, New York University
Enid Schildkraut, American Museum of Natural History and Museum for African Art

Learning the Hard Way

Masculinity, Place, and the Gender Gap in Education

EDWARD W. MORRIS

RUTGERS UNIVERSITY PRESS

New Brunswick, New Jersey, and London

Library of Congress Cataloging-in-Publication Data

Morris, Edward W., 1973–
    Learning the hard way : masculinity, place, and the gender gap in education /
Edward W. Morris.
        p. cm. — (Rutgers series in childhood studies)
    Includes bibliographical references and index.
    ISBN 978–0–8135–5368–9 (hardcover : alk. paper) — ISBN 978–0–8135–5369–6
(pbk. : alk. paper) — ISBN 978–0–8135–5370–2 (e-book)
    1. Sex differences in education—United States—Case studies.   2. High school
boys—United States—Social conditions—Case studies.   3. Men—United States—
Identity—Case studies.   4. Blacks—Race identity—United States—Case studies.
5. Academic achievement—United States—Case studies.   I. Title.
    LC212.92.M67   2012
    370.15′1—dc23

                                                                        2011048988

A British Cataloging-in-Publication record for this book is available from the British
Library.

Chapter 3 is adapted by permission of the publishers from "The 'Hidden Injuries' of
Class and Gender among Rural Teenagers," in *Reshaping Gender and Class in Rural
Spaces*, ed. Barbara Pini and Belinda Leach (Farnham, UK: Ashgate, 2011), 221–238.
Copyright © 2011.

Portions of chapters 3, 4, 5, and 8 appeared previously in "Rednecks, Rutters, and
'Rithmetic: Social Class, Masculinity, and Schooling in a Rural Context," *Gender &
Society* 22 (2008): 1–24.

Visit our website: http://rutgerspress.rutgers.edu

Manufactured in the United States of America

For Max and Esme

Contents

Acknowledgments

I have benefited from the help of many people in writing this book. First, I would like to thank the administrators, teachers, office staff, parents, and students of the high schools I call Clayton and Woodrow Wilson. While I am critical of much of the current structure of education, these schools reinforced my faith in the well-meaning educators and inspiring students throughout our public school system. I thank the schools for welcoming and accommodating me, and I also commend them for all the hard work they do to help future generations grow and succeed. I'd like to give special thanks to Kevin at Clayton and Corie at Woodrow Wilson (both pseudonyms), who granted me early interviews and helped me recruit more students to talk to. I hope both these amiable and thoughtful young men will capitalize on their enormous potential.

I originally designed this project as a beginning professor at Ohio University. I would like to thank my friends and colleagues there for their support and early interest in my research. I especially thank Leon Anderson, who helped me develop the ideas for the study design and provided invaluable guidance throughout the process. I also thank Cindy Anderson and Joseph De Angelis, who read early drafts of the research and provided very perceptive suggestions. After completing fieldwork I moved to the University of Kentucky, where I received further support. The participants in the interdisciplinary Children at Risk research cluster helped hone many of my ideas. I particularly thank Brea Perry, who read and provided great comments on early drafts of the research. I also thank the participants in the Rural Seminar Series, including Dwight Billings, Alan De Young, Keiko Tanaka, and Patrick Mooney, who offered insightful comments that significantly improved the project (especially my rural analysis). Shaunna Scott and Claire Renzetti also read drafts of the work and gave me terrific feedback.

Colleagues at other institutions have helped formally and informally as well. I presented my initial report from this research at an American

Sociological Association session and received thoughtful comments from Nancy Lopez, Rashawn Ray, and Jessica Fields, among others. Barbara Pini provided comments that greatly improved chapter 3. Chandra Muller was crucial in helping with the initial design of the project and securing funding. She also facilitated presentations I gave at the University of Texas, which helped me develop the research methodologically and conceptually. Christine Williams took a tremendous amount of time to give me her incomparable insights on early and later drafts of the work.

I thank the Spencer Foundation, whose generous grant allowed me to carry out the fieldwork for the study. I thank Ohio University and the University of Kentucky, both of which afforded research funding and course release time for the research. I also thank my editor at Rutgers, Peter Mickulas, and the anonymous reviewers of the manuscript, who added their time and expertise to improving the book substantially.

Finally, I could not have completed this book without the love, support, and patience of my family. As with all my work, my parents, Waymon and Deirdre, and sisters, Jennifer, Melinda, and Mary, offered great support and interest in the book. They have always challenged me to communicate my research in a straightforward way. My spouse, Jane, provided her insider knowledge as a teacher and school counselor along with her love and support, humbly requesting only that she "better get a big part in the acknowledgments." My children, Max and Esme, gave me unending inspiration and joy, which kept me going throughout this long, sometimes daunting process. This book is dedicated to them.

Learning the Hard Way

Chapter 1   Introduction

THE HEADLINE OF *Newsweek* magazine shouts with breathless urgency, "The Boy Crisis. At Every Level of Education, They're Falling Behind. What to Do?" This national cover story is just one of an avalanche of articles and books on what some have called the "new gender gap" in education: the significantly lower achievement of boys as compared to girls. These findings have produced heated debate. If girls are graduating from high school, completing college, and even entering graduate schools in higher number than boys are, what does this mean for gender inequality? Are boys and men now disadvantaged by gender?

This book examines the popular debate on the gender gap in education. It focuses on a long-term study of two low-income high schools—one urban and one rural—where girls noticeably outperformed boys. In contrast to most views of the gender gap, the findings of this book show that gender and achievement must be understood as intertwined with circumstances of race, class, and location. Moreover, my analysis reveals that, even in disadvantaged environments, boys' underachievement does not signify a reversal of gender inequality but a hidden cost of the power associated with masculinity.

I thought about masculinity and the gender gap one stark winter day as I entered Woodrow Wilson High School, located in a low-income, predominately African American community.[1] The school's entrance usually teemed with boisterous teenagers, buses, cars, and the occasional glowering school administrator. But today a thick layer of snow blanketed the vast field in front of the school, casting an uncanny silence. Laughter from a lone group of boys abruptly broke the calm as they sprinted past the front doors throwing snowballs. One snowball sailed over a boy's head and landed above the front doors on a wall peppered with graffiti. The frenzied writing and profane messages appeared to convey that Woodrow Wilson was indeed an inner-city school. An assistant principal soon emerged from the front doors, scowled at the boys, and curtly told them to get to class. Meanwhile, I peered back across the field and noticed another group of boys moving away from the school. Dressed in thick, dark coats, they leaped across the fence that bound school grounds and dashed into the adjoining neighborhood. During my fieldwork I had witnessed countless boys jumping over this fence to skip school but virtually no girls.

About seventy-five miles away from Woodrow Wilson lay Clayton High School. Clayton was located in a remote rural area, tucked away in the rolling hills of southern Ohio—a region adjacent to Kentucky and West Virginia known as Appalachian Ohio. The narrow road into town dipped and curved alongside a meandering creek often swollen from rain and snow. An abandoned shell of a brick building stained with coal soot marked the entrance to the city limits of Clayton. This building had once housed the high school, which had been heated with a coal furnace. It had been abandoned several years earlier when the district obtained a grant to erect a new high school building, but it was never demolished. The rise and fall of this community's coal-based economy seemed to be imprinted on the structure's darkened bricks and broken windows.

The new school building was located at the foot of a picturesque tree-studded ridge. The school was quite small—fewer than 350 students—and most people in the predominately white community it served came from low-income rural backgrounds. Inside the school's main office, an aide named Jessica sat behind the visitor sign-in sheet. As I signed in, the principal, a stout, ebullient man named Mr. Thomas, strode out from his office and asked, "Hey, Doc! How's the research going?"

Jessica suggested, "You should interview Preston McCormick. He's like the smartest person in this whole school."

Mr. Thomas offered his own advice, bellowing, "You need to interview Bucky Wagner. Now I'd really like to know what's going on with him!"

I mentioned that I needed permission forms for student interviews.

Mr. Thomas chuckled and said, "Yeah, well that might be a problem—Bucky told Mr. Perdue where he could put his permission forms the other day!"

I laughed as I walked out of the office and down the lustrous blue and white hallway, where the honor roll was posted on a bulletin board. What I saw was intriguing but did not surprise me at this point in my research: ten girls had made the "all A" honor roll, but just one boy's name was on the list.

These vignettes illustrate key questions in my study of gender at these two low-income high schools. Why did boys tend to show less interest in and more defiance toward school? Why did girls significantly outperform boys at both schools? Why did people at the schools still describe boys as especially smart? This book examines these questions. In the process it illuminates connections of gender with race, class, and place. My book is not simply about the educational troubles of boys but also about the troubled and complex experience of gender in school. It reveals how particular race, class, and geographical experiences shape masculinity and femininity in ways that affect academic performance. The findings and perspective add new clarity to the gender gap in achievement.

The Academic Gender Gap

Several writers have called attention to a presumed crisis for boys in school (see Weaver-Hightower 2003). Indeed, compared to girls, boys are disciplined, suspended, and expelled more often; have higher retention and dropout rates; are more likely to be classified with a learning disability; make lower grades, and have lower test scores in major subject areas except for math (Buchmann, DiPrete, and McDaniel 2008; Chudowsky and Chudowsky 2010). Such findings raise new and interesting questions about gender inequality.

People generally understand gender inequality in terms of unequal outcomes for women and girls, such as the fact that women on average make significantly less money than men do, even when studies control for education and work experience (Bobbitt-Zeher 2007). Studies of gender inequality in education have also followed this line of thought—for instance, by examining how schools shortchange girls (AAUW 1992; Sadker and Sadker 1994). This notion aligns neatly with the view that women and girls are generally disadvantaged in comparisons with boys and men.

But what should one make of the fact that boys are now falling behind girls academically? Some have used this information as fodder for discounting the notion of gender inequality for women and girls, arguing instead that boys are now suffering disadvantages at the hands of feminized schools and educational programs that are geared toward helping girls (Sommers 2000; Gurian and Stevens 2005; Tyre 2008). But are school waging a "war against boys" (Sommers 2000)?

This book attempts to reframe the debate over ge schooling. For too long this issue has been stretched into a facile "girls against boys" polemic. I assert that the notion that boys are falling behind must be contextualized in two ways. First, not all boys are suffering educationally, but in most areas of academic achievement and attainment, there are indeed evident gender gaps favoring girls. On the National Assessment of Educational

Progress test conducted by the U.S. Department of Education, girls score significantly higher in reading and just slightly lower in math (Mead 2006; NCES 2010). Women are more likely to enroll in higher education, comprising 56 percent of all undergraduates in 1999–2000 (Peter, Horn, and Carroll 2005). Women are also more likely to complete a bachelor's degree (Buchmann and DiPrete 2006). In high school, 65 percent of boys graduate in four years compared to 72 percent of girls (Mead 2006). Boys are more likely to be suspended, expelled, or held back in school, all of which are risk factors for dropping out of high school (Buchmann et al. 2008). In addition, the shift in this educational trend has been dramatic: in 1960, 65 percent of all bachelor's degrees were given to men; in 2005, 58 percent of all bachelor's degrees were awarded to women (Buchmann et al. 2008). Such data certainly make it sound as though girls are leaving boys in the dust.

However, these findings rely on casting girls and boys as discrete, monolithic groups and reporting their achievement and attainment in terms of averages. To add depth and clarity to these outcomes, gender must be considered along with students' race, class, and school location. Significant academic gaps do not appear among middle- or upper-class students (King 2000; Mead 2006). Plenty of men still obtain an M.B.A., an M.D., or a Ph.D. Young men attending elite universities such as Harvard, Yale, and Princeton do not appear to be in the midst of a crisis: enrollments at these schools continue to have equal numbers of men and women. The vast majority of people who run major corporations are men, and men continue to dominate in many areas of public life, including government. The educational crisis for boys is really only occurring among certain segments of boys (Kimmel 2000).

Indeed, perspective on the gender gap changes remarkably when one considers race and economic status. In general, African American, Latino, and low-income students demonstrate much wider academic gaps favoring girls (Carter 2005; Entwisle, Alexander, and Olson 2007; Lopez 2003; Mickelson 2003). Research in predominately minority, urban communities shows that girls in those contexts are considerably more likely than boys to make higher grades, graduate from high school, enroll in college, and aspire to higher-status occupations (Carter 2005; Lopez 2003). For example, four-year high school graduation rates by gender show a 5-percentage-point gap favoring girls among white students, but an 11-percentage-point gap favoring girls among African American students (Mead 2006). In 1999–2000, 64 percent of black college undergraduates were women, compared to 56 percent of white undergraduates who were women (Peter et al. 2005). That same year, 60 percent of low-income undergraduates were women, compared to 53 percent of high-income students (Peter et al. 2005).

These statistics suggest that studies of gender in education must take race, class, and school location into account. As a wealth of scholarship on intersectionality has revealed, gender cannot be abstracted from the racial, class, and geographical contexts within which it evolves.[2] It is boys in economically disadvantaged communities such as Woodrow Wilson and Clayton who are most likely to underachieve in school, not *boys* in a general sense. By studying gender in two low-income schools, one urban and predominately African American and the other rural and predominately white, this book underscores the profound ways in which race, class, and location intertwine with gender to influence education and thus provides a deeper and more textured understanding of the gender gap.

Second, this book emphasizes that boys' lack of academic success is actually consistent with contemporary sociological theories of gender inequality. These theories capture the complexity and irony entailed in how people enact and maintain gender. I demonstrate how boys disengage from schoolwork not because educators discriminate against them or teach in a feminized way but because certain boys in certain contexts associate school disengagement with the strength of masculinity. Schools guide the production of masculinities but in a way that centralizes rather than marginalizes powerful ideals of manhood. Prevailing discourses in both Woodrow Wilson and Clayton (although for slightly different reasons) framed true manliness as something that could not be achieved by paying attention in class or burying one's nose in a book. As I will explain, contemporary theories of gender offer the best framework for understanding these findings.

Explanations for Gender Differences in Education

BIOLOGICAL DIFFERENCES

One of the most common explanations for gender differences in education emphasizes the fact that boys and girls are biologically different. People generally assume that boys are naturally more active and aggressive and girls are more restrained and passive. Researchers have argued that such presumed natural tendencies place boys at a disadvantage in school. Michael Gurian and Kathy Stevens (2005), for example, contend that biologically based studies, including research on the brain, demonstrate that boys at an early age show more capacity for impulsive, aggressive behavior than girls do. The authors reason that schools fail to recognize these differences and force boys into overly controlled learning environments that contest their natural tendency for boundless activity.

As the parent of young children myself, I confess that this perspective appears to explain much of what I observe. At preschool the boys usually seem to be either running around feverishly, playing aggressively, or glumly sitting in time out because of disruptive behavior. Girls are active, too, but appear to be more careful and cooperative in their play. Because of such surface observations, many people understandably believe that gender differences are caused directly by natural sex differences. But it is hard to extract, even at this young age, the influence of society on how these children are learning and enacting gender (Messner 2000). Boys act out the roles of the aggressive superheroes that adults give them to play with, and boys quickly learn that others see such behavior as consistent with masculinity. Schools further act as gendered institutions that structure the activity of boys and girls differently, even shaping their bodily development and postures as early as preschool (Martin 1998). Moreover, when looking more closely at any group of young children, one sees that not all boys and all girls act in the same manner. Some girls are obstreperous; some boys are cautious. If gender differences were purely biological, such gender diversity should not appear because gender would be a direct function of categorical differences in sex.

In addition, a biological perspective fails to account for certain noticeable variations of gender differences in educational outcomes. In particular, it cannot explain the fact that the gender gap differs dramatically across race and class subgroups. One would have to argue that race and class additionally affect biological brain structure and natural impulses, which is something few commentators are willing to proffer. Such patterns suggest that gender differences are largely socially influenced and produced and that this process intertwines with race and class in complex and important ways.

GENDER SOCIALIZATION

Sex role socialization (or gender socialization, as it is often called) challenges a biological view of gender differences by suggesting that the distinct behavior of boys and girls is socially rather than biologically influenced (Mickelson 1989). This provides a powerful explanation for gender achievement gaps because girls are often socialized to be "good girls": to do what they are told, to sit still, to cooperate with others, and so forth. These feminine characteristics place girls at an advantage in the classroom compared to boys, who are socialized to be more active, risk taking, and defiant. Research in this vein has extended Mickelson's concept to document ways in which boys and girls are exposed to different social resources and risk factors because of gender. Some research suggests that parents are more likely to leave boys on their own, which makes them more vulnerable to negative peer influence (Downey and Vogt Yuan 2005; Ehrmann and Massey 2008; Entwisle, Alexander, and Olson 1994; Feliciano and Rumbaut 2005; Lopez 2003). Other work proposes that boys in mother-headed households suffer from a lack of male role models (Powell and Parcel 1997). Some research combines gender socialization with the framework of the late French sociologist Pierre Bourdieu (1984, 2001). Studies have found, for example, that girls engage in more activities that can translate into educationally useful cultural capital, such as going to the library and taking arts classes outside of school (Dumais 2002; Mickelson 2003).

Gender socialization appears to be an instructive theory of gender differences in achievement. It accurately depicts different behaviors, interests, and experiences of boys and girls that might have educational import while avoiding biological reductionism. However, I suggest that analysis of gender differences in education must move beyond both this socialization model and the biological view. Let me briefly outline several shortcomings of biological and gender socialization models, which open the door for the use of contemporary gender theory in bringing a fresh perspective to the gender gap.

First, biosocial and socialization-influenced research can cast gender categories as static, predetermined variables that have a specified effect on certain outcomes. The very findings and discussion of a gender gap reflect this perspective, which assumes that gender is a binary, preestablished, unchanging category that has a direct effect on educational outcomes such as grades, test scores, and graduation. This viewpoint sees boys and girls as unable to change, adapt, or resist their biological or social compositions. By contrast, contemporary gender theory, as I will explain, reveals gender as an ongoing social construction—an emergent outcome in itself rather than a preexisting, circumscribed category. This approach better captures the nuances, exceptions, and flexibility in boys' and girls' experiences (Thorne 1993).

Second, biological and socialization approaches downplay the role of power and inequality in gender. Gender differences are not just differences. They are differences created and maintained within an overarching context in which men in general hold power over women. Overlooking this context can lead, for example, to the somewhat bizarre conclusion that schools are waging a war against boys (Sommers 2000) despite the fact that men hold disproportionate political, economic, and domestic power (Connell 1987). Even within education, most people in leadership positions, such as superintendents or principals, are men (Williams 1995). Although less pugnacious than the "war against boys" pathos, a gender socialization perspective also tends to downplay gender as a site of continuing relational inequality. From this perspective, people are simply socialized to act in a certain (gendered) way, which maintains differences. But when these differences are couched in terms of inequality, we see how power infuses the process of gendered learning and ongoing enactment. Boys are not just taught to act differently from girls; this different behavior relates to and justifies greater social rewards and power.

Third, contemporary work on gender differences in education elides variation in the experience of gender. There are not singular masculine or feminine roles as sex role and socialization theories have posited (Connell 1995). Instead, manifold masculinities and femininities exist, shaped by social class, race, geographic location, and sexuality, among other factors. As Raewyn Connell (1987) makes clear, categorical theories that reduce all gendered experience to binary distinctions of male-female or man-woman do not account well for intersections of gender with other social categories of inequality and identity. These factors do not simply add an extra component of disadvantage (or advantage) onto gender; they fundamentally shape it. Such formations and resulting variation are not captured in analyses of differences in academic outcomes between boys and girls as distinct, homogeneous groups. Such data are important, but they do not tell the entire story. Boys and girls act in many different ways, lending important nuances to the concept of gender as it relates to education.

A Fresh Perspective on the Gender Gap

Theories of gender differences in education should account for agency, variation, and power in the production and maintenance of gender in society. In articulating a perspective that can accomplish this, I draw from the contemporary gender theories known as *doing gender* and *hegemonic masculinity* (Connell 1995; Messerschmidt 1997; West and Fenstermaker 1995; West and Zimmerman 1987). Combining these perspectives reveals how masculinity is accomplished in schools and how this accomplishment can be associated with power but also detract from achievement. Researchers in Australia, Canada, and Britain have begun to examine the construction of masculinity in schools and how it affects academic underperformance in those countries (Connell 1996; Mac an Ghaill 1996; Martino, Kehler, and Weaver-Hightower 2009; Skelton 2001). However, as Marcus Weaver-Hightower (2009) explains, these contemporary views of masculinity have not been applied to U.S. contexts. I add to this international research on masculinity in school through my comparative study of Clayton and Woodrow Wilson, which fleshes out intersections of gender with race, class, and place in intricate detail.

DOING GENDER

The theory known as doing gender helps us understand how micro-contexts and situations produce gendered meanings and how such meanings matter for school performance. The perspective frames gender as something produced by social actors through ongoing interaction (West and Zimmerman 1987). According to Candace West and Don Zimmerman (1987), "rather than a property of individuals, we conceive of gender as an emergent feature of social situations: both as an outcome of and a rationale for various social arrangements and as a means of legitimating one of the most fundamental divisions of society" (126). In this view, gender differences in education result from interactive processes through which students represent, and hold others accountable for representing, gender. Such an analysis of gender underscores social process. Instead of seeing gender as a preset cause of academic behavior, one can see academically relevant behaviors as vehicles for the dynamic production of gender. This approach asks how students' thoughts and actions produce gender in specific ways and how these productions have relevance for education. Doing gender calls attention to microlevel, everyday mechanisms of social differentiation that reproduce gender concepts and gender inequality (see Schwalbe et al. 2000). I will show, for example, how boys in my research approached education casually (which I term *contrived carelessness*), not because this behavior was biologically or socially ingrained in them but because discourses at both schools defined such behavior as consistent with masculinity. Boys did not take this approach because they were male; they did this to demonstrate manhood.

Because interactive processes circulate among certain actors, doing gender can take different forms depending on the situation. West and Zimmerman (1987) describe gender as a "situated accomplishment" to emphasize how it is a property of interaction, not individuals, and also how its emergence is linked to situational contexts (Fenstermaker, West, and Zimmerman 2002). As social contexts change, norms and perspectives on gender, resources for representing gender, and the impact of other social categories of difference on gender may change as well (West and Fenstermaker 1995). Gender for women and girls may be conceived of and accomplished differently in inner cities (Jones 2009), among college rugby players (Ezzell 2009), or among middle school cheerleaders (Eder, Evans, and Parker 1997). This highlights the malleability of gender and the personal agency underlying it. This book will show, for example, how urban and rural locations may encourage different enactments of masculinity and femininity, and how various boys and girls do gender differently.

Although influential, the doing gender approach has been critiqued for downplaying social structure. I believe that the theory can account for structural constraints, but it is worth emphasizing that men and women enact gender as a product of sociohistorical development that is deeply rooted in social institutions and predefined situations, which constrain and enable behavior.

For example, sports, even at the youngest levels, are often divided by gender and embedded with different expectations for how people will behave according to gender (Messner 2009). Even when youth sports are not formally gendered (such as with early levels of soccer), they informally promote and reproduce different expectations for boys and girls and men and women, such as the masculine coach and the feminine "team mom" (Messner 2009). Scholars have recently emphasized how the doing of gender occurs within such structured parameters, often rendering gender less of a performance and more of a reflex (Risman 2004; Yancey Martin 2003). According to Barbara Risman (2004), "we must pay attention to how structure shapes individual choice and social interaction and to how human agency creates, sustains, and modifies current structure" (233).

In this book, I consider how masculine and feminine actions, while always organized in terms of gender accountability, are funneled through prevailing social patterns of interaction and school institutional frameworks. I employ the concept of gender scripts, which boys and girls followed to constitute themselves as masculine and feminine in structured and locally normative ways, additionally molded by race and class. (See Yancey Martin 2003, 354, for an analogous concept she calls "gender practices.") I also use Connell's (1996) notion of a "gender regime," which exists at each school and reveals how "gender is embedded in the institutional arrangements through which a school functions" and how the schools as organizations "create institutional definitions of masculinity" (213). Thus, while gender may serve as an ongoing product of interaction at Clayton and Woodrow Wilson, this production often follows preset patterns and reinforces the presumed natural inevitability of such patterns. These institutionalized definitions, arrangements, and practices tend to reproduce gender and other inequalities.

HEGEMONIC MASCULINITY

For clarification on gender, power, and inequality, particularly as they relate to masculinity, I turn to the theory of hegemonic masculinity, which envisions masculinity as a system of power relations between men and women and between different men. This view proposes a plurality of masculinities that do not just reflect differences among men but constitute specific relations of practice. *Hegemonic masculinity* is defined as the contextually specific pattern of gender practice that "ideologically legitimate[s] the global subordination of women to men" (Connell and Messerschmidt 2005, 832). While this pattern of practice might bolster male dominance, it does not necessarily represent the most common form of masculinity. Instead, most men and women come to revere and accept it as an ideal of manhood.

Other masculinities are stratified vis-à-vis this hegemonic ideal. Connell (1995) specifically delineated subordinated, complicit, and marginalized masculinities. Subordinated masculinities include men who are oppressed by the very hegemonic definition of masculinity, such as gay men or men seen as effeminate. Complicit masculinities refer to men who do not necessarily embody or enact the hegemonic ideal but still reap benefits from it (the "patriarchal dividend," according to Connell [1995, 79]). Finally, marginalized masculinities refer to how some men face racial and class-based inequalities that shape their masculinity. I examine how boys at Clayton and Woodrow Wilson faced various inequalities that influenced their experience and interpretation of masculinity. Many boys, in efforts to manage race, class, and place disadvantages, followed local practices that defined manhood in ways contrary to school effort. Yet boys, girls, and adults at both schools did not see this as unusual or troubling, reinforcing notions that such behavior was indicative of masculinity.

One shortcoming in Connell's (1987) original formulation of multiple masculinities is that the framework can be construed as a static typology (see, for example, Connell and Messerschmidt 2005; Pascoe 2007; Schrock and Schwalbe 2009). Accordingly, the masculinities just delineated should not be read as psychological character types but as dynamic sets of actions. I find it helpful to think, as Douglas Schrock and Michael Schwalbe (2009) suggest, in terms of manhood acts that assert masculinity as a claim to power. This focuses attention more organically on "what males do to create, maintain, and claim membership in a dominant gender group" (Schrock and Schwalbe 2009, 281). Although my analysis reveals masculine identities in the schools, I do not simply list and rank them by importance. Instead, my analysis demonstrates flexibility and variation in the everyday ways in which masculinity is asserted and imbued with power.

Hegemonic masculinity also emphasizes that most masculinities are constructed in contradistinction to femininities. The achievement of masculinity generally involves a repudiation of femininity, implying that masculinity is both different from and superior to femininity (Pascoe 2007; Williams 1995). The notion of superiority drives the process of gender construction for men, but gender works differently for women. According to Connell (1987), there are high-status practices of femininity, termed *emphasized femininity*. These constitute revered features of femininity but are not hegemonic, Connell explains, because they do not assert and legitimate power over men. In fact, emphasized femininity tends to involve being supportive and receptive to men, thereby bolstering hegemonic masculinity. Thus, hegemonic masculinity holds its position by harnessing and defining revered practices of both masculinity and femininity and delineating which of these are appropriate for men and women to embody.

However, as with masculinity, alternative femininities may provide women with practices that resist and transform the existing gender hierarchy. Such resistance may occur through overt opposition to masculinity or express itself through indirect means of empowerment. In applying this theory of femininity to the gender gap in education, I show how girls at Clayton and Woodrow Wilson use educational achievement as a mode of resistance and empowerment, which I call *conscientious resistance*. In addition, I highlight how intersections of race and class provide girls with resources to accomplish this resistance that are different from the resources of boys.

RACE, CLASS, AND GENDER RESOURCES AND CHALLENGES

In many situations, race, class, and gender appear to be uncomplicated. As I have noted, people's representations of these categories occur without overt planning and performance. In other situations, however, a person's ability to represent one or more of these categories may be compromised. Under such conditions, doing race, class, and gender requires additional interactional work (Messerschmidt 1997; West and Fenstermaker 1995).

For example, scholars have found that under certain conditions masculinity becomes fragile and open to reproach (Kimmel 1996; Messner 1992; Williams 1995). This frailty encourages men to actively assert masculinity and, as mentioned, to seek expressions of masculinity that demonstrate superiority over women and other men. When traditional outlets of masculinity are blocked, men seek alternative means of shoring up their masculinity (Kimmel 1996, 2005). Michael Kimmel (2005) shows that in late nineteenth-century America rapid urbanization and an influx of female and immigrant labor created a "crisis of masculinity" for many white men (64). He argues that this crisis in work and family sparked the rise of "manly" leisure pursuits, including outdoor groups such as the Boy Scouts and sports such as baseball. From the perspective of hegemonic masculinity, this meant that when men felt emasculated in traditional areas of control such as work and family, they sought other constructions of masculinity that reaffirmed and displayed virtues such as toughness and physical vigor. Similarly, James Messerschmidt (2000) demonstrates that boys who are violent criminal offenders may use violence as a means to reassert masculinity in response to circumstances they perceive as emasculating.

Scholars have emphasized that inequalities of class and race profoundly intertwine with challenges and resources in doing masculinity or femininity. For example, Karen Pyke (1996) demonstrates how economic status in the family affects strategies of masculinity and femininity. Families in her research tended to emphasize the importance of the male career. For many men in her study, having a successful occupation was interpreted as being a "real man"; and for many women, supporting men in this pursuit was interpreted as being a "real woman." Under good economic conditions, these practices could be fluidly maintained. However, when men could not gain stable or successful employment, they sought more direct, forceful, and even abusive methods of demonstrating conjugal power. Such "compensatory manhood acts" (Schrock and Schwalbe 2009) compensate for perceived powerlessness by reasserting the dominance of masculinity. Thus, masculinity and femininity may serve as sources of challenge as well as resources from which other sources of challenge (such as race or class) may be deflected or negotiated. In this book I show how inequalities of class and race may influence students, providing them with scripts and incentives to follow certain modes of masculinity, including those that conflict with academic success. Such intersections suggest that the experience and expression of masculinity are altered by inequalities of race and class; and as I will describe, this may explain why the academic gender gap is wider among disadvantaged students.

EXPLAINING THE GENDER GAP AMONG DISADVANTAGED STUDENTS

Sociologists Prudence Carter (2005) and Nancy Lopez (2003) have documented broad gender gaps in achievement among disadvantaged minority students. In one chapter of her highly regarded book, Carter (2005) details gender disparities in achievement among low-income, minority youths and analyzes how they relate to perceptions of masculinity and femininity. She finds that boys in her study emphasized being "hard," which meant creating a tough, streetwise exterior (see also Anderson 1999; Dance 2002). Carter (2005) asserts that this emphasis on hardness distanced boys from school because they perceived school-oriented behaviors as effeminate: "In contrast to hardness, softness connotes the feminine forms perceived as compliant and nurturing. Sitting still and paying attention in class are imbued with feminine meanings and therefore might be avoided by students with more masculine identities" (86–87). Thus, constructions of hard masculinity may have caused these racial-ethnic and low-income boys to resist or not fully invest in schoolwork.

Similarly, Lopez (2003) analyzes the gender gap in academic attainment and achievement among Dominican, West Indian, and Haitian youths in New York City (all of whom had an African phenotype). She examines why a significant gender gap favoring girls exists among these groups. Using a variety of data sources, she finds that these youths experience profound racializing and gendering processes in popular culture, schools, and the family that shape their life goals and views of schooling. Within schools, she finds that boys tend to be interpreted as potentially dangerous and at risk. Girls, by contrast, tend to be perceived more positively and forge more productive relationships with teachers and school officials. Lopez emphasizes that to understand the schooling experiences of students of color and the yawning educational gap among racial minority groups, we must theorize race and gender as interconnected. The stereotypes that black Latino youth are subjected to, such as "mamacita" and "hoodlum," pertain not just to race but to gender. While neither stereotype is positive, a "hoodlum" perception implies a more confrontational stance for Latino boys, which pushes them away from school.

This book builds from the research of Lopez and Carter by closely examining how low-income and minority boys respond to schooling challenges. I expand on this work in a number of ways. My integrated framework of doing gender and hegemonic masculinity demonstrates how school-relevant behaviors are not only gender typed but also interpreted to indicate the presumed superiority of masculinity over femininity. I underscore how the school-defiant hardness described by Carter is maintained, even by disadvantaged boys, because of its associations with power. Boys in my study certainly contended with inequalities and stigmas of race and class. But many converted this sense of powerlessness into a (presumed) powerful masculinity (Majors and Billson 1992; Schrock and Schwalbe 2009), which based its accomplishment on behaviors such as defiance and carelessness that detracted from educational success. My analysis reveals microlevel processes such as contrived carelessness among boys and conscientious resistance among girls which served to maintain or resist gender inequality, producing very different academic efforts by gender.

This book further expands research on the gender gap among disadvantaged students to include a too-often neglected group: the white rural poor. Much of the academic concern with boys' underachievement in the United States focuses on urban African American boys. Few studies compare urban African American boys with white boys in similar economic conditions. This limited view might underlie the tendency to interpret the plight of black boys as specifically racial (stemming from "African American culture," for example, as many teachers at Woodrow Wilson said) instead of examining how complexities of place, class, and race are interwoven with gender. My ethnography includes Clayton, a predominately white, low-income rural school; and I find that educational outcomes favoring girls at Clayton were *virtually identical* to Woodrow Wilson, the urban school in my study. Both schools served areas with similarly depressed economic conditions but with different demographic profiles and histories. This comparative rural-urban design reveals the impact of place on shaping gender practices and outcomes. Emerging scholarship underscores the importance of place as a location and identity that intersects with gender, race, and class (Campbell, Bell, and Finney 2006; Lobao, Hooks, and Tickamyer, 2007; Pini, Price, and McDonald 2010). Indeed, while a similar gender gap emerged at both schools, this occurred, as I will show, for slightly different reasons, largely because of how rurality and urbanicity molded gender differently.

Research at Woodrow Wilson and Clayton

To plumb the complex relationship between social disadvantage, masculinity and femininity, and achievement at Woodrow Wilson and Clayton, I use the research method of ethnography. Broadly defined, this method involves the researcher experiencing daily life from the perspective of his or her research participants. In doing so, the researcher carefully documents what people in a certain site say and do. Ethnography aims for a "thick description" (Geertz 1973, 3) of social phenomena and thus draws data from a variety of sources to paint a deep social portrait that strives to reflect insiders' meanings. Over the course of one and a half school years I collected data from formal, audio-recorded interviews with students; numerous conversations with students; conversations and informal interviews with teachers and administrative staff; written field notes of happenings within classrooms, lunchrooms, hallways, and school events; school records (including achievement and discipline records from both schools) and school documents; and contemporary and historical newspaper articles featuring the schools. This gave me several different points of contact with students and teachers (along with other sources of information) across two different school years. These sources yielded more than 1,000 pages of data, which I systematically coded and analyzed.

Ethnography allowed me to gain close-to-the-ground knowledge, following social processes as they occurred and gleaning participant perspectives in considerable depth. Other methods, even some that might be qualitative in scope, do not provide insight into what people both say and do. Observations record only what people do; interviews and surveys record only what people say. Although both are valuable sources of data, each reveals a single angle of a social phenomenon. By synthesizing these angles, ethnography paints a rounded picture (although I do not believe the picture is ever complete). In analyzing and presenting data, I employ triangulation—drawing from a variety of data sources—to demonstrate validity and add texture to the book. The strength of ethnography lies in the depth and vividness of its analysis. I use this method not only to explain the gender gap but to convey the richness and intricacy of the experience of gender among these rural and urban teenagers. (For more information on methodology, please see the appendix.)

Organization of the Book

The remaining chapters trace and analyze the construction of race, class, gender, and place at Woodrow Wilson and Clayton in order to explain the gender gap. Chapter 2 provides a contextual overview of each school. I describe the communities that each school serves and include demographic and performance data from the schools themselves, noting differences and similarities. This chapter also examines adult and student interpretations of the schools and communities. We will see how students in both environments perceived stigmas attached to their schools and communities. Finally, the chapter describes the primary emphases for popularity at each school—a distinction I call *respect* and *respectability*. The peer culture of Woodrow Wilson emphasized being "known" and establishing "respect," whereas the peer culture of Clayton emphasized "family name" and establishing "respectability." These distinctions of place and peer culture provided different challenges and resources for enactments of masculinity and femininity.

In chapter 3, I explore deep connections between students' family background, gender, and school orientation. The chapter offers a concentrated portrait of two students from Clayton High School: Kevin and Kaycee. I focus on these two students primarily because of their moving personal stories. I examine how class background and family strife created "hidden injuries" (borrowing from Sennett and Cobb 1972) for each student and how gender as an ongoing accomplishment gave them different ways to manage these injuries. For Kevin, masculinity encouraged behaviors that defied school, whereas for Kaycee, femininity encouraged behaviors more consistent with school attachment.

Chapter 4 describes and examines the academic gender gap at both schools. I trace differences in academic outcomes by gender at each school and analyze how prevailing constructions of masculinity and femininity influenced these outcomes. The chapter documents how boys approached school casually, forgetting to bring learning materials to class, neglecting to do their homework or study for tests, and not completing assignments thoroughly. Rather than the result of natural absent-mindedness, such behavior stemmed from a contrived carelessness that boys affected because they defined it as consistent with masculinity. Many boys, such as Preston McCormick at Clayton, performed fairly well in school. But in order to do so and maintain an unquestioned masculinity, he (and others) framed themselves as possessing unique intellectual gifts, such as a photographic memory or high intelligence, which presumably mitigated the need for studying and academic preparation. The chapter further explores how boys tended to break or bend school rules— something documented in my observations as well as disciplinary statistics. People at both schools described such behavior as consistent with masculinity. By engaging in it, boys thereby asserted masculinity. The construction of masculinity through these behaviors enhanced a sense of superiority, even though it detracted from school.

In chapters 5 and 6, I examine masculinity at each school in more detail. Whereas chapter 4 notes similarities in the construction of masculinity across the schools, these chapters draw out distinctions. Both chapters examine how different practices of manliness engendered different degrees of connection or disconnection to school and how the schools as organizations reinforced hegemonic masculinity. The analysis documents how schools act as sites for the fabrication of gender in peer culture and set certain institutional parameters that guide that process. In both chapters, I analyze how race, class, and place influenced the interpretation and enactment of masculinity. At Clayton manual labor and familial power constituted the historical bedrock for hegemonic masculinity. Economic restructuring compromised that foundation, however, which encouraged boys to prove manhood in other ways. These methods were strongly shaped by class and place and discernable through social identities such as "redneck," "rutter," "prep," and "fighter." Masculinity in this setting emphasized physical toughness, and each of these identities represented this differently. The school institution furthered this emphasis on tough masculinity by favoring contact sports such as football. I also discuss alternative masculine practices at the school and what they meant for academic achievement.

In chapter 6, I examine masculinity at Woodrow Wilson. Masculinity in this setting also emphasized physical qualities but not as rigidly as at Clayton. Boys I interviewed at Woodrow Wilson, for example, were more likely to value book smarts and less likely to believe that the man should be the main provider for the family. Verbal skills coincided with masculinity at Woodrow Wilson, where boys commonly expressed themselves through practices that required a quick wit, such as "clownin'" and "riffin'." Boys at Woodrow Wilson placed high value on being known and achieving respect among peers but used different practices to attain this notoriety. Many saw athletics as indicative of high-status manhood (and as a potential career), others cultivated a gangster or street persona, and still others developed a class clown or hustler persona. The school institution and the peer culture provided more acceptable alternative outlets for masculinity than they did at Clayton—through music and band, for example. However, boys in this setting contended with the enduring weight of racism. I highlight how race and place infiltrated and shaped their production of masculinity.

Chapter 7 turns our attention to girls and femininity at both schools. Most analyses of the gender gap have focused on why boys are falling behind, but another way of looking at this relationship is to ask why girls are doing so well (Mickelson 1989). The chapter uses Connell's (1987) notion of empha-sized femininity to examine femininity and achievement. Race, class, and place offered girls at Woodrow Wilson and Clayton alternative pathways for the expression of femininity that were not connected to supporting men. In both locations, the girls I interviewed realized that their male counterparts would not necessarily fulfill provider roles. Thus, they firmly designed their own futures to compensate, seeking independence through educational suc-cess that would lead to a career. Race and place created slight differences in these practices. At Clayton, the ideals of emphasized femininity based on support of men and physical appearance held more influence. Girls there expressed self-deprecating views of their academic and other abilities, describ-ing themselves as "dumb" and acting in ways that appeared to deemphasize their intelligence. I analyze this in light of the seemingly contradictory finding that these same girls performed very highly in school. Girls at Woodrow Wilson projected more confidence and independence. However, both sets of girls took education seriously and engaged in effective practices to boost achievement, such as asking teachers for help and completing assignments thoroughly. I term this process *conscientious resistance*. Girls at both schools followed educational rules not because of natural or socialized tendencies to be docile but because they associated educational success with empowerment. They used education and rule adherence as a form of resistance to gender inequality.

In chapter 8, I examine fighting—a nonacademic area but one that I found significant to gender and academics. Fighting represented resistance to school and proved the dominance of tough, aggressive forms of masculinity. In interviews and observations, boys (and some girls) excitedly told me their fighting stories. For boys, especially those from lower-income backgrounds and those who felt blocked from school-sanctioned practices of hegemonic masculinity such as sports, fighting provided an important means of proving masculinity. Fighting obviously defied school rules; but through the demon-stration of physical toughness and refusal to back down or be intimidated, it conveyed masculine dominance in the rawest, most basic way. The chapter also examines girl fights at the schools. Although less common overall than boy fights, people appeared more interested in girl fights. However, teachers and students tended to describe them as lower status—crazier, funnier, and often over boys. I analyze how such framing of girl fights maintained the presumed superiority of masculinity even when girls took up this traditionally masculine practice. I end the chapter by tying fighting to masculinity and education, discussing how this most basic method of demonstrating masculine power represents opposition to school but reflects much of what schools and society promulgate about masculinity.

Chapter 9 summarizes my findings. The chapter returns to public concern over and discussion of the gender gap and considers what my findings tell us about this gap. I synthesize and expand the theoretical concepts from the book, emphasizing the importance of viewing gender as a situated outcome of interaction rather than as an inherent characteristic as well as the importance of analyzing class, race, and place as simultaneously constructed outcomes that profoundly shape gendered experiences. I also stress how, even for disadvantaged boys, masculinity has an allure and an expectation of power. The book closes with suggestions for new directions in research and policy concerning the gender gap in education.

Chapter 2 Respect and Respectability

GENDER IS SOCIALLY CONSTRUCTED. This perspective underscores the production of gender at the local level of interaction, shaped by particular social forces that manifest there. Thus, it was critical to my project to examine the contours of local context, or place, in enactments of masculinity and femininity at Clayton and Woodrow Wilson. The local history, conditions, and construction of knowledge at both schools created challenges for the education of students but in slightly different ways at each school, especially within the peer culture. At Woodrow Wilson, a large urban school, peers emphasized being known and achieving respect. At Clayton, a small rural school, everyone knew everyone else, and peers emphasized family name and respectability in the community. Both Clayton and Woodrow Wilson, however, suffered from broader negative perceptions of their schools and communities. These local place-based dynamics shaped gender at both school sites.

Two Communities: Rural and Urban

The two schools were different yet very much the same. I chose to study these particular high schools because of roughly similar economic circumstances in their communities but also because of differences in their location.

WOODROW WILSON HIGH SCHOOL

Woodrow Wilson lay on the south side of a large Ohio city in an area that had once been predominately white and middle class. In the neighborhood near the school, small split-level houses, many still sporting 1970s-era color combinations, dotted the streets at regular intervals. This community had the leafy, suburban feel of a neighborhood that no longer flourished but still held promise. Farther away from the school, predominately in one area across a busy city street, lay low-rent, government-subsidized apartments. Some had regal names and appeared to be well maintained, while others had darkened red bricks and a boxy, utilitarian design. Even on the coldest of days, groups of people throughout the community could be seen lingering in front of storefronts and apartment courtyards. The area radiated a sense of restlessness.

Street intersections around Woodrow Wilson were littered with signs advertising "We buy houses." These signs indicated that residential mobility in the area was high and that many people either wanted to move or could no longer keep their houses. Indeed, according to local newspaper reports, the community had experienced considerable economic and racial transition over the past fifteen years. As with many interpretations of neighborhoods in such transition, people linked these demographic changes to rising rates of crime (Farley et al. 1994; Quillian and Pager 2001). A 1991 article in the local newspaper reported on the shooting death of a student at Woodrow Wilson, describing residents as shocked by the shooting in this once "quiet neighborhood" and quoting a local demographer who stated that the neighborhood was undergoing transition from white middle class to African American and lower income. A 2005 article reported on another shooting death of a Woodrow Wilson student, noting that the homicide apparently involved stolen shoes and members of the Bloods street gang. This article mentioned no community surprise or outrage, implying the normalization—at least from the perspective of the mainstream press—of crime and gang activity in this area.

Despite rising crime and falling incomes, the area did appear to have more varied economic opportunities than the rural community surrounding Clayton. Table 2.1 provides an economic overview of the Woodrow Wilson attendance zone. These figures are derived from the U.S. Census Bureau's 2000 data and report the average from five census tracts that roughly matched the school's attendance zone. This match was imperfect, however, and there was fairly wide variation across the tracts. One tract in particular had a considerably lower poverty rate and considerably higher median income and educational attainment than did the others.[1] Moreover, the 2000 data were somewhat dated when I did fieldwork (2006–2007), so they should be interpreted with caution. The figures reported in table 2.1 show a community that was lower income but not desperately poor. Educational attainment in the area was limited, with few adult residents holding bachelor's degrees (17 percent); but the majority had attained at least a high school diploma.

The school itself appeared to be more economically disadvantaged than these census figures would indicate. As shown in table 2.2, 75.6 percent of Woodrow Wilson's students were economically disadvantaged, a figure that is

Table 2.1
Community Characteristics

	Woodrow Wilson (N = 16,176)	Clayton (N = 4,663)
Poverty (%)	14.7	26.3
Median income	$35,267	$25,135
No high school degree or equivalent (%)	11	20
Bachelor's degree or higher (%)	17	3.8

SOURCE: U.S. Census Bureau, Census 2000: American Fact Finder (http://www.census.gov).

Table 2.2
School Characteristics

	Woodrow Wilson, 2005–2006 (N = 937)	Clayton, 2005–2006 (N = 345)
Racial/ethnic group (%)		
African American	90.6	no data
White	5.7	98
Hispanic	2.2	no data
Asian/Pacific Islander	1.4	no data
Economically disadvantaged (%)	75.6	53.5
	Woodrow Wilson, 2006–2007 (N = 909)	Clayton, 2006–2007 (N = 313)
Racial/ethnic group (%)		
African American	90.7	no data
White	5.4	98.1
Hispanic	2.3	no data
Asian/Pacific Islander	1.3	no data
Economically disadvantaged (%)	78.3	62.3

SOURCE: State of Ohio, Department of Education, School Report Cards, 2007 (http://www.ode.state.oh.us).

NOTE: "No data" is due to small subgroup size. "Economically disadvantaged" refers to free or reduced-price lunch eligibility.

based on free or reduced-price lunch eligibility in 2005–2006 (the first academic year of my fieldwork, which began in January 2006). This rose to 78.3 percent in the second year of my fieldwork, 2006–2007. Despite a high disadvantaged student population, the school performed well academically, earning a respectable "Effective" rating from the state.[2] Teachers and administrators worked hard to make Woodrow Wilson an inviting, academically stimulating environment, but this goal was somewhat attenuated by the school building itself. Woodrow Wilson sat back from the road behind a grassy field where students often played soccer or football during lunch or before school. Its exterior was white and gray with a sprawling, irregular design plan. The students (and teachers) complained about the lack of windows, which consisted of a few narrow slits. The interior made up for the lack of natural light with blinding fluorescent lights throughout the school. The current school building, dating from the 1970s, had originally been constructed following an open-concept design with minimal walls to separate classrooms. It had since been modified to create classrooms with portable walls, which did little to buffer noise from adjoining classes and were pockmarked with holes students had punched in them.

Woodrow Wilson also had a palpable emphasis on crime control. The first thing one saw when driving into the school parking lot was a sign that announced in bold letters, "This is a Drug Free and Weapons Free Area." Surveillance cameras were visible in the corners of hallways and on the outside of the school. Woodrow Wilson had a school resource officer and several assistant principals and hall monitors who policed its interior and exterior, communicating on walkie-talkies. Students I spoke with did not seem to mind this emphasis on crime control, claiming it made them feel safer, but I must admit that it made me feel somewhat uneasy. Strangely, this did not appear to deter students from minor deviance such as skipping school or fighting. I observed—and spoke with—several students who jumped over the fence around the school parking lot and sprinted into the adjoining neighborhood. Numerous fights also occurred during my time at the school, including one brawl students referred to as "the riot," which drew extensive coverage from local media and led to the arrests of several students.

CLAYTON HIGH SCHOOL

The drive to Clayton High School signaled a stark difference from Woodrow Wilson. Instead of loud, congested city streets, a narrow road snaked through rolling hills and lush pastures, following a meandering creek. In the mornings, dense fog blanketed the road, revealing only the occasional wooden barn or double-wide trailer. An old pickup truck was typically parked outside one residence on the outskirts of town, emblazoned with a large bumper sticker that read, "Just Gettin' By." This motto seemed to announce the ethos of Clayton, where people struggled to make do in the face of steep economic decline.

The attendance zone of Clayton consisted of three small, contiguous towns, with dispersed pockets of houses scattered throughout the surrounding hills and hollows. The area was federally designated as "Appalachian" largely because of high rural poverty. I do not want my description of this rural community to appear demeaning or trite. However, the area felt isolated in both space and time. The vicinity had, for example, no cell phone service, no major retail stores, and only one national-chain fast-food restaurant. Clayton High School lay within the city limits of the largest town, also named Clayton. The downtown truly looked like a ghost town; I was shocked the first time I saw it. Rows of faded two-story wooden buildings stood along both sides of the main (and only) downtown street. These buildings appeared to have once housed thriving businesses, but now virtually every one lay vacant and boarded up. The only remaining businesses on the street were a gas station, a bar, and a small pizza restaurant. During the day the streets appeared to be abandoned, but activity picked up at night; and on the weekends families came from miles around to sell second-hand and homemade items from the sidewalks of downtown.

The streets of Clayton told the story of economic boom and bust in this area better than any book or set of statistics could. This area of Appalachian Ohio emerged in the early part of the twentieth century as a burgeoning region for coal extraction and production. In the early 1900s the town of Clayton actually appeared in a *New York Times* story about coal boom towns. It once boasted several bars, restaurants, stores, and even an opera house for vaudeville performances. These businesses thrived on the heels of a prodigious coal industry, with more than twenty mines within twenty miles of Clayton. More recent newspaper articles, however, lamented the area's now moribund coal economy. During the late 1980s and early 1990s, the coal companies had downsized precipitously, closing their area operations. Some residents traveled to neighboring West Virginia to work in the mines, but more stayed rooted in the community despite uncertain employment prospects. In an article appearing in a large Ohio newspaper, one area resident likened the swift, encompassing economic depreciation to somebody pulling the plug in a bathtub.

This proud working-class community struggled to maintain itself during such difficult economic conditions. Crime, especially drug use and distribution, spread throughout the area. I lived approximately fifteen miles away from Clayton during my research, and the people where I lived described Clayton as beset with drug use, ignorance, and sexual deviance. A drug raid at the end of my fieldwork led to the arrest of several suspected dealers, and police seized large amounts of prescription painkillers, crack cocaine, and marijuana.

Census figures reported in table 2.2 provide an economic overview of the Clayton community. As with the area surrounding Woodrow Wilson, these data reveal a largely working-class population. Overall, indicators show lower educational attainment and income than those for the Woodrow Wilson attendance zone (although data from two of the census tracts surrounding Woodrow Wilson were very similar to Clayton's). Of particular note is the low percentage of adult residents who had attained a bachelor's degree or higher (3.8 percent). Interestingly, while the economically disadvantaged population of Woodrow Wilson High School appeared to be higher than its surrounding community (at least according to 2000 U.S. Census figures), the economically disadvantaged population of Clayton High School was lower than its surrounding community would suggest. The table also shows the demographics of Clayton High School, indicating that the school had a lower proportion of students classified as economically disadvantaged than Woodrow Wilson did.[3] The school scored slightly lower than Woodrow Wilson on state academic indicators, earning a midrange "Continuous Improvement" rating in 2005–2006 and improving to an "Effective" rating in 2006–2007.

With fewer than 350 students in an environment in which virtually all teachers and students knew each other, Clayton High School had a more communal feel than Woodrow Wilson did. The school changed principals during my fieldwork, and the second principal, Mr. Thomas, put a greater emphasis on disciplinary control. Students nicknamed him "Hitler" for what they interpreted as an autocratic approach to school management. As at Woodrow Wilson, fights occurred on school grounds but more often immediately after school. The school building itself was fairly new and serviceable, although portions of the parking lot and gym flooded during heavy rains. Despite the decent building, school officials complained about a lack of resources because the school district purportedly had one of the lowest property values in the state and struggled to raise educational funds. The library was woefully outdated and understocked until the school finally obtained a grant to purchase more books. Textbooks in some courses were threadbare and in short supply: in English classes students sometimes had to share novels.

Perceptions of the Schools and Communities

Students and teachers at both schools believed that outsiders denigrated their schools and communities. For students, this perception of negative judgments from outsiders served as an enduring weight that affected their perception of education and themselves. Many students enjoy the unseen privilege of attending schools and living in areas that are widely recognized for excellence. Although Woodrow Wilson and Clayton both had much to be proud of, their schools did not tend to make headlines for achievement but for faults. Students at both schools appeared to think that, because of the poor conditions of their schools or poor judgments about them, outsiders did not want them to succeed.

At Clayton, students and teachers (most of whom lived in the community) reacted strongly to their perception of condescending outsiders, whose stereotyping of Appalachian communities as ignorant, backward, and quaint has a long, unfortunate history (Billings, Norman, and Ledford 1999; Stewart 1996). For example, one day, while I was observing a current events class, the teacher, Ms. Decker, showed the class a news segment from a Columbus, Ohio, television station. The segment concerned school funding disparities in Ohio and used Clayton High School as an example of one of the lowest-funded schools in the state. The report seemingly reiterated much of what I had heard teachers complain about regarding the lack of educational resources at the school. However, I was surprised to find that Ms. Decker did not agree with much of the story's content. After turning off the videotape, she led the class in fashioning a critical response letter to the television station, objecting to how the story portrayed Clayton. Ms. Decker disagreed with several assertions of the report: that some students at the school could not read and write, that Clayton was described as a "struggling school," and that its textbooks were shoddy and outdated. She also critiqued the reporter, mentioning that he had mispronounced the name of the school several times. After class, I asked Ms. Decker about the story, and she replied: "Yeah, well, people equate poor with stupid. People come down here from Columbus and they think everyone is stupid. . . . There is nobody here who can't read and write. We have some students that need basic skills, but you have that at any school."

Students at Clayton reiterated this perception of outsiders' negative judgments. A bright girl named Jamie said that she thought outsiders "look down on us" and perceive nothing but drug use and backwardness in the community. Harry, an excitable ninth-grade boy, said, "A lot of people are scared to come to Clayton." Students also appeared to accept a negative view of the school itself. Some of my interviewees said they liked the school because it was small and personable, but most used less sanguine descriptors. When I asked a girl named Chelsie how she would describe the school to someone who didn't know about it, she responded simply, "Poor." Kaycee, a student whom I describe more in chapter 3, said, "It's just kind of a rundown school. I mean we're not rich. We're gonna be taken over by the state sooner or later."

Students and teachers at Woodrow Wilson also intimated that others "look down on them" but for slightly different reasons. Their views of outsiders' perceptions centered on violence in the school and community and the physical state of the school facilities. When I asked students at Woodrow Wilson how they would describe the school to someone who didn't know about it, they typically mentioned the school's reputation for violence. LaMarcus, a reflective boy who played football for the school, said:

> Well, I mean, when I'm describing it, well, first off when you tell somebody about your school, like they usually hear about it. Because last year we had a big problem at our school. It was on the news and everything, about a big huge fight with about twenty people that broke out. So when people usually hear about Woodrow Wilson, they usually be like "Oh, that's a bad school! And people got arrested there! And there's all this fightin' and shootin' and killin'!" They hear about like people getting killed in front of the school and they don't want to talk about the school.

Students thought this reputation was not entirely deserved. Ivory, a high achieving, school-involved girl, said:

> I'll tell them it's not that bad of a school, 'cause like they hear things on the news . . . like a couple of years ago when I first moved here, there was a fight between [a rival high school] at a football game. And then last year there was the riot. So people are like, "Oh, you go to Wilson!" I'm like "It's not that bad!"

Woodrow Wilson students also commented on the poor state of the building and other facilities at the school. As I have mentioned, the school had a foreboding appearance enhanced by its crime-control emphasis. Ivory stated, "It looks like a jail! You walk up, you see barbed wire around the football field. . . . The school is just ugly!" Maintenance problems at the school included holes in the makeshift walls between classrooms; ripped, stained carpeting; missing ceiling panels; and an unusable athletic track, among other issues. When I first met LaMarcus, he relayed a litany of problems with the school's upkeep and insisted that I tell the district superintendent about the problems "because he needs to know." LaMarcus, an athlete, clearly saw disparities between Woodrow Wilson and suburban high schools during sporting events. He perceived these disparities as unfair and became despondent when speaking of them in our interview: "You go to [two predominately white, wealthy, suburban public high schools] and you look at their stuff—I mean their stuff is laid out. Brand-new stadium, new field, track is nice, they got an indoor track. You know, that's kind of . . . unfair." Students did not often directly link such disparities to race; most students I interviewed at Woodrow Wilson in fact made a point of downplaying the extent of racial discrimination. However, it was hard to not draw the conclusion that race

in this moderately residentially segregated city had something to do with it.
Ivory said:

> Like in this neighborhood it's mostly a black community, so you go to
> [a predominately white, middle-class suburb] and everything and see
> their schools and it's like, wow, why can't our schools be like that? . . .
> You see black schools and it looks like this. But then you go
> somewhere where it's a mostly white community and its like, wow,
> that's nice!

Like Clayton students, students at Woodrow Wilson perceived their school as
lower-status and stigmatized. As Quentin, a burly football player at Wilson,
put it, "This school is known for too many things. And not good things."

The stigma attached to both schools affected students' perceptions of
their education and position in society. Both groups of students perceived a
hidden message that their schools and communities were problematic in some
way. Students used adjectives such as *rundown*, *dirty*, *ghetto*, *gang-zone*, *poor*,
and so on to describe their schools and various neighborhoods in their
communities. As Erving Goffman (1963) elucidates in his well-known
book *Stigma*, such potentially discrediting attributes profoundly shape social
identity and social action.

Respect and Respectability: Striving for Credibility in the Peer Culture

Students at both schools contended with particular external stigmas, which
depended on the different locations of the schools. Perceptions of Clayton
reflected rural Appalachian stereotypes of backwardness, while perceptions of
Woodrow Wilson reflected urban African American stereotypes of violence.
Place-based differences also emerged in the peer cultures of the two schools.
The legacy of family name dominated Clayton, while achieving known status
held sway at Wilson. These different paths to peer notoriety wove their way
through the social landscape of the schools, and each path was motivated by
an abject social identity in the peer culture (see Butler 1999; Pascoe 2007).

WOODROW WILSON: AVOIDING THE "LAME"

Students in the pariah group at Woodrow Wilson were known as the lames.
Although students described the category as a social group, *lame* served as an
ideological concept more than a way to describe an actual group of people. For
Woodrow Wilson students, *lame* signified the inability to achieve social recognition and respect. This abject category revealed a driving desire within

the student culture to garner respect by attaining known status. Woodrow Wilson students placed utmost importance on being known, or recognized, by peers. Students claimed that it did not much matter what a person was known for so long as they had a respected reputation in the school.

Initially, I thought that the word *lame* was simply a proxy for *nerd*, but students emphasized that high academic achievement could actually be an acceptable way to be known. As a girl named Courtney explained, "you gotta know everybody, and everybody gotta know you." Instead, *lame* implied a lack of social affinity; it was applied to students who were not outgoing and did not "like to have fun," in the words of a girl named Alicia. Several interviewees described lames as "just there," meaning that they attended school, came to class, and went home in relative anonymity. Describing one student called lame, a boy named Corie mused, "I wonder what his life is like. . . . I wonder if he has a job or something. . . . He's just there."

Students took pains to underscore that the *lame* label was bestowed solely on those who "kept to themselves." However, it was clear that certain students could avoid lame status easier than others could. Those who played sports, were affiliated with gangs, won fights, and achieved high grades were all described as known. Lame also encompassed a hidden social class component through possession of expensive, fashionable clothing. Candace said, "[Lame] means nobody knows you, you don't dress nice, your shoes aren't nice. Basically it's your appearance and who you talk to." LaMarcus discussed at length the importance of clothing in the peer culture, stating that people are called lame if they "don't have the latest gear." He said that if one wears expensive clothing, "people are gonna pay attention to you. The only way people pay attention to you if you don't have very expensive stuff is if you're really known. . . . It's just the actions you take." Thus, while the *lame* label could be affected by expensive clothing, my interviewees insisted that poorer students could become known and respected through social achievements or "the actions they take."

Achieving known status also earned a student much-sought-after respect, according to students. According to Elijah Anderson (1999), "in the inner city environment respect on the street may be viewed as a form of social capital that is very valuable; . . . not only is it protective [but] it often forms the core of the person's self-esteem" (66). Anderson and other authors (such as Bourgois 1996; Jones 2009), have vividly described the importance of respect, which typically connotes the achievement of recognition and deference in urban areas. This was certainly true at Woodrow Wilson.

Different paths for attaining respect existed at the school, one of which was the toughness associated with gang membership. According to David, gang members were well known and respected among peers: "Some people they only think about being known, they only think about protection, they only think about being talked about and stuff like that. It's just all about respect. . . . Like all the gang members are popular." Of course, the attainment of respect through toughness and intimidation—especially for boys—tended to impede school attachment and achievement. A few could achieve known, respected status by getting high grades, but girls pursued this avenue far more than boys did. Many boys cleverly sought respect and popularity through clownin' and quick wit, which gave them masculine credibility without directly defying authority. However, even this route to recognition, as I will show in chapter 6, negatively affected boys in school by irritating teachers and distracting the boys from learning.

The emphasis on being known and achieving respect grew largely from place-based context, including intertwined factors of race, class, and urbanicity. As an inner-city school with a stigmatized reputation, students perceived an enhanced need to assert themselves and demand recognition. My research underscores how urbanicity, in addition to race and class, con-stitutes a major contextual and motivational factor in seeking respect. Urbanicity encouraged the drive to be known. As a school in a populous, residentially mobile area, students were not immediately known and thus had to establish themselves socially. For example, Courtney, who was African American and low income but grew up in rural Mississippi, distinguished her former rural community from Woodrow Wilson: "Where I'm from there ain't no such thing as lame and popular—it's just as one. Everybody know you. 'Cause I'm from a small town, and everybody know everybody." The urban environment of Woodrow Wilson sparked the drive for recognition and respect.

CLAYTON: REJECTING THE "RUTTER"

Rutter was the local pariah category at Clayton. The term was fascinating in its peculiarity. According to students, it originated from a local family with the surname Rutter who lived in deep poverty and depravity, refusing to "take care of themselves." It eventually devolved into an invective, with students calling each other "rutter" as an insult. The term was not used beyond the immediate local area of Clayton. (I lived about fifteen miles from Clayton during my fieldwork, and people where I lived did not recognize the word unless they were from the Clayton area.) Like *lame* at Woodrow Wilson, *rutter* represented the opposite of what students strove to achieve in the peer culture. At Clayton, social efforts centered less on being known, because everyone in this small community already knew everyone else. Instead, they reflected a desire to portray a respectable—that is, economically stable and honorable—identity.[4]

On its face, *rutter* referred to those in severe poverty. An engaging student named Zack explained, "The ones that people call rutters, they usually wear all black and their clothes kind of have holes in them and things like that. They're less fortunate." Students often distinguished rutters from wealthy preps, who wore fashionable clothes, participated in school sports and activities, and were seen as popular. Zack continued, "And then the preps, they wear all the name-brand clothes and that kind of stuff. They dress real nice. They don't get dirty."

Zack was one of the only students I interviewed who referred to rutters as unfortunate. Other students showed less restraint in their assessments. Jamie said, "You're just a rutter! Like dirty. Like you live in a really nasty house. You wear the same clothes over and over again without washing them. You don't take baths." Harry claimed that the peer culture was bifurcated between "cool people" and "rutters." He described rutters as "people who are disgusting, never brush their teeth; those people . . . they don't take care of themselves." He said "cool" people avoided rutters because of this lack of hygiene and lack of popularity. As I have examined elsewhere (Morris 2009), the concept of the rutter referred not simply to having less money but to a lazy, willful form of poverty. Few of my interviewees felt sorry for rutters. Instead they were seen as victims of their own personal choices. Students described rutters as those who "don't care" and have little self-respect. Kaycee explained that rutters could have better hygiene and attire if they wanted to: "[If you're a rutter,] you just don't care about yourself. Why wouldn't you bathe? Because you can." A high-achieving girl named Lyndsie thought that rutters did not care about school: "I think rutters would rather not be here. I think the rutters would rather be at home drinking or something."

Although related to poverty, in the local imagination *rutter* represented more of an achieved than ascribed status. Students at Clayton underscored the immorality and indolence represented by rutters more than their unfortunate economic circumstances. According to this view, a rutter did not live in poverty by chance; he or she lived in poverty because of a lack of responsibility. In other words, students emphasized that rutters lacked not just money but, more precisely, respectability. They drew moral boundaries of social differentiation that paralleled—and, for many, supplanted—economic boundaries (Lamont 2000). Moral standing in this community served as a form of capital, as researchers have noted in their findings about other rural areas (Sherman 2006). Indeed, strong themes of personal responsibility, hard work, and morality infused my interviews and field notes at Clayton. Students said that many people in the community "don't care," are "lazy," or "don't want to work." Rebecca, an amiable girl who worked hard academically, complained about some students' lack of school effort:

> They don't care. Their parents aren't really . . . I know it sounds
> mean, but their parents aren't anything. They sit at home, they don't
> have a job, [students are] used to watching that from their parents and
> stuff. And they think, "[My parents are] on welfare, I'll just be on
> welfare." And they don't have to do anything with their life, . . . like
> "I'm gonna be what Dad and Mom are."

As Rebecca indicates, family achievement and reputation were strongly valued at Clayton. Travis stated, "Family name is everything here." This agrees with findings in other rural locations (Batteau 1982; Duncan 1999), where tightly knit communities calcify a timeless (and largely unfair) division between "good" families and "bad" families. At Clayton *family name* composed a primary resource in hindering or enabling one's establishment of respectability. Preps typically came from the few wealthy families in the area, who (unsurprisingly) held positive moral reputations. Kaycee, as I will discuss in chapter 3, came from a family with a bad name. Yet she lauded good families for helping the school:

> Cole Watson—he's a really good person, but I think his mom has
> donated a lot of money to the school. . . . And the Mitchells, they
> donate a lot of money so they got a really big name here. And the
> Stoorses. They donate money and stuff for the school. And like the
> Mitchells aren't bad people, even though they get favoritism.

The enduring legacy of family name thus shaped the drive for a respectable local reputation. The concept of the rutter, originating from a local family, emblematizes this local importance of family name. Students also mentioned that rutters came from families with discredited reputations. (No one at the school, interestingly, had the surname Rutter.) The quest for respectability and differentiation from local stigmas of the rutter and family name both motivated and constrained students at Clayton but affected boys and girls differently. As I will show, many boys responded to the threat of class and reputational disempowerment by embracing tough, defiant masculine scripts such as "redneck" and "fighter." Some boys who suffered reputational or economic disadvantages challenged the ingrained respectability hierarchy by demanding the respect garnered through physical toughness and intimidation, which I detail in chapters 5 and 8. In this sense, *respect* and *respectability*, while reflecting different social contexts and dynamics, represented the same goals for students at both schools: acceptance and dignity.

Placing Gender

Intersectional analyses typically highlight race, class, and gender but less often consider geographical context. Yet place, as a major structural and perceptual factor, intertwines extensively with other forms of inequality (Cresswell 2004; Lobao, Hooks, and Tickamyer 2007). In *The Sociology of Spatial Inequality*, Linda Lobao and colleagues (2007) argue that place is crucial for the study of race, class, and gender because it channels these categories of inequality, "sometimes constraining, sometimes amplifying their effects" (10). Indeed, at Woodrow Wilson and Clayton, local context profoundly and inextricably guided constructions of gender.

The rural and urban locations in my study show certain structural and economic similarities. However, they also show important differences. Each place created different challenges for students to attain credibility, and each propagated different gendered scripts for overcoming these challenges. As Woodrow Wilson students intimated, predominately minority, inner-city areas stereotypically represent social disorganization and high crime (Farley et al. 1994; Quillian and Pager 2001; Wilson 1996). Perceptions of rural areas such as Clayton tend to be less fearfully negative, but (especially for Appalachia) can still indicate pathologies such as drug and alcohol abuse, incest, and ignorance (Billings et al. 1999). Beyond this, the concept of *urban* in general tends to represent sophistication and restive activity, while *rural* suggests a connection to nature and simplicity (Campbell, Bell, and Finney 2006; Corbett 2007). Such perceptions influenced masculinity and femininity at both school locations. As I will show, at Woodrow Wilson stereotypes of dangerous African American boys and assertive African American girls affected how students there enacted gender. At Clayton, local ideals of stoic, physically capable men and deferential, domestic women affected how students there enacted gender. Moreover, these place-based circumstances influenced gender and academic achievement. For some boys at Woodrow Wilson, becoming known and asserting urban masculinity put them at odds with school authorities. For some boys at Clayton, achieving respectable rural masculinity necessitated physical labor and prowess rather than seemingly pointless academic bookwork. For other boys at both schools, gaining respect through tough, rebellious acts such as fighting challenged various stigmas of race, class, and family but strained school attachment.

For students at Clayton and Woodrow Wilson, place deeply affected their lives, including their gender practices. The rural and urban locations provided different resources and challenges for accomplishing gender, race, and class. Despite these distinctions, students in both disadvantaged and

vilified communities basically sought the same outcomes: recognition, belonging, and dignity. Both sets of students grappled with the perception that
outsiders viewed their schools and communities in negative, stereotypical
ways and that their fellow students might view them as lame or a rutter. Such
perceptions influenced how these eager young men and women constructed
academic and gender identities as they strove to achieve respect and
respectability.

Chapter 3

The Hidden Injuries of Gender

Students at Woodrow Wilson and Clayton faced many difficulties and disadvantages, and their gender ideals and pathways to becoming a man or a woman developed within these challenging contexts. Their gendered responses to life challenges produced different outcomes. Masculinity was consistent with school distancing while femininity was consistent with school attachment, and each enactment had different implications for education.

In this chapter I focus on two students at Clayton High School, Kevin and Kaycee. Although I realize that such a concentration makes the book somewhat asymmetrical, my rationale is twofold. First, the approach contrasts the masculinity and femininity of two students with similar backgrounds in the same school context. Second, Kevin's and Kaycee's personal experiences greatly struck and affected me. As a sociologist, I am trained to divine group-level patterns, but unfortunately this often entails losing people's personal stories. This chapter, then, is an attempt to communicate those narratives and showcase the fact that my research was about people, not simply abstract concepts and patterns.

The narratives demonstrate what I call the hidden injuries of gender, a phrase modeled on Richard Sennett and Jonathan Cobb's (1972) lyrically titled *The Hidden Injuries of Class*. In their classic text, they write, "[the] fear of being summoned before some hidden bar of judgment and being found inadequate infects the lives of [working-class] people; . . . it is a matter of a hidden weight, a hidden anxiety, . . . a matter of feeling inadequately in control" (33). Sennett and Cobb refer to such hidden injuries throughout their book, showing how class status affects the dignity of poor and working-class people and how they carve out a sense of self-respect in reaction, constructing "badges of dignity" that deflect perceived degradation (84).

35

Gender can be a framework for interpreting and responding to social challenges that threaten to impugn dignity. Like Sennett and Cobb, I found that social class, family background, race, and place-based stigma threatened the dignity of students in my study, prompting them to carve out a sense of respect and efficacy. Kevin and Kaycee managed challenges from their family backgrounds by following distinctly masculine and feminine scripts. Other students at Woodrow Wilson and Clayton faced both similar and different challenges, but all interpreted such hidden injuries through the lens of gender and devised gendered responses to heal these injuries.

Kevin

I first met Kevin in a ninth-grade English class at Clayton. He had thick, sandy-blond hair and deep-set eyes. He rarely smiled, and his brow was often furrowed into what approached a scowl. Despite this sullen exterior he was highly personable. He was one of the first students I met and talked to during my fieldwork, and he later helped me recruit additional students to interview. Students and teachers seemed to like him but also viewed him as a little different. Students occasionally made fun of him, and teachers viewed him as potentially troublesome. When I got him out of class for his interview, I asked the teacher, Ms. Galloway, if I could get any makeup work for him. She replied, "Well, you can get it, but the question is, will he do it?"

Kevin and I walked down the hall to a private room, his white high-top sneakers squeaking loudly on the concrete floors. When the interview began, he told me that he lived in a house with his parents, his younger brother, and occasionally his sister and seven-year-old nephew. His mother worked as a secretary for an electrician and, as he described it, got "paid pretty good." Kevin's father was fifty-four years old and disabled. He had dropped out of school in the eleventh grade and was collecting disability assistance at the time of the interview. Kevin seemed to vacillate between feelings of pride and shame regarding his father:

> KEVIN: He's said to only have an eighth-grade education through IQ
>   tests. . . . But he's a smart guy. He can't really do bookwork, but if you
>   go out and you give him lumber, he can build a porch. Like he built
>   most of our house with my Uncle Jon before he was disabled. . . .
> E. M.: Okay, so he can do things. As far as bookwork—
> KEVIN: As far as bookwork, he's not great at it. He can read and write
>   decent. About an eighth-grade level—read and write. He can't read
>   huge long words, and he can't spell 'em out.

Kevin was a pretty good student with around a B average. He wanted to go into construction like his father but own and operate the business himself: "Well, I like [construction]. I mean it's easy for me. I'm just—you know, cut wood, hook up the gutters, nails, 'cause I helped build our whole entire house, the one we live in now." Kevin wanted to get a two-year degree to help him with this career goal. But he viewed education as more of a necessary hurdle than something that would provide him with useful knowledge. He preferred to learn from his uncle, also in the construction business: "I could just learn everything from him. I wouldn't have to go to college or anything." He described this view as something common to boys and consistent with his understanding of masculinity: "Like most the guys [at Clayton], they're like, well, what's the point [of school]. I can drop out right now and do work with my uncle doing construction and be brought up right underneath his wing."

Kevin viewed this career plan as a way not only to have "a big house and a nice wife" but also to demonstrate masculinity through physically vigorous work. In describing his life plans, he underscored bodily attributes:

> I have good plans ahead of me and I'm young and I'm in shape pretty
> much as good as I'm gonna get right now. I mean I have fat, but I
> mean it's muscle underneath there. . . . Otherwise I wouldn't be able
> to box—I'd get wind knocked outta me. And so I'm in good shape,
> my arms are in good shape, I can run a mile, you know, I can do
> everything that I'm required to do at my age physically. And I have
> a good career plan.

At Clayton, hegemonic masculinity (Connell 1987) emphasized physical qualities such as strength, pain management, and endurance. Many boys expressed this through their interest in manual labor. In directing their thoughts and behaviors in this way Kevin and other boys enacted a working-class masculinity. The stable employment and sense of usefulness they hoped to gain from blue-collar work reinforced the dignity associated with this class position. The physical vitality of the work further confirmed their masculinity.

It was clear that Kevin crafted such plans in response to the limited economic resources he perceived. He did not want to end up like his father, who could not bring in much income and could not demonstrate masculinity through physical labor. As I described in chapter 2, Clayton teenagers denigrated those whom they perceived as impoverished by virtue of their own lack of initiative, using the local slur "rutter." Kevin interpreted his life goals as dependent on his own will power and contrasted this attitude with that of other low-income kids in the area, whom he perceived as indolent: "It just makes me mad that people just want to throw their life away like that and not accomplish anything. Like when I'm twenty and I'm out there runnin' a small business or something, they'll still be on the street rubbin' two quarters together, you know, tryin' to make seventy-five cent with two." This sense of will power was a rational, self-efficacious response to depressed economic circumstances in the area and in Kevin's own background.

Kevin felt the hidden anxiety of trying to represent a stable, dignified class position despite a disadvantaged background. His planned career lay several years away, but his anxiety expressed itself in everyday life through the peer culture of the high school. For many teenagers, clothing serves as an important emblem of individuality, belonging, and status. Although low-income in general, the peer culture at Clayton emphasized such outward appearance. Yet Kevin described his restricted resources for achieving such status:

> E. M.: Are [the preps] trying to act like they're better or—?
> KEVIN: Yeah, pretty much 'cause—they got money. Like Meghan, she's got like all kinda money. She's got like name-brand clothes, and shoes, and brand-new shoes any time she wants to get 'em. And shoppin' all the time. . . . I don't do that shit. I mean look at these things. [Looks down; pulls off some of the surface from his peeling shoes; puts his finger through holes between the upper part of shoe and the sole.] I've had these things since the beginning of the year. I paid like forty bucks for 'em. That's not a lot for shoes. And they're comfortable. I don't give a shit what they look like. People can call me what they want. I can stand up for myself. But I mean like I got good clothes on, I mean I had this shirt [a plain gray short-sleeved t-shirt] since last year. It's got a little stain on it from where I had lunch but, you know, it's nice.
> E. M.: So some of it has to do with money, and they're sort of trying to be better?
> KEVIN: [Nods head to indicate yes; continues staring down at his shoes. His face has reddened, and he looks upset.]

Kevin quickly composed himself and continued:

> I mean these are Loves right here [picks at his shoes again]; these are a good brand of shoe. But I got 'em at a discount store, so fake leather, you know, it peels off. But this part up here [points to the upper part of the shoe]—I mean it's still white. [Pause.] And I'd probably go out and buy the same pair but just not wear them out as much like I used to. When I got these I was wearin' 'em all over, you know? But if I got a pair and didn't wear 'em anywhere but school they'd look brand new every day.

He described how kids from wealthier backgrounds are not forced to be as careful with clothes and shoes as he is:

> I mean, it's just the way people take care of things. Rich kids and preps and everything—I don't think you see 'em with the same shirt on in a month. I wear this shirt just about once a week. I have like six, seven nice shirts and then I have crappy ones I wear around the house. . . . [Speaking slowly] I don't have a lot of nice clothes . . . but I wash my own clothes because I gotta have stuff clean. 'Cause my mom just had surgery—she had to get her gallbladder taken out—she doesn't do much. She never did do much anyway.

Kevin went on to describe how he had to plan what to wear and when to wash it so he could alternate his few nice shirts and pants every week. He anticipated being ridiculed for wearing the same clothes. He was ashamed of his squeaky, peeling shoes but appeared to blame himself for being too rough on them.

In the same way that work status and notions of success compromised respectability in Sennett and Cobb's study, clothing and peer group status created hidden injuries for Kevin. The daily stress must have been taxing. He responded to these challenges in several positive ways—he established life goals, performed adequately in school, and was socially outgoing albeit not entirely popular—yet he clearly approached life with a sense of trepidation and distrust. According to him, he had achieved a bad social reputation that inevitably lingered in this small town: "I've been outcasted since fifth grade." Kevin had several close friends; and as I have mentioned, most people I talked to seemed to like him. But he described how some students made fun of him:

> I get recognized as one of the people ever'body just wants to pick on. And that's the way I'm just recognized and some people are just like 'at. I know three or four guys that are just like 'at. They just see me and they see a target. I don't know why, seein' as how I box, and kickbox, and don't do anything to make them mad—it's just—that's the way they feel and—I can't be in any more trouble in school anyway so—

Kevin was referring to his several suspensions for fighting and other aggressive behavior. While not one of the most disciplined students at Clayton, he got into a fair share of trouble. One day, when I was signing in at the school, I noticed that the principal was chewing out Kevin in the office. As I turned the corner to walk down the hallway, Kevin emerged from the principal's office. I asked him how he was doing. He responded, "Pretty shitty. I just got sent to the principal's office for fuckin' talkin' about a test! It's fucked up—for no other reason than talking about a dumb test!"

Kevin admitted, however, that he could let his anger get the better of him in school:

> I mean I've cussed out a teacher a couple of times, but that wasn't because I didn't wanna do my work. I mean I was really mad, havin' a bad day and they didn't make it any better by like, one time a [teacher's aide] wouldn't let me use my bathroom pass. And I said no—I have to go to the bathroom, let me go to the bathroom or I'm a walk out. And we got in a big argument about it and I ended up cussin' at 'er and walkin' outta the room.

He described himself as having a problem with his temper: "I'm a nice guy, but if you piss me off, I can get pretty angry. It runs on both sides of the family—temper problem, you know. Yeah, I mean there's really not much to say, I'm a nice guy and I talk nice and I act nice to people and do right most best I can in life." Although Kevin tried his best to do right, he often responded aggressively to a sense of being belittled either in classrooms or among peers. This defensive response, often noted in other research on boys (Keddie 2007; Messerschmidt 2000), is consistent with hegemonic practices of masculinity. Such responses not only alleviated boys' sense of belittlement but affirmed masculinity. Yet they had hidden academic costs.

Kevin got into trouble for insubordination, and he often got into fights at school. Such academic costs were less salient to him than the necessity of standing up for himself and reconstituting masculinity through fighting. He thought fights allowed him to demonstrate his superior toughness over other boys:

> E. M.: Well, since you've been in a couple [of fights]—what started those fights?
>
> KEVIN: A guy tryin' to think he's tough, takin' food off my tray and sayin', "Oh, this is mine, you ain't gonna eat this are you?" Well, you know, I took him outside after school and I beat the piss out of him. . . . And [another day] he goes again. I told him if he didn't quit I was gonna get up and hit him. And he hit me in the head with a spoon. So I got up and I walked over toward 'im, and I told him to stand up. And this was like—from the door to you like where he was standing if he was you and you're him, and he didn't stand up so I walked up and, you know, I blasted 'im in the nose [makes a punching motion toward me]. And I hit 'im in the side of the head, and they said I hit 'im about four or five times, I don't really remember much. I just hit. I just swung. But he had marks all along his head and his eyes were all black and his nose was all busted up. I mean, I beat the piss outta him twice! [He laughs.]

Kevin viewed fighting as a free space in which he could demonstrate superiority unencumbered by the limitations of social status. As I will describe, fighting for students at both schools represented this freedom. Fighting allowed Kevin an emotional release in a context in which men were supposed to be emotionally stoic. This release is consistent with masculinity, however, because it occurs through physical action: "I just hit. I just swung." Fighting confirmed Kevin's masculinity, proving his toughness and superiority over other boys.

In a more indirect way, fighting among boys also conveyed their difference from and superiority over girls. As I will show in detail, girl fights at both schools, although relatively common, were not often viewed as real or serious fights. Kevin expressed this view:

> Like me being a guy, I wouldn't really fight over a girl, but girls fight over guys all the time. And then girls fight over stupid shit like arguments. Like they'll get in an argument and fight over it. Like just words. I've never fought over just words. It's always—it's something physical, you know.

Kevin interpreted fighting as a means of physical expression that is more consistent with masculinity and demeaned girl fights as stupid and often over boys. He thus asserted the superiority of boys over girls: even when girls engaged in the masculine idiom of fighting, he cast their actions as insignificant or for the purpose of being available to boys.

Because Kevin perceived that his financial background and limited athletic ability hindered him from pursuing school-sponsored outlets for physical masculinity such as sports, he turned to alternative means of demonstrating masculinity such as fighting and boxing at a local gym. When I asked him who his role models were, he said his only role model was Tommy, a local man who was once a professional boxer and operated a small boxing gym in town that Kevin frequented. Kevin described how he used boxing to relieve the stress of his home and personal life: "I get out my stress, and I just forget about what went on at the house or with my girlfriend, if we had an argument. I mean, I just get away from the world—dealing with reality. It's a good getaway."

Aggressive contact sports such as boxing are often seen as a means of stress relief and a way to release aggression. But studies find that such activities actually increase the chances of further aggressive behavior, including physical fights at school (Kreager 2007; Messner 1992). This was the case for Kevin, who (although he was a competent student) got into trouble for being verbally and physically combative at school. For him, this behavior served as a compensatory manhood act, meaning that it helped compensate for and solidify his masculinity in response to a sense of powerlessness (Schrock and Schwalbe

2009). As with many such compensatory acts, however, Kevin's aggressive behavior produced costs, resulting in suspensions that stunted his educational progress and shaped how teachers and administrators at Clayton viewed him. In the words of one teacher, "[Kevin] has a bad attitude. He's gonna be trouble down the line."

As I have mentioned, Kevin performed adequately in school but did not put much effort into schoolwork. He viewed school as simply a necessary hurdle to overcome in order to meet his goal of running a construction business. He interpreted high academic achievement and striving as pointless and annoying. He also aligned school effort and "office jobs" with femininity, which he perceived as lower status and not "hard work":

> I think it's a lot easier for girls to have that "wanna go get a good grade" spirit. And wanna . . . get their grades up and go to college. Girls don't think about fightin' or think about hard work. They're thinkin' office jobs, you know. Accounting, business, stuff like that— the easier . . . type stuff.

As we will see, many boys at Clayton viewed the bookwork of school in a similar way. They, like Kevin, perceived physical labor as more useful and important. Although boys at Woodrow Wilson showed more affinity for book smarts, boys at both schools interpreted school effort as something more common for girls and therefore as lower status. Kevin's disavowal of school effort, along with his presumption about the superiority of manly work, thus became avowals of masculinity.

Kevin's family background and peer status created hidden psychological injuries. Masculinity emphasized a stoic independence in managing these emotional tolls. It further provided a specific outlet for challenging these injuries—primarily through aggressive verbal or physical outbursts, often in defiance of school rules, and a self-made path to manhood (Kimmel 1996) that did not focus on academic effort. In this way gender itself produced a hidden cost. By accessing and forming masculinity to challenge and relieve sources of stress in his life, Kevin used aggression and independence, which limited his attachment to school.

Kaycee

Kaycee was a vibrant, outgoing girl who always appeared to be in a good mood. She had dark hair, brown eyes, and an olive complexion. Her wide, toothy smile was infectious. But when I interviewed Kaycee toward the end of my fieldwork, I was surprised to find that her bright personality masked some hidden shame regarding her family background.

Kaycee's parents were no longer together, and her father was unemployed. As she put it, "my dad doesn't really have a job. . . . He just like does carpentry on his own." Her mother had worked as a cashier at a grocery store for more than twenty years but had been recently laid off. Kaycee's mother had a high school diploma, while her father had dropped out of school in the tenth grade. Kaycee's older brother, his girlfriend, and their child (Kaycee's nephew) lived in Kaycee's house, which she did not like. Like their father, her brother did not have a job: "My brother is . . . unemployed. He's twenty-one and he's just kinda—[She laughs.]"

It soon became clear that Kaycee was experiencing considerable tension in her home, both at the time of the interview and earlier in her life. When I asked her what she thought about school, she gave an interesting answer:

> I like school. Yeah, I like school. I . . . get away from the drama at my house. [She laughs.] When I come to school, I like it. I remember one day last year, like my family is a really disoriented family. Like we're weird. Like I'm not, but I'm the only sane one in my family. And one day I walked out of school with a big smile on and looked over and there was my mom sitting in the car and my brother's truck was parked next to her and my brother wasn't in his truck. And I got in the car and my brother was over there and his knuckles were all bloody [from hitting a wall during a fight with his girlfriend]. And I thought, [her voice becomes sarcastic] "Great, now I'm out of school." Yeah, so school is kind of a place that I like to go to.

Most students I interviewed said they did not really like school or qualified what they liked with many negatives about school. Kaycee, by contrast, perceived school as a welcome respite from a turbulent home life.

Although she had developed a pro-school attitude, Kaycee admitted that family turmoil affected her in school:

> E. M.: Now, is it hard though when something like that happens? . . . Is it hard to concentrate in school?
>
> KAYCEE: Oh my gosh! The other morning my brother's girlfriend woke at like . . . that night they got in a fight and then the next morning . . . like her family won't take her back in 'cause she hit her dad upside the head with a phone. So he kicked her out and then she moved back in with us and . . . she had nowhere to go. So that night she came back after my brother and her just got in a fight. So that that morning she woke up and rolled over and like. . . . said

that she was gonna take my nephew and move back to New York.
And then that started a huger fight. And that was right before
school, so . . . and I was like "Mom, I'm leaving."

This and other problems had earned Kaycee's family a bad reputation in the
community. As Kaycee described it, "I don't have a good last name." But she
wanted to overcome this reputation through school achievement:

Like one time I went up to my cousin, and her boyfriend said, you're
gonna change the McCleary last name. Like you're gonna change
what people think about it. 'Cause I'm going to college and I've
already planned what I want to do and everything and I don't do
drugs or anything, but the rest of my family does. And he's like you're
gonna change the McCleary name and I'm like, okay. Because that's
what people think about us around here.

Kaycee struggled not only with the tension in her family but also with the
stigma her family had acquired in the community. As I discussed in chapter 2,
family name and reputation carried heavy weight in Clayton. This was a small
community where everyone knew everyone else, and many families had lived
in the community for generations. Students from "bad" families such as
Kaycee's perceived that they would have to work constantly to overcome this
reputation.

As Kaycee mentioned, drug use and unemployment perpetuated part of
her family's negative reputation. She told me about her father's being monitored by local police officers and having his car searched. She also poignantly
recounted times when she had to manage the repercussions of her father's
addictive behavior:

One time my mom dropped me off like at my dad's house for the day
and he was passed out and his head was busted open. I was scared to
death. I couldn't wake him up. I thought my dad was dead, and I
couldn't get to school. I think I was like ten or eleven. And I was
gonna go over to my next-door neighbor . . . but [the neighbor] ended
up coming over. It was like a miracle that he just came over and
knocked on the door and I just bawled and ran over and gave him a
hug and was like "Something happened to my dad!" And he went
over and tried to wake him up and couldn't wake him up, so he took
me to school, and I went to school squalling.

It is interesting that in this example Kaycee was concerned not only
about her father but also about getting to school. One might think that such a
troubled family life would have hindered her educational progress. But on the

contrary, she used school as a space and a method for healing these injuries. She described how school had comforted her when she was younger:

> KAYCEE: My parents were off and on for—a long time. Like they got in fights and stuff and it sucked. I don't like my childhood, I hated it. . . . But I thank a lot of my teachers because I would come into school one day and they could see that I was upset and I had my own little cot in a corner where they'd see that my parents had been fighting all night and I hadn't gotten any sleep and I couldn't do anything so they just put me in a cot in the corner and they'd just let me sleep during school. So [school's] been like real good for me—
>
> E. M.: So you feel like the school has always like cared about you in a sense?
>
> KAYCEE: Yeah. And I told my mom one day, "You know what? Kids my age hate school! I'm not supposed to like school!" But I do.

Instead of encouraging a defiant stance toward school and other people, as they did with Kevin, the frustrations of her family background made Kaycee more attached to school. For her, school did not present a further threat of belittlement but an opportunity to escape: "I feel . . . protected here. I don't feel like my drama can come here. I just drop it." Kaycee used this attachment to perform well in school: she had a high B average and was planning to attend a four-year college and major in elementary education to become a teacher.

Femininity, as a socially defined pattern of action, facilitated her ability to translate family troubles into concerted school connections. Instead of keeping problems to herself only to have them eventually boil over (as Kevin did), Kaycee sought connections with others as a way of mitigating problems. Early in her life, school had provided caring adults in the form of teachers whom Kaycee could confide in, suggesting that emotional connections to others were not only acceptable but consistent with demonstrating femininity (Connell 1987).

Kaycee's enactment of femininity also facilitated her school achievement. Although she performed well in school now, she told me that she had had trouble reading early in her educational career because her parents did not regularly read to her at home:

> My mom tried, like my mom was a really good mom. Like my mom is my hero. And my mom worked like two jobs when my dad was like an alcoholic and a drug addict. So I mean—But my mom would try to read to me but she would leave the TV on and I would get up and take off. And she told me half the time she would read to me and I'd stare at the TV and she'd be like "Are you paying attention?" And I'd be like "Uh-huh" and just stare at the TV!

Perhaps drawing from these early experiences, Kaycee described herself as "not real smart." Emphasized femininity in Clayton historically placed women in supportive, dependent roles within the home while men worked in coal mining or other manual labor jobs. Perhaps because of this, girls at Clayton appeared to be uncomfortable about demonstrating superiority. As I will discuss in chapter 7, girls such as Kaycee tended to minimize their academic ability. Conventional views suggest that this lack of confidence should limit girls' educational progress (AAUW 1992; Sadker and Sadker 1994). But instead of debilitating her, these perceived disadvantages impelled Kaycee to exert more effort: "I have to like really, really try [in school]." She accepted herself as "not real smart"; but instead of stifling her academic self-efficacy, this perception actually encouraged it.

While this historical submission of women to men in the family was not as strong at Woodrow Wilson, I found that girls there were also less likely than boys to be described, and to describe themselves, as "smart." This apparent disadvantage propelled the achievement of girls at both schools by encouraging academic effort. Kaycee explained the importance of effort for girls:

E. M.: Would you say that girls do more studying than boys?
KAYCEE: Yes.
E. M.: Why is that, do you think?
KAYCEE: I don't believe that guys are smarter than girls but I think
that it just comes to them naturally. I don't know what it is! [She
laughs.] . . . Like Tom Jackson, he is so, so smart, like he is probably
one of the smartest guys in our school, and he doesn't study. But
Annie and Torrie Patterson, they have to study, they're the smartest
girls in our grade, but they have to study.

Kaycee interpreted boys as possessing more natural intelligence. Even smart girls, she claimed, have to study to do well academically. This gendered view, while seeming to accept an inherent gender hierarchy, buoyed her persistence in studying and trying hard to do well in school. In chapter 7, I show how similar interpretations sparked girls' achievement at both Clayton and Woodrow Wilson. Girls did not rest casually on notions that they were smart and could sail through school without effort. Instead, they focused on their demonstrated achievement and used effort as a means of ensuring that achievement.

Kaycee seemingly accomplished femininity in rather conventional ways consistent with the emotional, supportive, and submissive tenets of emphasized femininity. She minimized her academic ability compared to others, especially boys, and she actively sought supportive, caring relationships through the school to protect against family trauma. Yet this very production of femininity, although conventional in many ways, provided a school-focused pathway that encouraged academic success. Based on Kaycee's family background and what she told me about her early problems in school, her educational career should have suffered from a distinct home-based disadvantage (Lareau 2000). But she had been able to overcome this disadvantage. Some of her ability to do so stemmed from personal qualities, but some stemmed from the interactional construction of gender. Femininity in our culture and at Clayton tends to emphasize being forthcoming with emotions and forging relationships as a means of emotional support. This allowed Kaycee to become attached to school and to enjoy it. She interpreted school as a caring, supportive environment because she approached it that way. Kaycee also performed better in school than one might expect, based on her background and her self-deprecating view of her own ability. Here again, femininity provided unexpected tools that facilitated school achievement. Because she lacked confidence in her innate ability, something she interpreted as more common for girls than for boys, she put extra effort into schoolwork. In constructing femininity, Kaycee simultaneously constructed positive school attachment and performance.

Conclusion

The stories of Kevin and Kaycee are emblematic of broader themes I encountered in my research—in particular, the way in which gender composes a pathway of action that individuals use to respond to challenges in their lives. In constructing gender, individuals follow scripts of femininity and masculinity that are deemed socially appropriate. Following such scripts allows them to maintain gender accountability (West and Zimmerman 1987) but also influences how they contend with feelings of shame and approach social institutions such as school.

Both Kevin and Kaycee performed their gender in socially expected ways. Kevin enacted a tough, gritty masculinity; Kaycee exhibited a bubbly, emotive femininity. These enactments of gender meant that they managed their hidden injuries of family background differently. Both students carried distinct but similar scars from this background. Kaycee's self-concept notwithstanding, both students were smart, and both maintained B averages and took upper-level classes. However, they had divergent experiences with school. Kevin had difficulty staying out of trouble. When he sensed that someone had belittled him, he reacted aggressively, through either physical or verbal confrontation. Although I believe Kevin will perform well in high school and attend a two-year college (as was his expressed plan), his behavior in school showed signs of thwarting this progress. School suspensions and misbehavior are important predictors of subsequent high school dropout (Hammond, Linton, Smink, and Drew 2007). For Kaycee, perhaps the emotional turmoil of her family will catch up to her and encumber her academic career. At the time of the interview, however, she had been improving academically and she appeared to be focusing on doing well in school and enrolling in a four-year college. In contrast to Kevin, she had no disciplinary history at the school and was actively involved in school sports and clubs, which serve as protective factors against high school dropout (Hammond et al. 2007). She also developed strong relationships with teachers, which is an important springboard for social mobility (Hardie 2011).

A closer look at the experiences of Kaycee and Kevin reveals hidden injuries not only of family economic and emotional background but also of gender. Kevin asserted masculinity in overtly dominant ways, such as through fighting and boxing. His aggressive and at times indifferent behavior expanded the rift between him and the school. His intelligence and commitment to obtainable life goals may allow him to bridge this rift, but at the time of our interview it was certainly a widening obstacle. Available patterns of feminine practice provided Kaycee with more useful tools to forge a pro-school orientation. She approached school as an opportunity to develop supportive relationships. Femininity did encourage her to disparage her academic skills; but instead of enervating her academic effort, that self-concept actually fueled it. With Kevin and Kaycee we see the outlines of broader patterns of school achievement and attachment, which differ by gender. In the following chapters I examine these patterns more completely, revealing how the construction of gender at both high schools explains the gender gap in academic achievement.

Chapter 4　　　　Too Cool for School

Masculinity and the
Contradictions of Achievement

Donte, a tenth grader at Woodrow Wilson, approached life with effusive optimism. He was relentlessly outgoing—constantly talking and joking with other students and teachers and instantly befriending me early in my fieldwork, even though he hardly knew me. The more I hung out with Donte, the more impressed I became with his energetic, positive demeanor and his ability to insert levity into the most quotidian school routines. When I interviewed him later in my fieldwork, I was further impressed with the surprising depth of his thinking and his buoyant dreams of success, despite growing up with seven other siblings in poor living conditions.[1] Yet Donte's spirit and goals changed when he confronted school. Education did not appear to factor into his plans to become successful in business, and his youthful exuberance chafed against academic exercises required in classrooms. He appeared to be unconcerned with school. Sure, he knew it was *supposed* to be important, but he simply neglected to invest his seemingly boundless energy into things such as reading, completing math homework, and answering questions (seriously) in class. Donte was not alone. After following students at Woodrow Wilson and Clayton through ninth and tenth grades, I found that boys at both schools approached education casually but with a certain contradictory purpose to their casualness. Such practices, which I term *contrived carelessness*, hindered achievement but aided representations of masculinity. In a phrase, many of these boys were simply too cool for school.

When constructing masculinity, boys at both Woodrow Wilson and Clayton interpreted pro-school behavior as inconsistent with or irrelevant to manliness and interpreted much anti-academic behavior as indicative of the power of masculinity. This general statement is, of course, seriously complicated by differences in class, race, and personal choice (not all boys acted in the same way). However, I noted similar discourses at each school that framed manliness as empowered and superior but tended to separate masculinity from high achievement.

Gender and Achievement

When I began my research, I did not know that Clayton and Woodrow Wilson had salient gender gaps; but once I became immersed in the schools, I quickly recognized the importance of gender and noted that girls at both schools appeared to be more academically conscientious than boys were. Although the schools were very different in many ways, the gender educational outcomes were the same: girls, on average, outperformed boys.

At Woodrow Wilson, the discourse regarding gender was overt. In my first visit to the school I met with Mr. Shultz, the school's testing and data coordinator. While we were talking in his office, a polite black girl wearing a pink track suit came in and asked him for information about postsecondary credits, a program in which students could take college courses and receive credit for them. Mr. Shultz gave the girl some papers describing the program, and after she left I asked him about it. He replied that more girls than boys took advantage of the program, adding that girls at the school also graduated and went on to college more regularly. To demonstrate his point, he pulled up the current class rankings on the computer. He told me that, in the senior class that year (2005–2006), eight of the top ten students were girls and that, of the top twenty, only four were boys.

Teachers and other administrators at Woodrow Wilson were aware of this gender discrepancy and were concerned about it. Many attributed the difference to race and culture. Mr. Shultz echoed this view when I asked him about the gender discrepancy, saying, "I think it has a lot to do with culture. The gender gap is biggest among African Americans, and that's true in the top ten. There is a perception among the boys—and it sounds silly—but that school isn't 'cool,' so a lot of it's a cultural thing." Indeed, on the surface it seemed as though this gender difference was peculiar to predominately African American urban schools. Suburban schools proximate to Woodrow Wilson did not show such stark gender differences. For example, one predominately white suburban high school nearby had five boys and five girls in its top ten seniors; another had eight valedictorians—four boys and four girls. This contrasted with class ranking and graduation rates at Woodrow Wilson, which, based on the data

Table 4.1
Class Rank and Graduation Rates by Gender, Woodrow Wilson
High School, 2006–2007

	% of Top 10	% of Top 20	Graduation Rate (%)
Seniors			
Boys	20	25	82
Girls	80	75	89
Sophomores			
Boys	30	25	n/a
Girls	70	75	n/a

SOURCE: School records, 2007.

I collected in the second year of my fieldwork (2006–2007), showed a wide gender gap (see table 4.1). My findings also aligned with data on a national level, which demonstrates that the largest gender gaps in education occur among African Americans (Mead 2006). Such data have impelled researchers and educational practitioners to publicize the plight of black boys in school and devise programs to keep them educationally connected (Delpit [1996] 2006; Ferguson 2000; Noguera 2003; Sewell [1997] 2000).

My research supports some of Mr. Shultz's explanation for gender disparities—in particular, the perception among boys that school-focused behavior is not cool. But my data fail to support the assertions that this perception originates from African American culture. When studying a large urban area, one might conclude that boys' underachievement stems from race because mostly white suburban schools do not have such evident gender gaps. But ironically, this explanation minimizes the role of gender. African American girls share the same culture and live in the same neighborhoods as boys do, so why would they develop different perceptions of education? The explanation also minimizes the potential roles of social class and location. Aren't there white boys who also succumb to perceptions that school is not cool?

I carried these questions to my other research site, Clayton High School. As I have mentioned, while Clayton's economic circumstances were similar to those of Woodrow Wilson, the student body of this small rural school was 98 percent white. In contrast to Woodrow Wilson, Clayton had no overt discourse on gender differences in achievement. Most people there stressed economic factors such as school funding (the district had one of the lowest average property values in the state) and family poverty. According to the first principal, Mr. Abel, many of the students at Clayton struggled in school because they valued manual labor and wanted jobs in fields such as construction,

Table 4.2
Class Rank and Graduation Rates by Gender, Clayton High School,
2006–2007

	% of Top 10	% of Top 20	Graduation Rate
Seniors			
Boys	20	25	81
Girls	80	75	90
Sophomores			
Boys	10	15	n/a
Girls	90	85	n/a

SOURCE: School records, 2007.

which required little education. But because such occupations employ pre-dominately male workers, Mr. Abel implied that boys in particular eschewed education in favor of working-class jobs.

Indeed, as at Woodrow Wilson, boys at Clayton appeared to be uninterested in school. I obtained class rank and graduation rates at Clayton (2006–2007), shown in table 4.2. Based on my observations to that point, I was not surprised to see a gender disparity favoring girls: eight of the top ten in the senior class were girls, and there were just five boys in the top twenty. Remarkably, these figures were nearly identical to those at Woodrow Wilson during the same year, even though Clayton was composed almost entirely of white students. And the senior class of Clayton was not just an anomaly: similar differences appeared in other grades, including the sophomore class, where I focused my observations. Further, I checked with administrators at four schools near Clayton that had similar rural, low-income populations, and all but one reported similarly wide gender differences favoring girls in class rank and graduation.

So why did girls outperform boys? The answer is complex and, as I will show in subsequent chapters, requires unpacking intersecting issues related to class anxiety, racialized experience, and place-based social dynamics. Here, however, I emphasize commonalities of gender experience and expression across the schools, focusing on microlevel processes through which gender difference and inequality were produced in everyday school life (Schwalbe et al. 2000).

Contrived Carelessness: Masculinity and Academic Nonchalance

Contemporary gender theory views masculinity as a socially constructed out-come rather than an internal characteristic (Butler 1999; Messerschmidt,

2000, 2004; Pascoe 2007; West and Zimmerman 1987). From this perspective, boys at Woodrow Wilson and Clayton employed educationally relevant behavior as a vehicle for the construction of masculinity. Hegemonic masculinity was defined slightly differently in each school setting. However, across both schools boys consistently affected an unruffled, carefree attitude toward schoolwork. Girls tended to direct considerable care and effort to academic work. Boys, by contrast, took great pride in their lack of academic care and effort. Their contrived carelessness took the form of a publicly displayed absence of academic diligence and planning. Boys' semi-purposeful flouting of school requirements gained them notoriety but hampered their ability to succeed academically.

"TEST?!"

My field notes document numerous situations in which boys were unprepared or unwilling to learn. Boys at both schools often lacked writing utensils, paper, books, and other required materials , and many seemed surprised to find out about quizzes, tests, or assignments in classes. Boys often joked about their lack of preparation for class. For example, one day early in the second school year of my fieldwork at Woodrow Wilson, I observed a tenth-grade English class taught by Ms. Williams, a young white teacher. I sat in the back of the classroom just behind two African American boys named Rashawn and Jarod. I said hello to them, and they acknowledged me briefly but continued talking to each other about some money Rashawn had won. Rashawn was energetic, excitedly regaling Jarod with the news of his winnings, while Jarod silently smiled back at him. As they talked, Ms. Williams announced, as loudly as her small frame could muster, that she was now going to hand out a vocabulary test.

Rashawn abruptly stopped his conversation to exclaim, "TEST?!" which made Jarod and several others laugh.

Ms. Williams replied seriously, "Yes, we have a test every Friday, remember?"

Seemingly surprised, Rashawn said, "Oh." He then resumed his conversation with Jarod until Ms. Williams came around to pass out his test. Rashawn ignored her when she arrived at his desk, so she said "Rashawn, you ready to go?"

He seemed surprised again and asked, "To the office?"

Jarod laughed, but Ms. Williams seemed to be annoyed. "No, to take the test," she said.

Rashawn replied, "Oh, yeah, I'm ready!" and got out a pencil.

Girls, of course, also forgot assignments and were occasionally disengaged and unprepared during class. However, they did not flaunt their lack of preparation as the boys did. Some boys appeared almost proud of these behaviors, using them to construct an indifferent, non-school–focused persona, as in this example from Clayton, which I captured in my field notes:

> At around 10:15 I go down the hall to Ms. Collins's tenth-grade English class.
>
> Ms. Collins, a soft-spoken, veteran teacher, tells students that they will be working on their writing assignments in class that day.
>
> A boy wearing a red shirt named James is just sitting there in his desk near me, not writing or doing much of anything. Ms. Collins asks him if he needs help getting started. James mentions that he will do it later, but Ms. Collins says, "I don't want you just sitting there doing nothing." James says, "Sure, okay," but he does not have any paper with him. Ms. Collins goes to get him some notebook paper.
>
> Some girls in front of James are working and talking about something they call "writer's hand." One girl says, "I hate writer's hand" as she puts her pen down, rubbing her hand and wrist. James interrupts, asking, "What the heck's writer's hand?" The girl explains that it is when your hand gets sore from writing. James says, "Well, I never write, so I don't have it!" and laughs. He sits there for the remainder of the period with the paper Ms. Collins gave him, looking around the room, but not writing anything.

For boys such as James at Clayton and Rashawn at Woodrow Wilson, this portrayal of disorganization and lack of attention seemed to be purposely produced, similar to Erving Goffman's (1959) notion of *presentation of self*. Goffman argues that people organize their behavior in order to convey a particular self-image and identity to others. James and Rashawn publicly announced their lack of concern for schoolwork. Rashawn did not appear to be troubled about the test he was unprepared for, and James bragged to the girls about how he never writes anything. Both cases represent contrived carelessness: these boys willingly and contentedly projected a semblance of inattention to school.

Contrived carelessness also appeared when boys came to class late and failed to complete class assignments and homework. Even in math classes, where homework was expected virtually every day, girls completed it much more often than boys did, as shown in this excerpt from my field notes at Woodrow Wilson:

> Ms. Gerrard, a quick and stern geometry teacher, warns me that the class I am observing is "kind of crazy." I see a quiet boy from the Spanish class I have just observed and say hi to him. A girl comes in and announces that she has done her homework.

There is one white boy in the class. Ms. Gerrard asks him to get his homework out. He says he doesn't have it.

A black boy comes in late, and Ms. Gerrard says she is marking him tardy. The boy, named De Angelo, says, "I'm not retarded!" Several students laugh. Ms. Gerrard gives him a stern look.

A group of three boys sit in front of me and say hello to me as they come in. None of them has finished his homework. Ms. Gerrard tells one of the boys, "You need to try."

The boy says, "But I did try—I couldn't do it."

Ms. Gerrard says, "Well, try harder." She turns to a portly boy named MarShawn, and says, "You did the first one [problem] right; you need to do the others."

She moves to the other side of the room. A girl named Brittany has no homework. A boy named Tareek, who sleeps for most of the period and who, I later learn, has just returned from a juvenile detention center, says, "I forgot we had it." The other students, the majority of whom are girls, have completed their homework. . . .

Toward the end of class, Ms. Gerrard mentions homework for next class, which Ross, a lanky basketball player, doesn't like the sound of at all. "Ohhhh, we have homework?" he asks with disgust.

Ms. Gerrard says yes.

"Man, it's the weekend!" Ross says.

"You still have it," she replies.

"Well, I ain't doin' it," Ross mumbles.

Observations of boys' tardiness and reluctance to complete schoolwork saturated my field notes from both schools. As the previous example reveals, boys publicly exhibited these behaviors rather than hid them. De Angelo made a joke out of being late, and Ross announced that he was refusing to do homework. Boys derived plenty of humor from this attitude, and their falsely innocent surprise was indeed often funny but did not convey a sense of academic seriousness or preparation.

"GO WITH THE FLOW"

This indifference was shown further in the concern that boys and girls exhibited about schoolwork. Boys in general appeared less troubled than girls were about the necessity of completing assignments on time and coming to class prepared. Many boys put minimal effort into completing assignments thoroughly. For example, I often observed a tenth-grade biology class at Clayton taught by a nice but somewhat taciturn teacher named Mr. Prather. Three students whom I later interviewed, Kevin, Jamie, and Roger, were in the class, along with the notoriously "bad" Bucky Wagner. I sat next to Jamie and Kevin, and they asked what I was studying for my book. I told them I was learning what life is like for high school kids.

Jamie immediately replied, "It sucks!" as she frantically took out her notes to study for an impending test in the class. I told her I could get her out of class sometime for an interview, and she said, "Not this class—I'm failing it!" She began poring over her notes.

Kevin told me he would like to do an interview, and at that point Mr. Prather came around to collect homework. Kevin turned in his; and after Mr. Prather had collected everyone's work he asked Kevin in front of the class what the answer to number 5 was.

Kevin replied loudly, "I don't know!" and the class laughed.

Mr. Prather said, "I thought you did your homework."

Kevin said that he had done some of it but had never finished. Mr. Prather then handed out a test, telling students they could use their book and their notes. Kevin finished his test very quickly without looking at either the book or any notes. He started to talk to me, but I warned him that he should check his answers. He said, "There's no use checking. I know they're wrong." Jamie, meanwhile, checked her answers fastidiously, changing some of them after consulting the book and her notes. After she finished, she drew on the back of her test.

Eventually all the students had finished, and Mr. Prather took the tests and gave the students some free time. After the bell rang, I talked to him about the class. He seemed frustrated and discouraged: "Eleven in that class are failing. They just don't care. It was an open-book quiz, and there were only three seven-out-of-sevens." Even though Jamie told me she was failing the class, Mr. Prather said that she was actually doing fairly well. Kevin, on the other hand, had gotten a four out of seven on the quiz. Mr. Prather said, "He didn't want to check his answers. A lot of them are just happy getting a B or even a C, and they just expect you to leave them alone."

Many boys at both schools were content to put minimal effort into school and receive decent but not exceptional grades. This does not mean that boys saw grades as unimportant and that they resisted school entirely: most did not want to appear stupid. For example, although boys tried to appear uncon-cerned, at times their lack of preparation exposed them in classrooms. Once they had been called out by teachers, many had little prior work to rely on for help in answering questions. Rashawn at Woodrow Wilson, for instance, was also in Ms. Gerrard's geometry class; and one day I observed her ask him a question that he could not answer. When such incidents happened, boys often made jokes or tried to appear unconcerned about not knowing the answer, but this time Rashawn failed to conjure a quick face-saving strategy (Goffman

1959). Instead, he blankly stared ahead at the problem written on the board. Ms. Gerrard, perhaps feeling his potential embarrassment, enjoined him to look back at his notes. Rashawn stared down at the unopened book bag on his desk and then back up at the board. Sensing an opportunity to ease the tension as well as tease Rashawn, Ross yelled, "Yeah, look at the notes you never wrote!" This incited laughter from much of the class, including Rashawn.

In my observations and interviews, boys did not denigrate the attainment of good grades. Similar to Roslyn Arlin Mickelson's (1990) notion of an attitude-achievement paradox, in which students place high value on education yet do not translate this positive attitude into achievement, many boys in my study simply did not do the work required for exemplary performance. When exposed in classrooms for ignorance, as in Rashawn's case, they appeared to be uncomfortable about their lack of diligence. But perhaps because such exposure rarely happened or because, when it did, boys were able to save face by turning their lack of knowledge into a joke, they continued to project a carefree attitude toward schoolwork.

Contrived carelessness was not merely an individual strategy of masculinity. While boys did tend to flaunt their lack of academic concern, they did not enact this performance with an expressed intention of proving their manliness. Instead, it functioned more subtly as a socially embedded expectation for boys' behavior (Risman 2004; Yancey Martin 2003). Other students, and even teachers and administrators, normalized such behavior as simply part of what boys do. For example, Ms. Henderson, the guidance counselor at Clayton, averred, "Girls seem to have more of a plan of what they want to do. Boys are more 'go with the flow.'" As I will demonstrate, boys maintained their casual attitude because the social context of each school defined this pattern of behavior as indicative of masculinity. The "go with the flow" mentality regarding schoolwork represented the distinction as well as the power of manhood.

Academic Behavior and Definitions of Masculinity

ACADEMIC DILIGENCE, MASCULINITY, AND FEMININITY

Both boys and girls associated trying hard in school, especially doing more than what was required, as more common to girls than to boys. For example, one day during Ms. Collins's English class at Clayton, the students were working with partners to construct shadowboxes depicting different scenes from a John Steinbeck novel. Most of the class went to work in the library, but two groups wanted to stay behind and work in the classroom. I agreed to stay with these groups—one with two boys named Jimmy and Robert, and the other with two girls named Kayla and Jessica—while Ms. Collins helped the remainder of the class in the library. Once Ms. Collins had left, Kayla and Jessica worked on their shadowbox while Jimmy and Robert started playing hangman on the board. Once the boys grew bored, they wandered around the room hitting each other on the arm, joking with the girls, and eventually sitting down to talk to me. I asked if they could show me their shadowbox since I thought that they were supposed to be working on it. Jimmy removed it from the top of a cabinet, while Robert explained that it was already finished. Yet they certainly had not worked on it thoroughly: they presented me with a dilapidated plain-brown cardboard box containing some withered figures cut from construction paper. None of it was decorated, which was a requirement of the assignment. I asked the boys why Kayla and Jessica had a much more elaborate and interesting shadowbox. The girls had decorated the entire box, including having pictures cut out of magazines in the background, and they continued to work on it while we were talking. Jimmy and Robert looked at the girls' shadowbox and then back at me, seemingly nonplussed. Eventually Jimmy replied, as if the answer should be evident, "Because—they're girls! That type of stuff is what they're all about!"

Neither Jimmy nor Robert performed well in school, and this example indicates that their lack of school effort was perceived as more consistent with masculinity than femininity. For Jimmy, spending time working on and decorating a shadowbox (which was a requirement of the assignment) was something more appropriate for girls than for boys. Jimmy presented an interesting case because his older sister, a senior at Clayton, performed very well in school and in fact had the fourth-ranked grade-point average in the senior class. Jimmy, by contrast, ranked fifty-third in the sophomore class out of eighty students. Teachers frequently described him as smart but also as someone who refused to apply himself. Clearly, based on his sister's success, observers might assume that Jimmy could have performed much better. But his framing of conscientious effort in school as something more "for girls" perpetuated his underachievement. In defining and distancing himself from femininity, Jimmy (like Kevin in chapter 3) denigrated following academic rules and exerting academic effort. Indeed, Ms. Collins later told me that Jimmy was struggling in the class because he rarely completed any of his assignments thoroughly.

"I GOT LIKE A PHOTOGRAPHIC MEMORY"

As the examples from Jimmy, Rashawn, Kevin, and others reveal, prevailing notions of masculinity discouraged boys from a conscientious approach to schoolwork. Of course, many boys at both schools completed assignments and performed well in school. However, because of social norms for masculinity, even boys who performed better academically had to project an image that they did so without any concerted planning or effort. They had to maintain contrived carelessness. For example, a boy named Preston at Clayton was described by several teachers and students as the "smartest person in the school." Yet Preston only had a 3.15 grade-point average (out of a possible 4.0). He described for me the gender differences in educational behavior at the school:

> Well, it's almost stereotypical for boys around here to not do anything
> and the girls to do stuff. But like everybody is trying to get the guys to
> keep doing their work and get As, but they just sleep! [He laughs.]
> They don't listen, just sleep. The girls—they'll listen, they'll take the
> notes, they'll do well on the tests. And then there are a few people
> like myself who will sleep through class but still hear everything kind
> of [he laughs], take the occasional notes, do my worksheets, ace all the
> tests. [He laughs.] . . . So I mean there are some people who can like
> not really pay much attention and get by.

Preston revealed that the ultimate goal of schoolwork for many boys at Clayton was to just "get by." Further, he framed himself as having a unique ability to perform adequately in school without exerting much effort. This was a common theme for boys at both schools: an insouciant approach to schoolwork coupled with a perception that they possessed superior intellectual capacity.

For example, as I have mentioned, few boys I interviewed reported that they studied or did much work outside of school. When I asked why, several of them said that they did not need to study. Many boys described themselves as having a superior memory, such as Zack at Clayton:

> I have a photographic memory pretty much. I mean it's more for like
> audio type stuff. If a teacher says something about it, I'll be reading it
> on my test, I'll read the question and then I'll remember what the
> teacher said about it. . . . It's kinda unique [laughs].

Zack did perhaps possess a keen memory—at the time of the interview he was one of two boys in the top ten of the sophomore class at Clayton. However, even lower-performing boys gave this explanation for not studying. At Woodrow Wilson I interviewed a boy named Quentin who played football for the school and told me that he struggled to keep his grades up to be eligible for school sports. At the time of the interview he was making Cs, Ds and Fs. Yet Quentin did not perceive studying as a way to improve these grades:

> E. M.: If there's like a test or something like that, do you study for it?
> QUENTIN: Naw, I don't study a lot.

E. M.: And why is that?

QUENTIN: Because I got like a photographic memory. When I read
something I can remember it in my head.

E. M.: Okay, so you don't need to?

QUENTIN: Naw, I don't need to.

But Quentin's perception that he had a photographic memory meant that
he did not study for tests and quizzes, resulting in mediocre to low grades.
Quentin's confidence in his superior memory actually stifled the academic
behavior that could have improved his grades!

"SMART BUT LAZY"

This seemingly unfounded confidence in the ability to perform well in school
without exerting effort did not emerge out of thin air. It stemmed from discourses at both schools surrounding masculinity. Differences emerged in how
students and teachers discussed gender and academically oriented behavior,
which framed girls as more conscientious and boys as naturally smart. In
describing themselves as gifted with innate intelligence, boys merely echoed
these sentiments. Travis at Clayton described academic behavior, but not
intelligence, as a feminine characteristic:

> [Girls are] doin' a lot more studying and more work. Anybody can be
> smart. Anybody can get good grades in school, they just gotta do it.
> Guys . . . are lazy. They don't wanna do anything. They just wanna
> sleep all day, and most of 'em can't wait to get out of the school. Girls,
> they do all the work. I guess if you get the right kinda girl, she'll do all
> your work for you!

As Travis's comment exemplifies, boys' laziness confirmed and reinforced
their sense of superiority. His idea that "the right kinda girl [might] do all your
work for you" parallels hegemonic practices of masculinity in both families
and corporations, where men expect women to take care of their needs
(Risman 2004, Yancey Martin 2003). As in those venues, this dynamic in
school symbolized masculine superiority. Boys sensed that they already had
social power through their gender; they did not have to prove this power by
doing pedantic work. Girls were framed as successful because they worked
hard, not because of their intellectual ability.

As several authors have noted (for example, Williams 1995; Yancey
Martin 2003), women in organizations contribute, often unwittingly, to
unequal gendered patterns. Similarly, in my research, girls thought that they
needed to study but that boys did not. Recall that in chapter 3, Kaycee said

that school comes to boys naturally and that girls need to study more to do well. A girl named Rebecca at Clayton expressed a similar perception:

> I have friends who study all the time, like Jamie [a girl]. And then Preston don't really study. He just gets As on tests and does not even look at his paper! Me and Jamie study, and Chelsie Rankin, and Tracey. . . . Now people like Preston, he don't even have to look at the book and he knows everything! . . . I don't know, Preston, he just freaks me out how he can do that stuff.

Thus, despite the academic dominance of girls at both schools, both boys and girls described boys as especially smart.

This was true of teachers as well (see also Sadker and Sadker 1994). For example, I observed an algebra class at Woodrow Wilson, which, based on class engagement, did not appear to show strong academic differences between boys and girls. But the teacher, Ms. Lee, told me that she found it more difficult to keep the boys focused in class. She said she tried to keep the attention of one boy in particular, Jonathan, by asking him questions in class, explaining that he was "really smart but lazy. He doesn't try that hard." Mr. Terry, another teacher at Woodrow Wilson, was one of many teachers at both schools who described boys as inherently smart but unmotivated:

> There are some boys who seem really smart but just don't do well or don't turn things in. [Mr. Terry mentions the one Latino boy in the class, Carlos, who was answering most of the questions the day before, when they were looking at political cartoons.] He was answering all the questions, and these were like advanced critical-thinking type questions, so he's pretty sharp. But he has an F in here right now, so I just don't know what's going on.

In many cases teachers distinguished between girls, who did their work and boys, who were academically lazy. A teacher at Clayton named Mr. Wolf described Rebecca (whom I have already quoted) as "not the smartest, but she'll make sure she does her work. She'll make sure she does okay on the OGT [the state graduation exam], so I'm not worried about her." He then described a boy named Brent: "He's smart, but doesn't do anything. He may pass the OGT but not the class itself because he doesn't turn anything in and sleeps most of the time." Teachers' descriptions of such boys reflected the boys' own perceptions of masculinity and helped to reinforce them. By accepting and partially expecting a nonchalant attitude, teachers indirectly encouraged boys' behavior. Further, as I will discuss in chapters 5 and 6, both schools lauded the accomplishment of masculinity in nonacademic areas, especially sports.

This is not to say that boys who succeeded academically were uncelebrated, but often their academic success coincided with their sports success or, as I have shown, was framed as the result of superior innate intelligence more than hard work.

At both schools, teachers' and students' discourse on masculinity and achievement reflected Raewyn Connell's (1987) notion of hegemonic masculinity. Natural intelligence, ironically coupled with an expected lack of academic effort, composed a core part of the dominant definitions of masculinity. Boys' confidence in their special ability to get by academically without exerting much effort was tied to a risky impulsiveness that represented manliness. A willingness to take chances has been shown to underscore manly bravery in various contexts, and this bravery is part of what discursively elevates hegemonic masculinity above other masculinities and femininity (Connell and Messerschmidt 2005; Messner 1992). While certainly not involving the physical risk that is often characterized as bravery, academic gambling lent an aura of danger and aloof preeminence, a sense of being above pedantic academic rules and regulations.

On the other hand, one could see the boys not as gamblers but as protectors of a fragile claim to superiority in an educational arena where girls were making inroads and steep gains. In some cases boys did possess the ability to get by academically; but more often, like Jimmy (mentioned previously in the chapter), they found themselves falling further and further behind. Yet their lack of academic effort, while hindering their performance, ironically maintained their sense of superiority. If they had tried hard and had still underperformed, they would clearly have dropped into a lower position; but if they had refused to try hard, they had a safety valve, whether or not they had succeeded. According to Preston, "people who are called quote unquote 'not cool'—they're like the people who will actually try but not do good [in school]." His view echoes research on boys in Britain, who derided boys who worked hard in school as "swots" (Jackson and Dempster 2009). My findings from Clayton and Woodrow Wilson reinforce the notion that cool masculinity can solidify dominance. Academic risk taking and insouciance can be seen as shoring up masculinity under challenging conditions (Kimmel 1996). Thus, boys (with the indirect help of teachers and other students) carved out spaces and strategies in which the dominance of masculinity could be symbolically maintained beyond reproach. Framing oneself as not needing to study was part of the strategy of contrived carelessness that helped insulate boys from any admission of vulnerability and thereby preserve their sense of dominance in the face of challenges to manhood within school.

Rules Are for Girls

Although lack of attention to schoolwork directly impeded boys' academic progress and outcomes, other factors affected their academic careers more indirectly. One concerned their tendency to get into trouble and to demonstrate behavior that openly defied or cleverly manipulated school rules. As research has shown, taking risks and flouting conventions are often interpreted as constituting masculinity (Carter 2005; Ferguson 2000). In my study, boys generally expressed and exhibited disdain for strict rules. However, the schools were saturated with such rules, which tended to place boys at odds with school-sanctioned comportment and activities. For example, I asked Kevin if he ever thought about wrestling for Clayton's school team since he enjoyed boxing and had told me in elaborate detail about how he wrestled with his friends and older family members. He replied, "No, I don't like that many rules. I'd rather be street fighting. . . . They'll let you go at it for a while before they break it up."

Such disregard for rules distanced boys from school. More boys than girls regularly slept or had their heads down on their desks during class, although those behaviors were technically against classroom rules. Teachers also disciplined boys more often than girls. Research shows that boys, especially African American boys and those from lower-income backgrounds, tend to get into trouble frequently in school, whether that trouble is limited to minor reprimands in classrooms or expands to more serious suspensions and expulsions (Sadker and Sadker 1994; Skiba, Michael, Nardo, and Peterson 2002). Table 4.3 shows discipline statistics from Clayton and Woodrow Wilson. At both schools, boys substantially outpaced girls in numbers of disciplinary infractions, including more serious offenses resulting in out of school suspensions or expulsions.

Table 4.3
Disciplinary Occurrences by Gender, Woodrow Wilson and Clayton High Schools, 2006–2007

	Clayton	*Woodrow Wilson*
Boys	77	984
Girls	11	654

SOURCE: Ohio Department of Education, 2008 (http://www.ode.state.oh.us).

NOTE: The difference in discipline counts across the schools stems partially from differences in school size.

Teachers and administrators often singled out boys as problem students. At Clayton, this tendency was more visible than it was at Woodrow Wilson. For example, the room for in-school suspension (ISS) was inside the library and had a large glass window so that anyone in the library could see which students were in ISS—virtually always boys. Similarly, because the principal's office was connected to the main office, one could often see and hear him disciplining students. (Clayton did not have any assistant principals to fulfill this role.) One day, during the second year of my fieldwork at Clayton, I heard the principal at the time, Mr. Thomas, lambasting a boy named Isaac, who had seemed to be well behaved in the classes I had observed and had also appeared to be academically engaged, consistently answering questions during class and apparently genuinely interested in what I did as a professor and in the process of writing a book. Isaac seemed to have some behavior problems, however. I heard Mr. Thomas tell him sarcastically, "Oh, you never do anything. . . . I'm sure everybody in jail didn't do anything either. Don't come in here again. If you show up one more time, you're out!" I observed similar trends at Woodrow Wilson.

Much of the recent literature on boys and discipline emphasizes how categories of race and class shape perceptions of masculinity (Ferguson 2000, Morris 2005). From this perspective, racial- or ethnic-minority and low-income boys tend to be stereotypically perceived as unruly, dangerous, and recalcitrant and disciplined accordingly. I certainly do not deny this perspective: as I will detail later in the book, race and class influenced the perceptions, experiences, and motivations of boys at Clayton and Woodrow Wilson. However, I wish to emphasize here how some boys responded to perceptions that they were dangerous by enacting a tough, defiant masculinity (see also Anderson 1999; Black 2009; MacLeod 1995).

"I DON'T LIKE PEOPLE TELLING ME WHAT TO DO"

Although I observed girls getting into trouble and disobeying teachers, boys more commonly defied teachers in an openly confrontational way. One Clayton student, Travis, had been labeled *unruly* and had actually been placed under house arrest for fighting and insubordination. When I asked Travis why he rebuffed teachers, he responded:

> I just don't like people telling me what to do. It's not that—it's just that
> I don't like people yelling in my face and stuff and that's—they yell at
> me and—I don't know, I just can't stand it. So I say something back
> to 'em and get in trouble, or I just blow up and start punching something
> and walk out of the classroom and then get in trouble, so it don't
> matter where I go. But I just don't punch anything anymore 'cause if I
> break it, I'm gonna get in more trouble, so I just yell back at 'em.

Boys such as Travis found it difficult to yield to authority and could respond with physical aggression. Although not all boys exhibited this degree of hypermasculinity (Pyke 1996), many confronted teachers both verbally and physically. As my field notes from a social studies class at Woodrow Wilson illustrate, some boys appeared to enjoy challenging teachers:

> The class is doing presentations on their projects. Mr. Sampson, the teacher, starts by trying to get the class focused. The most difficult is a boy named Darrell. He was relatively quiet when I observed the class earlier in the year but now has developed more of a rambunctious streak. He is joking around loudly with some girls, and Mr. Sampson is telling him to be quiet and sit back down at his desk. Judging by his tone, Mr. Sampson seems quite aggravated with Darrell. I suspect there has been something going on there.
>
> Mr. Sampson says, "Sit down now or I'll write you up."
>
> Darrell responds, "C'mon, Sampson—you know we down! You know you're my favorite, ah, English teacher."
>
> Mr. Sampson says, "Whatever, Darrell." He tells the first group to go up and do its presentation.
>
> The first group consists of Darrell, a tall girl named Shamika, and two other girls who have African accents. Their project is about the 1980s in the United States. Shamika describes aspects of popular culture then. Darrell goes next and basically makes a joke of the whole thing. I suspect, however, that he is actually nervous about getting up in front of people. He stands at the back of the group and was the last one to go in front of the room. He is not as polished in his speaking as Shamika is and makes little jokes such as "And that's how it was back in the day!" His portion lasts only a matter of seconds and much of it just repeats what Shamika has already said. Two girls sitting in front at the opposite end of the room from me think he is hilarious, though, and laugh at him enthusiastically.
>
> After this group finishes, Mr. Sampson moves the girls who were laughing to the other side of the room. They continue to laugh at Darrell after he sits down, and Mr. Sampson says with considerable contempt, "Darrell, you're this close to getting sent out of here."
>
> . . . The groups finish, and Mr. Sampson sums up the presentations for the class. He says they were good overall but adds, "It's important when you're doing a presentation to be professional about it. Don't just get up there to make jokes and clown around."
>
> Darrell says, "I wonder who was doing that?" The girls laugh hysterically. (I chuckle too.) There are no more presentations, so there is time for the class to hang out. Darrell is yelling across the room, so Mr. Sampson walks over to tell him to be quiet. Instead of

complying, Darrell suddenly stands up and faces Mr. Sampson
directly. Mr. Sampson is much taller and he just stares down at
Darrell but seems somewhat surprised by this maneuver. Darrell sits
down laughing and says, "You got scared when I stood up Sampson—I
saw that!"

Mr. Sampson walks over to his desk and says, "Yeah, I'm shaking
in my boots." Darrell continues to chuckle.

After class Mr. Sampson tells me that Darrell has been a "big
problem" recently. He says part of it is because "those girls laugh at
him all the time, which just gets him going."

In other words, because Darrell received the girls' recognition and encouragement for disobeying school rules, his behavior became as a way to portray a
desirable, heterosexual masculinity.

Even high-achieving boys often accomplished their masculinity in a
rebellious way, but for them such actions were often more benign. Boys in
Advanced Placement classes, for example, often played the role of class clown.
Compared with boys in lower-level classes, they did so with more aplomb,
perhaps because they could draw on their cultural capital (Bourdieu 1986;
Bourdieu and Passeron 1977). Sometimes the strategy actually endeared them
to teachers. For example, I observed an Advanced Placement science class at
Woodrow Wilson in which boys chided the teacher, Ms. Murphy, an eccen-
tric, gray-haired woman, with impunity. Under the dim lighting of an ancient
overhead projector, Ms. Murphy led the class in a discussion of an ecosystem.
She asked the class to name something that feeds on trash. A boy named
Kamani, who was sitting in the middle of the room, shouted, "Daniel!" (the
name of another boy in the class), which made everyone laugh.

Ms. Murphy waited for everyone to quiet down and then looked at
Kamani, saying simply, "Kamani. Stop." She then continued the lesson, using
the analogy of working for a paycheck.

Kamani interrupted her to interject, "What's a paycheck?" The class
laughed uproariously again.

This time Ms. Murphy ignored him and continued with her paycheck
analogy: "They take things out like taxes, insurance—" Blake, a long-haired
boy who sat in the front of the room, picked up Kamani's lead and added
"child support" with approving laughter from the class.

Ms. Murphy then asked a series of questions about carbon in the air,
which were answered by Daniel and a girl named Shana. Daniel then
mentioned global warming, which triggered Ms. Murphy to lament the rising
price of gas.

"I'm walking to school!" Kamani shouted.

Ms. Murphy then digressed to talk to the class about how people should walk or ride bikes to school. Finally, she realized that the class period was nearly over and attempted to resume the lesson, asking, "What would we plant to put nutrients back in the soil?"

Kamani shouted "Dead animals!" which met with laughter from the class but a deadpan "no" from Ms. Murphy. Thinking quickly, he changed his answer. "Feces!" he yelled. This prompted hysterics from the class but another deadpan facial expression from Ms. Murphy. The bell then cut off further discussion.

When I asked Ms. Murphy about the class, she explained, "They were a little crazy today, I don't know what it was. But they are my best class academically. You can tell when they kid around and stuff. You don't hear the language [profanity], and it's just more silly."

Especially in upper-level classes at both schools, I noticed that students joked freely with teachers. The situation was reminiscent of what Foley (1990) calls *making out games*, in which more favored students are able to distract the teacher from their lesson. Boys such as Kamani appeared to be ringleaders in this process; girls certainly made jokes in class but not nearly to the same degree as the class-clown boys did. These higher-achieving boys got away with more because their behavior did not directly confront authority: it bent rules rather than broke them. But it still brought them social rewards. As with Kamani, clowning placed boys at the center of classroom attention. Such subtle defiance solidified their masculinity by allowing them to cleverly mock and demonstrate disregard of rules and authority.

MAINTAINING SOCIAL MASCULINITY

Both girls and boys saw open defiance as particularly endemic to masculinity. Some, such as Alicia at Woodrow Wilson, suggested that it was more difficult for boys to handle school because they had difficulty following rules:

> It's harder for boys [in school]—they don't like to pay attention, they're too stubborn! And it goes back to that gangster thing. They think, "Oh, well, if I listen, I'm a lose my rep" or something. So they like "Man, get outta here with that," and they try to disrespect their teachers and all that. I heard on my bus this boy was like "This teacher tried to tell me what to do," he was like "I'm a grown dang man, dog, you ain't gonna tell me what to do! I'm eighteen years old, no!" Whatever. I'm like if that's what you want to do with your future, I mean go ahead. It's not me. I know I'm going somewhere in my life. So I think it's harder for boys because they don't like to listen and they're stubborn!

Alicia then told me a story about a boy in one of her classes:

> This one boy, Mr. Adkins started like "Well, get off the computer, step off, you ain't gettin' on the computer now because you lied."
> [The boy] was like "I ain't lie, I ain't lie!"
> [Mr. Adkins] was like "Yeah, you did lie."
> He was like "No, I didn't."
> [Mr. Adkins] was like "You better back down, you better back down," or whatever.
> And he was like "I'm not backin' down for nobody."
> Then [Mr. Adkins] was like "Well, you can just leave," so he left, and I don't know what happened after that. So boys are just stubborn.

According to Alicia, it was common for boys to defy their teachers because complying could harm their reputation and their masculinity. For instance, the boy who considered himself a "grown dang man" cast the accomplishment of masculinity as inconsistent with school compliance. As in Alicia's story of the boy who refused to back down, choosing instead to get into more serious trouble, many boys responded defensively when teachers directly confronted them. We saw similar reactions from Kevin in chapter 3, behavior that further detached him from school but bolstered perceptions of his toughness.

Students and teachers at both schools typically described such behavior as emanating from something inside boys: a natural essence or a personality trait. But as Alicia makes clear, boys flouted rules because following them might harm their reputation. This behavior was enacted by boys, and expected by others, as part of the accomplishment of masculinity. Breaking or bending rules demonstrated the confidence, toughness, and independence associated with masculine power (see Schrock and Schwalbe 2009). Indeed, boys received social rewards for doing so. Girls giggled approvingly at boys who made jokes in class at the teacher's expense. Other boys respected tough boys who refused to bow to authority. Boys did not uncontrollably display this behavior; they willfully enacted it within a social context that rewarded and expected it as part of manliness.

My interview at Woodrow Wilson with Corie (whom I introduced in chapter 2) made this performance of masculinity explicit. Corie, a quietly pop-ular boy with long braided hair, had the potential to be a very good student. Both his parents had completed some college courses, although he was living with only his mother at the time of the interview. Corie was probably one of the most thoughtful students I interviewed at either school, yet he struggled with his performance, often skipping school and not completing assignments.

The guidance counselor described him as "very intelligent, but one of those that's feeling the pull of the thug life." Although generally easygoing, Corie could get into trouble and had been suspended for getting into a fight. He thought it was important for boys to maintain a masculine image in school:

> E. M.: Do you think it's easier for girls in school, or is it easier for boys in school—to do well in school and be a good student?
>
> CORIE: It's easier for girls. 'Cause guys, we have to keep up a certain— social masculinity, I guess you could call it—
>
> E. M.: And what does that mean?
>
> CORIE: If I go into class and just sit in the back and be all quiet—you know, away from everybody, just do my work, and not say anything the whole class period—then, you know, I'm not really doing anything for my reputation. . . . And so, I mean, like in order to keep up our social masculinity, we would have to, you know, get smart with a teacher, or skip a class, or not come to school, you know, just like do things that show people like, you know, we are cool, quote unquote—
>
> E. M.: And by doing that, you're being masculine?
>
> CORIE: Yeah.

In this interview, Corie cast masculinity as a public performance, noting that rule breaking must be enacted under the gaze of others if one is to effectively accomplish "social masculinity." As he made clear, noncompliance did not stem from the biological or socialized impulsiveness of boys but composed a strategy of action that facilitated their accomplishment of masculinity. Consistent with a "doing gender" framework (West and Zimmerman 1987), many boys at both schools employed anti-academic behavior not because it percolated from them uncontrollably but because it was defined and used as a resource to represent manliness.

Monitoring Masculinity

"EVERYTHING YOU SAY SOUNDS GAY!"

Contrived carelessness and other masculine practices were group-level gender constructions. The social contexts of the schools played a profound role in defining the boundaries of gender-appropriate practice by monitoring masculinity. For example, policing masculinity through insults reinforced the enactment of non-school–oriented masculinity. As Donna Eder, Catherine Evans, and Stephen Parker (1997) find, adolescents often use insults to configure and maintain status boundaries. For boys, these insults tend to have homophobic and effeminate overtones, such as "pussy," "fag," "gay," or "queer" (Eder et al. 1997; Pascoe 2007). Although the terms are certainly homophobic, Pascoe (2007) argues that they ultimately represent a feminized male, something boys tend to interpret as the lowest embodiment of masculinity. Thus, they direct such epithets at each other to shore up and define their masculinity as different from and superior to femininity.

While this discourse on feminized, lower-status masculinity was important in the everyday construction of gender, I found that it also occurred through academics. Academically oriented behavior tended to be seen as unmasculine. Recall the field note in which Jimmy at Clayton depicted working meticulously on a project as something common to girls. Soon after that remark, he noted that, for boys, exhibiting similar behavior could compromise manliness:

> At this point the other kids from the class come into the room, led by a boy named Connor in a wrestling letter jacket. He is carrying his shadowbox project. The project is not as elaborate as Kayla and Jessica's but does have some cutout paper decorations over the front. Jimmy immediately points at the project, laughs boisterously, and says to Connor, "You're gay!" Connor tells him to shut up.

As I have discussed, boys who succeeded because of so-called natural intelligence were seen as acceptably masculine. However, if they succeeded because they were careful, organized, and committed to schoolwork, their masculinity was called into question. Boys perceived as nerdy—often those who put effort into schoolwork and were involved in school activities—were likely to be called "gay" or "pussies."

> E. M.: Are there any students here that are considered to be like nerds?
> REBECCA: Yeah. [She laughs.] Well, kinda. Like Tom Jackson—they kind of call him names. Um, that's because he hangs out with a whole bunch of girls so—we're kinda worried about him, but—
> E. M.: So there's some concern that he—?
> REBECCA: Might be gay, yeah!

Rebecca went on to describe how boys made fun of Tom for being gay, especially after he played the flute at a school assembly. Tom was a member of the school band and had the highest class rank of any boy in the sophomore class at Clayton. As Rebecca made clear, peers scrutinized the masculinity and sexuality of boys who, like Tom, performed well academically, hung out with girls, and were involved in non-sports–related school activities such as band. This pressure compelled many to avoid exhibiting academically oriented behavior or, if they did, to shore up and display their masculinity in other ways, such as through sports and fighting, which I will discuss in subsequent chapters.

Boys at Clayton were particularly prone to viewing effort directed toward high achievement as negative and feminized, as the following excerpt from my fields notes shows. In this instance, I was hanging out in English class with Kevin and his friends Roger and Warren, helping them with a ballad they were writing on a topic of their choice.

> Kevin has decided to write about boxing. He says his story will be about fighters who "got beat." I ask if he can mix it up a little, like think about if one fighter was losing at first and then came back to win. He tells me that this never happened [in the fight he was watching]. Instead, the person who won was the best from the opening bell. I suggest that maybe he can make up the story a little bit to make it more compelling.
>
> Kevin replies, "Naw—I don't want to put in a lot of extra effort like that. I'll just do the basic stuff and get a B. I got an 87 in here," he adds proudly.
>
> Warren chimes in: "Yeah, I hate these pussies who make like an A minus and then they whine about it."
>
> Kevin says, "Yeah, it's like 'Why do you care? Why does it have to be better?' Nothin' wrong with a normal grade!"

Both Kevin and Warren preferred to put minimal effort into school. Kevin even associated getting higher grades with trying to be better than necessary, suggesting his cynicism about high achievement, which Karolyn Tyson, William Darity, and Domini Castellino (2005) also observed among low-income rural white students. But the boys' expression of resistance to high achievement was also gendered; when Warren described academic strivers as "pussies," he evoked the specter of a feminized male (Pascoe 2007). In his view, academic striving reflected a concerted, conscientious interest in high achievement, something that compromised the masculinity that boys worked to cultivate.

Boys did not necessarily see good grades as inconsistent with masculinity, but they did see academic behavior and striving as inconsistent. Indeed, as I have mentioned, students at both schools expressed a fondness and respect for high achievement. Although some commentators suggest that African American students, especially boys, resist high achievement, interpreting it as "acting white," I found little evidence that boys at either school purposely rejected achievement.[2] However, they did criticize the school-oriented focus and behaviors that tend to result in higher achievement. Boys who remained attentive in class, assiduously followed school rules, admittedly studied, and prepared academically were most likely to be called "gay."

At Woodrow Wilson, for example, I met a boy named Abdi, whose family had emigrated from Somalia. A lanky boy with glasses, Abdi tried hard to fit in with his African American peers, even trying to use the same cool jargon and speech cadences. However, he spoke with a slight accent, which distanced him from peers. This distance was exacerbated by his overt interest in his schoolwork, which, as I have noted, was not common for boys at Woodrow Wilson. As my field notes show, Abdi's "proper" style of speech and behavior prompted teasing:

> As I am coming into [Mr. Sampson's social studies classroom], some boys, including a Latino boy named Ernesto and an African American boy named Kalin, are throwing a girl's purse around. She is trying to get it back while the boys laugh. She seems somewhat upset but is laughing as well. A desk is knocked over in front of me in the process, and I help her put it back up.
>
> I say hello to Abdi, a Somali boy I have seen before and who remembers me, and a girl named Riana who sits in front of me. . . .
>
> Kalin turn around and starts making fun of Abdi. "You are so gay!" he says. Abdi tries to ignore him. Ernesto again tries to snatch the same girl's purse. "Stop!" she yells. . . .
>
> After some review, Mr. Sampson hands out a vocabulary worksheet. Abdi finishes his sheet very quickly—the first in the class. Mr. Sampson comes over to check it and says that a couple of the answers are wrong. Abdi frowns and then looks the sheet over again, changing the answers.
>
> Meanwhile, Ernesto announces that he is finished. Mr. Sampson looks it over and says, "Perfect," giving him back the sheet.
>
> Kalin protests, saying to Ernesto, "You used your notes, fool!"
>
> Ernesto puts his hands up and says, "What notes?" implying that he hasn't taken any notes. And indeed, there is nothing on his desk. Kalin seems to accept this and leaves him alone.
>
> The girl with the purse turns around and asks Abdi for one of the answers. The other students gradually finish.
>
> The kids then have some free time to hang out. Students in the group in front of me are throwing a used Juicy Fruit gum wrapper at each other. The girl with the purse throws it at one of the boys, but it ricochets off a desk and hits me on the leg. This causes a great uproar among the kids. The girl says, "I'm sorry, I was throwing it at him," pointing to one of the boys. I tell her that I'm not exactly injured, but she seems slightly embarrassed.
>
> Abdi talks about the gum package to someone and says, "You be lickin' it."
>
> Kalin laughs hysterically at this and says, "That sounds so gay— 'you be lickin' it!' Everything you say sounds gay!"

Kalin teased studious Abdi about being gay but did not taunt Ernesto in the same way, even though Mr. Sampson had openly praised his "perfect" work. The praise did cause Kalin to raise questions, but Ernesto effectively deflected criticism by bragging about not using notes and by having already taken part in physical play with Kalin and other students. Ernesto's active behavior, lack of strict adherence to school rules, and lack of academic diligence solidified his masculinity. He performed masculinity in a way that allowed him to make a high grade but avoid criticism for being effeminate. Abdi, however, who presented a less physical, more academically focused persona, could not evade questions about his manhood.

Boys thus monitored academically oriented behavior and focus as one means to police masculinity. Rebecca explained this connection well: "It's easier for girls because they don't get made fun of if they make good grades. Well, I don't know about boys [being made fun of for] making good grades, but if they see these boys studyin' up all the time, then they think different of them. If they're not all out runnin' and playin' football instead of here in the library readin', then they look at them different sometimes." Her perspective underscores the role of academically relevant behaviors and the everyday interactive processes through which boys and girls constituted themselves as gendered beings. Although one might be tempted to draw a direct link between sex categories and achievement using a biological or socialization approach, my findings reveal that this link was mediated through behaviors and meanings representing masculinity and femininity. This active production of gender, rather than preexisting differences in academic capacity, resulted in lower academic outcomes for many boys.

Conclusion

Evidence from Woodrow Wilson and Clayton deepens and clarifies our understanding of the academic gender gap. This gap did not emerge from African American culture, biological traits, or discrimination against boys. Instead, the underachievement of boys at both schools stemmed from the contextual construction of masculinity and the relationship of this construction to perceived superiority. This is not to say that other factors might not have played some role. I do not want my argument to be misinterpreted to indicate that these boys—many of whom struggled against the daunting effects of poverty and racism—did not endure serious inequalities that hampered their educational opportunities. However, my task requires explaining why, under the framework of such inequality, girls outpaced boys in educational performance and aspirations. A common persuasive argument for this gap concerns biologically based sex differences (Gurian and Stevens 2005). Higher levels of testosterone might enhance the impulsiveness and rambunctiousness of boys. Their brains might be hardwired in a way that places them at a disadvantage in much of the written and verbal work now required in schools. Although few studies (mine included) possess the data to directly test and isolate the impact of such factors, my data do reveal that such differences, whether they exist or not, would not sufficiently explain the academic gender gap. The importance lies not within the biological categories of male and female but the daily interactional labor that boys and girls conduct to forge masculinity and femininity.

Similarly, on the basis of my findings, I argue against a sex-role socialization explanation of boys' underachievement. As the products of continuing socialization, certainly boys and girls learned slightly different modes of behavior and appreciation. I emphasize, however, that such practices were created, reproduced, and negotiated through continuing interaction and social sanction. A socialization approach suggests that boys defied rules and failed to bring materials to class because they had been taught such behaviors and that this teaching was ingrained as part of their gender identity. I do not deny that socialization is important, but my perspective differs in emphasizing the ongoing process through which such actions are defined as consistent with masculinity and are accomplished not just as difference but as a way of representing masculine power.

In contrast to the notion of distinct gender roles, my data reveal that not all boys (or girls) acted in the same way. What I found instead is that boys and girls actively policed and defined the parameters of behavior that were seen as appropriate to each sex category. Masculinity at the schools was thus in flux, an emergent quality that students and adults actively and continually constituted. First, students—especially other boys—criticized boys who acted beyond the boundaries of what was seen as appropriate masculinity. The school-oriented practices of boys such as Abdi at Woodrow Wilson or Tom at Clayton tended to be interpreted as unmanly and branded with a sexualized epithet such as "gay" or "pussy." Thus, social context, especially the peer culture, held boys accountable for their representations of masculinity (West and Zimmerman 1987). Second, boys received social rewards from girls and other boys that channeled their masculinity in non-school–oriented directions. Behaviors socially associated with being a real man and encompassing the toughness, bravado, and assertiveness of hegemonic masculinity tended to be at odds with school rules and authority. Boys did not enact these behaviors because of inescapable urges. In fact, many specifically employed resistance to authority as a method for demonstrating masculinity, characterizing refusing to submit as an indicator of being a grown man or establishing one's social masculinity. Such behaviors solidified a strong masculine reputation among boys and, especially when conducted in a humorous way, tended to be cheered on by girls. Thus, academic defiance or disinterest composed expedient paths of action that fettered boys in school but enabled their accomplishment of gender.

My findings underscore that the accomplishment of masculinity in these settings was not just about the social creation of gender difference. Instead, this difference was animated by the notion and need to demonstrate masculinity as superiority. In his classic *Learning to Labor*, Paul Willis (1977) describes how a group of working-class boys he calls "the lads" resisted education and wonders why these boys refused to use education as a vehicle for upward mobility. Willis reasons that masculinity played a significant role because the boys' perception of blue-collar (as opposed to academic) work better coincided with the toughness and physical utility they associated with being a man. Similarly, I find that for the boys in my study, the superiority associated with masculinity lured them away from school. Many viewed school-oriented behaviors as feminine and therefore devalued them and granted them lower status. This perception was most apparent in criticism of academic care and striving as something characteristic of being gay or a pussy. Such behaviors, especially when represented by a male body, threatened the perceived superiority of hegemonic practices of masculinity.

This perceived superiority could actually signify itself academically. However, it was accomplished through an association of masculinity with native intelligence instead of academic hard work. Boys used contrived carelessness to present themselves as academically unruffled. They were expected to go with the flow without exhibiting any outward effort, even if they did perform well. Thus, their academic results appeared to reflect innate skills instead of assiduous care and effort, thus anchoring the preeminence of masculinity even if boys did not necessarily obtain good grades. Lower grades could simply indicate that they were "smart but lazy."

This finding supports and expands on previously published research (Jackson and Dempster 2009; Morris 2008). Using data from Great Britain, Jackson and Dempster (2009) provide evidence from several boys in college and the equivalent of U.S. middle school (thirteen- and fourteen-year-olds), who bragged about their ability to perform well in school without serious effort. Thus, contrived carelessness among boys may not be peculiar to Clayton and Woodrow Wilson but may indicate a broader, possibly even global, practice of hegemonic masculinity. Boys with rich resources from cultural capital and wealthy family backgrounds (Bourdieu 1986; Lareau 2000) can enact such strategies and still succeed academically. (Indeed, this even serves to naturalize their success.) Most boys in my research, however, had few such resources to help them succeed. Contrived carelessness and the presumed power of masculinity had grave side effects for boys at Clayton and Woodrow Wilson.

When bending or breaking school rules, boys exhibited a lack of concern for school prescriptions and authority that elevated them above the system. Many fancied themselves as independent, rebel critics who resisted compliance and submission. Their refusal to subordinate themselves gave them a sense of power. But even the clever, artful, rule-bending boys perceived that they were smarter than the system and could circumvent school rules or the need to study while still getting by. Flouting or manipulating school rules gave boys an additional pathway to demonstrate masculinity, along with a powerful projection of independence. This academic nonchalance parallels Patricia Yancey Martin's (2003) findings in the corporate workplace, where women perceive that men often spend time socializing instead of doing actual work but maintain advantages over women precisely because of their socializing and casual approach. In presenting themselves as academically unconcerned, boys at Woodrow Wilson and Clayton took a similar approach to masculinity, one that gave them a veneer of informal control and superiority. However, in contrast to powerful men in corporate offices, the boys in my research ultimately suffered for following this masculine script because it fettered their academic efforts.

Boys did not engage in such practices constantly and uniformly. Rather, these practices were construed as hegemonic and therefore shaped a particular discursive project of what comprised real masculinity. This project should not be seen as a fixed character type indicative of a majority of boys at the school but as a set of practices that boys enlisted situationally. Sometimes such patterns were taken for granted as "what boys do" (Yancey Martin 2003). At other times, boys enlisted more overt manhood acts (Schrock and Schwalbe 2009) that asserted masculinity as a claim to power. As Corie explained, he might occasionally have to exhibit defiance to authority to reestablish his "social masculinity." Boys used these social tools to construct masculinity instead of seeing masculinity as an inherent, personality type (Pascoe 2007). Thus, as a situated outcome of social practice, gender was fluid and variable. This fluidity also explains why a larger gender gap emerges in schools such as Clayton and Woodrow Wilson than it does in wealthier schools: masculinity may be defined and achieved differently and produce different impacts depending on the context, especially in response to a sense of powerlessness.

Chapter 5   Redowrocks and Rutters

Rural Masculinity and Class Anxiety

WHEN COMPARED TO GIRLS, boys at both Woodrow Wilson and Clayton affected a more casual approach to schoolwork, resulting in less academic diligence and lower performance. This contrived carelessness was a way of doing masculinity, a response to perceptions that anti-school performances represented masculine power and independence. In this chapter I look deeper into why masculinity acquired such connotations and patterns of action, focusing on the rural context of Clayton. Theories of doing gender and hegemonic masculinity are contextually based; so to understand such processes in school, we must learn more about the settings in which masculinities and femininities evolve and how they intersect with other modes of difference and inequality. According to Connell and Messerschmidt (2005), hegemonic masculinity should be understood as locally situated and "embedded in specific social environments" (839). At Clayton, rurality, economic restructuring, and the exigent demands of achieving a respectable social-class position molded local definitions of masculinity and scripts for masculine performance.

The local circumstances affecting masculinity and education became apparent to me on one rainy day during the second year of my fieldwork at Clayton. As the guidance counselor, Ms. Henderson, and I sat in her office talking, she had to interrupt our conversation to take a phone call. While she was on the phone, Tim, a dark-haired boy wearing a brown sweatshirt, came in and sat next to me. I had not had much contact with Tim during my research, but he seemed to be nice and quiet. I asked why he was seeing the counselor, and he said that he needed to change his schedule to get out of Spanish class. "It's too hard," he complained. "I don't know what's going on."

I told him that I thought students needed at least two years of foreign language.

He replied, "Yeah, my sister said that you need that to go to college, but not to graduate. I just can't handle [Spanish] right now."

Ms. Henderson finished her phone conversation and asked Tim why he was there. He said he wanted to transfer out of Spanish. She asked him directly if he wanted to go to college.

"Maybe one day," he replied plaintively.

Ms. Henderson informed him that he would need to complete Spanish if he wanted to go to college.

Tim replied, looking down, "Yeah, I know, but maybe I can take it later."

Ms. Henderson accepted that decision and asked Tim what other class he would like to take.

He lifted up his head and immediately replied, "Woodworking." Ms. Henderson switched him into the woodworking course.

At the risk of hyperbole, I venture to say that this one brief encounter may have altered Tim's life. Perhaps he will eventually try his luck with Spanish and go to college, but at the time he appeared far more interested in taking woodworking, a class he would undoubtedly enjoy but that would not give him the credits he needed to pursue a degree after high school. After Tim left, I asked Ms. Henderson about his decision. She said that such decisions were typical among boys in the area: "Around here, a lot of boys see their fathers or uncles doing trades, and they want to do that. A lot of boys are more tied to the family and the area and don't want to leave. The girls are more willing to get out."

What Tim's experience and Ms. Henderson's words showed, I eventually realized, was the definition and persistence of local hegemonic masculinity at Clayton. Boys were connected to manual labor and the families and community that historically revolved around such labor because it was defined as crucial to manhood and represented the strength of masculinity.[1] In a largely working-class, coal-mining boomtown, being a man meant demonstrating a capacity for arduous and dangerous physical labor. And as in other coal-mining areas, class relations through the mining industry promoted gender relations that privileged male labor power and established the economic dominance of men (Yarrow 1985).

Of course, Clayton had evolved considerably since the heyday of the coal industry and, as I have mentioned, saw this industry evaporate in the late 1980s.

This change created complex and shifting definitions of both masculinity and femininity. The working-class bedrock that had established the strength of many men in the community eroded, leaving behind class-based uncertainty. Teenagers at Clayton did not think in such socioeconomic terms, but they did think about future employment and experience the manifestations of economic limits in their families, community, and peer groups. In the face of such class-based anxiety, many of the basic sensibilities associated with being a man, such as demonstrating physical vitality and toughness, working with one's hands, valuing common sense, and being plainspoken, remained intact. While boys, girls, and adults continued to associate such attributes with masculinity, none of those attributes aligned well with schoolwork. The same boys who jumped at the opportunity to saw wood in woodworking class wilted listlessly when completing vocabulary worksheets in Spanish.

In the peer culture, boys located masculinity within class-inflected parameters, which appeared through social identities such as *redneck, fighter, prep,* and the pariah category known as *rutter.* In chapter 2, I introduced some of these identities and explained how they were motivated by attempts to maintain local respectability. Here I more closely examine how they animated local constructions of class-based masculinities and how such constructions often diverged from academic interests. In addition, I note ways in which the school organization helped establish a gender regime at Clayton that defined multiple forms of masculinity in a hierarchy (Connell 1996).

Gender, Work, and Power in the Community

When I told teachers at Clayton about my interest in student gender differences, many described girls' high academic performance as ironic because they perceived the community (and most of the teachers lived in the community) as traditional and patriarchal. According to a math teacher named Mr. Clark, "overall I'd say there are more girls excelling [in math]. That's really interesting because in this community—and this is just my perception because I'm not from here—but in this community my perception is that male chauvinism runs rampant, so you wouldn't expect the females to do so well." When I asked Mr. Cale, an English teacher, if he saw any gender differences among the students, his eyes brightened and he replied:

> The interesting thing is, there is a very traditional system around
> here. The male is definitely seen as in charge. He is the head of the
> household, he makes all the decisions, pays the bills and is supposed
> to be the provider, and women are supposed to defer to him. This

place is in some ways like stepping back fifty years. I've seen it in parent-teacher conferences. The man will talk and the woman won't say anything—she'll just sit back and nod and look concerned, but will let him take charge. The men are very controlling. And there are a lot of very traditional ideas about what men are supposed to be like—in charge, strong, head of household.

The patriarchal views described by teachers were also described, and seemingly replicated, by boys. Boys and girls perceived family roles differently. Boys tended to see the man as the primary leader and provider within the family (although all of the girls I interviewed thought male and female householders should be equal). A boy named Zack expressed his perceptions in an interview:

> E. M: Do you think the man should be the main provider for the family?
> ZACK: Oh, yeah! I think it's just kinda stupid how girls have to go to work. It happens a lot around here. You have it so the girls have to go to work. I don't like that.
> E. M: Okay, so you think it's kind of a problem that that has to happen?
> ZACK: Yeah.
> E. M.: And that happens a lot around here?
> ZACK: Happens quite a bit. Most of the time it happens around here, it's not because it has to happen. It's because people—the guys are too lazy. We got a lotta lazy people in our community.

Like other boys I interviewed, Zack affirmed his belief in the traditional male role of breadwinner, but he added a unique twist: he indicted men in the community as being too lazy to fulfill that role properly. Zack was one of the highest-performing boys in his grade, and his interpretation of local problems in family life appeared to have provoked him to work hard in school to obtain a good job (which he intended to do by going to college and joining the military). Many other boys, however, did not see this same connection and continued to eschew academics. For example, I interviewed a boy named Brent who slept through his classes, often got into trouble, and had repeated ninth grade. Although he had little interest in education, he nonetheless thought that the man should be the main provider for the family: "The way I see it, the man should support the women in child care with the income." I asked him if he had ever thought about what he would do if he could not be the primary breadwinner. He would not accept this as a possibility, replying, "I'd have to survive. You gotta manage one way or another."

Girls, on the other hand, disagreed with traditional man-as-provider family roles. A girl named Lyndsie sought empowerment through economic self-sufficiency:

> E. M.: Do you think that the man should be the main provider for the family?
>
> LYNDSIE: It should be like equal. I mean, because I would never want to just stay at home with the kids. Not that—I mean, I love kids and I want kids, but I'd want to work and feel like if I needed to get something I wouldn't have to go to my husband and be like "Oh, I need money." Like I would have money myself that I would make. But—no, I think it should be equal.

As Lyndsie made clear, earning an equal income could be, for girls, a path to empowerment and self-reliance. With relatively good-paying, coal-based jobs, men had once been able to be the main providers for the family even without much education, but those jobs no longer existed in Clayton. Girls appeared to have adapted to that change by focusing on educational success as a route to a good occupation. Some boys, such as Zack, also followed this path, casting laziness and inability to support one's family as the true failure of masculinity. Many boys such as Brent, however, still adhered to a sense of masculine entitlement that centered in industrial labor and familial economic power, and they continued to take little interest in school.

Academic Behavior, Physical Attributes, and Masculinity

I suggest that few boys saw education as a means to economic success because local definitions of masculinity centered not necessarily on economic results of labor but on men's *labor power*—their physical capacity and vitality, which represented the more basic power of manhood. Especially in rural areas, economic mobility (which typically requires moving away from the area) is not necessarily valued (Corbett 2007; DeYoung 1995). Instead, rural communities tend to emphasize bonds to place (which includes the local community and the natural environment) as well as interest in hard "honest" work (Campbell, Bell, and Finney 2006; Corbett 2007; DeYoung 1995; Sherman 2006). This connection to place and to certain forms of work that partially symbolize *the rural* is also gendered. The association with nature and the physically demanding work revered as foundational to rural communities tend to be seen as male domains and practices (Bye 2009; Campbell et al. 2006). Within such a context, boys and others at Clayton located masculinity primarily within the body and physical forms of ability, power, and resilience. The mines had all closed, but this continuing emphasis reconstituted itself through a number of practices at Clayton.

BOOK SMARTS AND COMMON SENSE

Like Tim, many boys at Clayton preferred vocational rather than academic pursuits, a preference that translated into future aspirations. I obtained surveys regarding plans after graduation, which a guidance counselor had distributed to outgoing seniors in 2006. Of the students who reported that they had no plans for any sort of college, 84 percent were boys and 16 percent were girls. Of those reporting that they planned to attend four-year colleges, 33 percent were boys and 67 percent were girls. Many young men reported an interest in manly blue-collar jobs requiring no college or at most a two-year degree, such as auto mechanics, construction, and loading trucks. Some young men simply reported "no plans" or "nothing" after graduation, although just one young woman reported "no plans" after graduation, and the counselor had written on her survey that she had a young baby.

One reason for girls' and boys' divergent career plans concerned perceptions of the behaviors required in an academic setting. Girls at Clayton were more likely to value or at least tolerate the types of behaviors and attributes that could lead to academic success, while boys eschewed them. Student perceptions of book smarts serves as one example. As I will show in chapter 7, virtually all the girls I interviewed responded that they thought book smarts— that is, the knowledge and competencies gained from books—were important to success.[2] Few boys at Clayton thought that book smarts were as important. Instead, they tended to value common sense and working with their hands. A boy named Robert, who had repeated two grades in school, described both behaviors in our interview:

> E. M.: What is your favorite class?
> ROBERT: I'd have to say woodworking.
> E. M.: And what is it that you like about it?
> ROBERT: I like to work with my hands. We get to do things, not just sit there listening to someone talk the whole time.

To boys such as Robert acquiring book knowledge required boring, inert activities such as reading or "listening to someone talk the whole time." In contrast, he and other boys considered nonacademic, blue-collar work such as woodworking or construction to be more active and enjoyable. An interest in the common, practical knowledge and skills required for such work undergirded this predilection. Robert, for example, emphasized the importance of common sense over book smarts:

> E. M.: Do you think that book smarts are important to be successful?
>
> ROBERT: Book smarts—no. . . . There's other ways—just knowing what you're doing, you don't have to have a lot of book knowledge.
>
> E. M.: So there's other things that you think are more important—like what?
>
> ROBERT: Well, like just common sense. That's just as important. And some people are smart but they don't have common sense.

Brent gave a similar answer, seeing himself as street smart rather than book smart and stating that street smarts are more important:

> BRENT: Actually I have no book smarts. See, I can't comprehend like that. I'm a hands-on person and I have a lot of street smarts. . . . I say street smarts is all you need really.
>
> E. M.: Okay, so street smarts are really more important?
>
> BRENT: Yeah, I say so.
>
> E. M.: Okay, so what are street smarts?
>
> BRENT: Knowing how to do things. It's like common sense pretty much.

Boys often mentioned their fathers when discussing the distinction between book smarts and what they saw as more practical knowledge. Harry, a wiry, enthusiastic, ninth-grade boy, had a father who operated a company that built supercross tracks for racing. I asked him about book smarts:

> HARRY: I never had any success reading a book and getting better at anything! . . . No, books [are] not, reading's not my thing. I mean, I'm a good reader, but it's just time-consuming and I just don't find it relaxing or anything like that.
>
> E. M.: So you think there's ways to be successful basically without—
>
> HARRY: Oh, yeah. My dad never did. I don't know how. [He is] makin' like 25,000 dollars a week. It's just doing what he does and he never read a book, I don't think! [He laughs.]

These examples suggest that boys not only gravitated to manual labor and away from book knowledge because of male role modeling but also because they perceived it to be better, more important, and more useful. Repeatedly in my interviews at Clayton, boys said that they preferred and valued hands-on educational and occupational activity. This was a concerted way to practice and represent masculinity, and a sense of importance motivated this representation.

"GUYS DON'T HAVE TIME TO DO HOMEWORK"

The dismissal of book smarts and academic behavior thus constituted a means through which boys enacted masculinity. Gendered interpretations of academically focused behavior emerged in my interviews, especially by associating girls with studying. Harry told me:

> I think girls have a God-given talent to study! [He laughs.] Personally, I cannot study. I've tried it. And I just cannot sit there for three hours and study. I just can't do it. I've tried—it just gets boring. And I'm not learning anything. Except I do pass my tests somehow. And I just [he laughs], I really do just think girls are meant to study. I can't study though. At all.

I heard similar comments throughout my interviews with boys. Travis said, "Girls go home and just study all night long. Like especially smart girls— that's all they do is study." Such sentiments connected femininity, not masculinity, to academic behavior such as studying. But boys did not dismiss studying simply because they perceived it as feminine; they also perceived it as an unnecessary waste of time. Harry claimed that he did not learn anything from studying and that he still somehow passed his tests. Later in our interview, he added: "I just got more important things to do, I got other things that needs done. . . . I think it takes up way too much time, like you come home and—I mean, I have to pack firewood in the building all day after school, 'cause we have one of those wood burners that heats the house."

For boys such as Harry, doing "more important things" such as loading firewood took priority over homework and studying. But even when boys did not have a specific chore at home they could use as a rationale, they implied that other things were more important than schoolwork. Travis, for example, said, "Guys don't have time to do their homework. . . . They just go home and—always got somethin' to do like weightlifting, or—I ride—I race four-wheelers—I ride a lot and that's pretty much all we do." Several boys at Clayton enjoyed racing four-wheelers, an exciting but risky activity. As Will Courtenay (2006) reports, such risk taking results in much higher rates of injury for men and boys in rural areas but remains popularly consistent with dominant rural masculinity. Such physical activities, along with weightlifting and sports, which many boys mentioned, provided scripts for the local enactment of masculinity. Doing these things constituted and authorized "boys to be boys," while homework and studying could not. Boys did not have more work to do than girls did; they simply chose to emphasize accomplishing the nonacademic chores and activities associated with masculinity. Further, by framing these activities as more important than studying or cultivating book smarts, boys positioned such presumed masculine behaviors as superior to presumed feminine behaviors.

WORKING WITH YOUR HANDS

Boys' fondness for physical, hands-on activity and learning emerged most clearly in the vocational classes I observed. One day, for example, I observed Tim, along with a couple of other boys, in an English class and a biology class before they entered a small-engines class taught in the school's small vocational wing. Tim lethargically endured the English and biology courses, alternating between putting his head down on the desk and glumly staring out the window. In the small-engines class, however, he became a different person. I captured an observation of the class in my field notes:

> There are eighteen kids in the class, three of whom, surprisingly, are girls. Several of the kids are wearing camouflage, including two in camouflage caps. I notice that a large boy near me with dark, shaggy hair already has dirty hands. After a brief discussion, Mr. Russell, the industrial arts teacher, lectures the students on getting all the tools put back in the right place.
>
> Mr. Russell, a tall, brash man, says they can go into the shop next door. As we walk over there, he tells me, "Most of these kids will be asleep and screwing around in other classes, but you see they'll come here and go right to work." Indeed, I notice Tim and some other boys from the biology class I just observed. In biology, Tim was asleep virtually the entire time, and the teacher even made a joke about it at the end. In this class he jumps to put on a smock and eagerly works on repairing motors with a couple of other students.
>
> [After talking to Mr. Russell,] I drift over to a group of two boys putting together a motor. One wears camouflage pants and a baseball shirt, and the other wears a gray, oil-flecked shop smock. I ask the one in the smock if he likes this class, and he says yes. I ask if it is one of his favorites, and he just laughs and nods affirmatively. These boys and most of the others are working quickly and diligently. The exception is a boy with blond, spiky hair wearing ripped jeans with American flag patches. He is floating around the room doing mostly nothing. He plays with the drills, uses a piece of wood as a baseball bat, and tries to disrupt the other boys' attempts to fix the motors. At one point he comes near me and slams a hammer down hard on a repair manual sitting on the table, laughing at a couple of boys who were startled by it.
>
> The only other students that are not in the shop working are, interestingly, the three girls. They are in another room near the

classroom, either working on something else or not doing anything.
I ask Mr. Russell about this. He says, "Oh, well, they don't have their
team leader here today. [Each group is assigned a student leader.]
Usually, they'd be in here in their own group working away."
Mr. Russell, though, makes no effort to help the girls and incorporate
them into the class. Instead, he simply leaves them to talk quietly in
the other room. [A large window allows visibility into the adjoining
classroom.]

As this field note shows, vocational courses such as small-engines and
woodworking classes (taught in the same location by the same teacher)
engaged many of the boys who torpidly slogged through academic classes such
as biology. They seemed to find new life and focused energy in the familiar
space of hands-on shop classes. The field note also demonstrates that industrial
arts classes were a definitively masculine space. This shop class actually had
more girls than most did, but the girls congregated in a separate group and on
this occasion did not do any classwork. As several authors have found,
although schools are ostensibly gender-neutral, they implicitly encourage the
creation of gendered spaces that facilitate the production of stereotypical
gender practices (Connell 1996; Pascoe 2007; Thorne 1993). Often, school
officials either encourage or fail to discourage such gender divisions. This was
the case with Mr. Russell, who neglected to lead the girls in class activity and
had a gendered view of vocational education in general, telling me, "We need
to have them drop out and get a job early if they want, especially the boys.
That's what they do in other countries."

Indeed, boys appeared to gravitate toward hands-on and vocational
education largely because such pursuits were defined, even within the school,
as manly. Further, in the face of deindustrialization and movement toward
a service-based economy, such interests actually seemed to represent a rural,
working-class, protest masculinity (Connell and Messerschmidt 2005).
Vocational education is often interpreted as an anachronistic relic of a moribund industrial era. The principal during the first year of my fieldwork at
Clayton, Mr. Abel, partially evinced this view. While he saw the importance
of hands-on education, he also emphasized the importance of matching it with
academic credentials: "What if you want to be a manager one day? You can't
be sixty-five years old, breaking your back doing construction. You need some
school to be a manager." As I discussed in chapter 4, people at both schools
associated masculinity with rule defiance and resistance. The loud, mechanical,
physically active space of the shop allowed boys a masculine space for resistance to the effete, stilted demands of academic classes, which through the
advent of state-mandated assessment testing, had expanded in magnitude.

This sense that "working with your hands" functioned in opposition to the seemingly feckless, elitist world of academics could also be seen in interpretations of speech. Many boys valued being plainspoken, which meant using simple, direct speech. Some appeared to enact the stoic, laconic image that often symbolizes rural masculinity (Campbell et al. 2006). In fact, this image even affected my ability to talk to boys and get interviews. One boy, for example, declined to interview with me, explaining, "No—I'm not much of a talker." *Plainspoken* did not really mean being silent, however; it meant being direct and unequivocal. Brent, for example, said, "I speak my mind. Whatever is on my mind I'll tell you, you know? I'm not afraid of telling people what I think." Being plainspoken also implied an interest in action over speech. The shop teacher, Mr. Russell, appeared to exemplify this direct speech and action. Several boys in my interviews said that he was their favorite teacher, and they looked up to him, describing him as big and bold, commenting that he would often cuss in class. To Robert, Mr. Russell's capacity for direct action and anger made him more revered: "He can get mad, though. He gets real mad if we don't use goggles with the band saw. I've seen him smash somebody's project for doing that one time. And I've seen him throw a lawnmower across the room one time. It was cool! . . . You know you better not mess with him!" Even the teacher of shop classes represented a tough, aggressive, physical masculinity that many boys sought to emulate, reinforcing such classes as a powerfully masculine space and such behaviors as indicative of manliness.

Sports, Toughness, and School-Centralized Masculinity

Of course, not all boys at Clayton showed an interest in shop classes and manual labor. Thus, any assertion that they resisted schoolwork simply because they valued manual labor would be an attractively facile explanation. A similar dynamic has been shown elsewhere, notably in Paul Willis's (1977) research in Great Britain. Willis's argument rested on the immediate availability of manufacturing jobs that required little education. As I have mentioned, however, Clayton had a dearth of such jobs, which points to the importance of a more nebulous, more complex legacy of masculine power based on the demonstration of physical vitality. This vitality, as well as a capacity for risk taking and pragmatically intelligent know-how, constituted local hegemonic masculinity at Clayton. Boys coordinated their behavior and interests to represent this masculinity through several different strategies and practices. One of the most prominent and potentially useful was participation in school sports.

Sports often constitute a school-sanctioned pathway for demonstrating the power of masculinity (Eder, Evans, and Parker 1997; Messner 2002), and this was certainly true at Clayton. Sports appeared to have a deep community meaning, which enhanced their importance along with the importance of this representation of masculinity. As I have mentioned, I lived close to the school in an adjacent town during my fieldwork. People where I lived who had children participating in sports would often joke about how competitive people at Clayton were about even primary school sports. High school sports were a serious business indeed. People of all ages flocked to high school sporting events, especially football, which, like Douglas Foley's (1990) "great American football ritual," was a popular community experience (28). At one game I attended, two gray-haired women wearing school sweatshirts sat in the front row of the stadium and screamed themselves hoarse by the end of the game. They directed their comments not at the referees so much as at Clayton's own players. "They're just arm tackling!" one of the women complained. "Are you afraid of gettin' hit?"

Clayton's success in sports countered the regional stigma attached to the school. As I discussed in chapter 2, many outsiders and insiders interpreted both the community and the high school as backward and deviant. Sports, especially football, provided a sense of pride in the face of such stigmatization. A girl named Emily said, "We may not have some of the most nice [she laughs] rumors about us, but I think Clayton's a really good school. . . . We have a really good football team!" Sports were more than just an activity; they served a broader school and area function of instilling community pride and accomplishment. As Robert said, "it's more about sports here I guess 'cause they don't have much else."

Within this context, boys who played football could expediently produce a highly revered, powerful masculinity. This masculinity represented not only the physical power and toughness that was locally emphasized but also elevated boys to school and community heroes and carried the school's vehement endorsement. The school institution contributed to the preeminence of sport- and especially football-based masculinity. The first thing one saw when driving onto school grounds was a large board announcing athletic events and including supportive messages for the athletes. Aside from reminders about state-mandated testing, this board rarely displayed non-athletic information. In addition, the inside of the school was saturated with sports imagery. A large trophy case boasting past sporting triumphs occupied a prominent place on a wall immediately across from the school entrance. Both principals during my fieldwork had been former high school football coaches, and they adorned their offices with football and other sports paraphernalia.

To be sure, bulletin boards throughout the school announced and celebrated academic and other non-sports events, but the emphasis on sports, especially football, was unmistakable.

THE HIT STICK

In my observation of both schools, Clayton's hit stick was the most evocative symbol of the hegemonic masculinity achieved through sports. The hit stick was a large paddle festooned in the school colors that was carried around the school by whichever football player had achieved the best hit, or tackle, in practice or a game that week. As if such school visibility were not enough, a large poster documenting that year's hit stick recipients was prominently displayed outside the school's main office. In fact, I first noticed the hit stick when I looked at this poster, which included individual pictures of several different football players holding it. Instead of smiling, these boys snarled back at the camera menacingly, some holding the stick as if they were about to actually attack someone with it.

The hit stick clearly represented the prestige that the school conferred on certain athletic boys as well as the prestige conferred on a certain type of masculinity. Even though only a few boys could actually achieve the hit stick in any given year, it centralized and glorified a tough, athletic masculinity attained through an activity reserved exclusively for boys. Zack, who played baseball for Clayton but not football, criticized the popularity and meanness of many of the school's jocks and preps but still expressed awe over the hit stick:

> ZACK: That's how you get popular here—athletics. If you're good at sports, you get pretty popular.
>
> E. M.: And you would say football is like the big one, the big sport?
>
> ZACK: Yeah. Oh, yeah. We have this thing for football, it's called the hit stick. And whoever gets the hardest hit during the week gets to carry it around school. It's pretty cool. It comes around in football season. It's pretty nice looking too. . . . It's like, it's kinda like the things kings carry around. It's pretty sweet.
>
> E. M.: Like a scepter? [I laugh.]
>
> ZACK: Yeah, except it's about that big. [He measures out several feet with his hands.) It's like white and blue, has a little badge on it, has a little C on it. It's pretty cool.

The hit stick conferred a powerful, kingly status, not just on the particular boys who carried it but on the particular masculinity these boys exemplified. Even outside of football season, the hit stick poster stayed up on the wall to remind everyone of the importance of the tough and violent masculinity it celebrated. Moreover, in the spring, the football team used the Ironman competition to reinforce their school prominence and physically strong masculinity. This competition gave football players "grades" for achieving certain weightlifting and fitness goals in the spring. While the Ironman competition was not as central to school life as the hit stick was, its poster also appeared in a prime location near the main office, and a team coach announced the winners over the school's intercom system. Clayton as a school clearly colluded in asserting the hegemonic status of the physically tough, vigorous masculinity represented by football.

Not only did football help construct hegemonic masculinity, but it also helped subordinate other masculinities. Courtenay (2006, 152), citing the work of Will Fellows (1996), quotes one gay rural man as saying, "I really hated football, but I would try to play because it would make me more of a man." At Clayton, other school-related activities, such as band or academic achievement, simply did not connote the same degree of manliness and sometimes even called masculinity into question.

> TRAVIS: I mean, in this school—it's all about football. Football, football, football. Not band. Band's gay!. . . . The guys [in the band] act different too. They act kinda gay. So that's why they're picked on. But the girls [in the band] ain't really said nothin' to.
>
> E. M.: . . . You said they act kinda gay. Now, does that mean, do you think they're actually gay, or are they just acting in a certain way that kinda—?
>
> TRAVIS: They just don't act normal . . . so [other students] just make fun of them.

While football represented the paragon of hegemonic masculinity, band represented a subordinate and abnormal masculinity (see also Foley 1990).

In addition, boys used the hegemony of football to diminish women's sports. Although many girls at Clayton participated in sports and enjoyed successes similar to the boys', especially in basketball and volleyball, students interpreted girls' sports as being less significant. For example, on one warm spring day toward the end of the school year, I observed a sophomore English class. As the class completed a vocabulary quiz, several students stared longingly out of the windows at the newly green grass. An excitable boy named Warren shouted, "You know what we should do? We should go outside today!"

Zack, who was also in this class, endorsed Warren's suggestion: "Yeah, we should go outside. We could go out there and play football!"

The teacher, Ms. Collins, chuckled and asked, "Why play football?"

A girl named Ashley, who played volleyball for the school, said, "Yeah, why not play volleyball?"

Zack and Warren looked at each other in momentary bemusement. Then Zack quickly replied, "Because—football is a real sport!"

Warren laughed heartily and added, "Yeah, volleyball is gay!" Ms. Collins then cautioned Warren on using "that word" and began going over the group projects, which ended the discussion.

Connell (1995) notes that hegemonic masculinity forms in contradistinction from other masculinities as well as from femininities. Hegemonic masculinity holds status over other masculinities precisely because of its claim to be the most effective means to enact and legitimate the power of masculinity over femininity. Clearly, football had this status at Clayton. Even boys who did not possess the talent to play for the school team (such as Zack and Warren) used the powerful masculinity it represented to achieve and convey a toughness that subordinated those boys who refused to play (such as those in the band) and most girls, who were channeled into and grew to prefer non-contact sports such as volleyball.

The toughness and honor associated with school sports allowed athletic boys to demonstrate masculinity even if they performed well academically. Cole Watson, star quarterback and erstwhile recipient of the hit stick, was actually one of two boys among the top ten students in the senior class. No one made fun of Cole for being "gay." However, this pathway to revered masculinity and high achievement was extremely limited: only select boys had the athletic ability or the financial means to participate in varsity sports. (Athletes were required to purchase much of their own equipment.) Further, aside from Cole, few of the football players excelled academically. For example, the two boys among the top ten students in the sophomore class did not play football. And the boys who participated in sports still approached school with contrived carelessness: students said that football players received decent grades just so they could remain on the football team, often due to special treatment. According to Robert, "the teachers all give them good grades and they get away with more stuff." This should not suggest that teachers necessarily did favor the athletes but that students' perceptions that athletes received good grades without really trying remained consistent with hegemonic notions of masculinity.

Rednecks, Preps, Rutters, and Fighters: Class and Masculinity in the Peer Culture

Class-based anxiety in the economically depressed area of Clayton animated the construction of masculinities and femininities. Particular practices of masculinity within the peer culture of students thus carried class connotations. Such practices did not just forge masculinity but also reflected and enacted social class. Although doing gender and hegemonic masculinity both focus on gender, they emphasize the interrelationship of gender with race, class, and other inequalities. Masculinity and femininity are constructed differently based on race and class, and positions within the gender order differ according to the particular version of masculinity or femininity that is being constructed. Some men, particularly white, middle-class, heterosexual men, tend to hold the most powerful positions, over both women and other men. Other men, such as those who are disadvantaged by race or social class, do not enjoy as much overall social power. These men might still find some rewards within this system by expressing masculine qualities that display overt dominance over women, such as aggression, physicality, and control. However, this power is limited and ultimately reinforces and legitimizes the power of upper-class men (Pyke 1996).

Within this context, students at Clayton worked to represent not only masculinity and femininity but also a respectable class position. Constraints of family economic background and community reputation strongly shaped such representations. Some students, by virtue of economic and reputational family capital (Sherman 2006), achieved high status as jocks and preps. Students at Clayton used the two terms interchangeably but most often referred to school sports stars as *preps*. The sport-oriented preps often came from higher-income backgrounds, although the group included a few students of lesser means who had outstanding athletic ability. Preps dominated the popularity contest at Clayton, and people described them as well dressed, smart, and athletic. In this low-income environment, preps differentiated themselves by their stylish, clean, name-brand clothing. As Zack said in chapter 2, preps "dress real nice" and "don't get dirty." Cole Watson, star senior quarterback, was the quintessential prep. His family also contributed money to the school, and he had extensive cachet among both students and teachers. For example, the school yearbook sponsor, a vibrant English teacher named Mr. Tanner, told me that Cole tended to dominate the yearbook's coverage: "We had to change many of the original picture layouts they had because just about every picture they did had Cole Watson in it. He's like the big stud football player, 4.0 student, and all this stuff. I told them they need to change it to show some other people!"

In classes, Cole appeared to embody an assured sense of entitlement. At his desk he took up as much room as possible, often with his arm hanging over the desk behind him. He also (like many other students in his upper-level classes) received a considerable amount of slack from his teachers and joked freely with them. When I first met Cole, he introduced himself to me in an Advanced Placement physics class, shaking my hand and saying, "Hey, dude, I'm Cole Watson." When he left in the middle of class for a student council meeting, he walked past me again, saying, "Later, dude." Cole's masculine popularity was confirmed not only by athletic ability and his relaxed classroom demeanor but also by his relationships with girls. His attractiveness to heterosexual girls appeared to be further enhanced by the notion that he was especially nice. Kaycee commented that he not only "dresses real nice and looks real nice" but was also a nice person: "Like at prom, it was so nice. There's this girl that like she never had a boyfriend her whole entire life and like she was sitting over there and Cole went over and asked her to dance with him. But like he has a girlfriend, but like the whole time he slow-danced with her and like talked to her the whole entire time and we were like that's really nice."

Most students I interviewed, however, did not describe preps as nice but as condescending or mean to other students. As Rebecca said, "all the cheerleaders and the preppy people—they think they're better than everybody." Students said the preps most often made fun of the group called the rutters. As I mentioned in chapter 2, these economically disadvantaged students represented poverty, lack of ambition, lack of cleanliness, and moral depravity. Preps and rutters occupied separate poles on the student popularity continuum.[3] While students often described preps as wearing clean, name-brand clothing, they described rutters as wearing dirty, generic, tattered clothing. In terms of class anxiety, the imagined concept of the lowly, otiose rutter signified the depths of poverty, immorality, and backwardness that teenagers in this economically stricken area desperately wanted to distance themselves from (Morris 2009). At the same time, many students also tried to differentiate themselves from the preps, who could be perceived as snobby and elitist. Some, especially the girls, attempted to do this by describing themselves as "in between" preps and rutters: as someone who would talk to anybody. Boys, on the other hand, took more of a protest route to navigating these class identities (Connell and Messerschmidt 2005), often by way of the working-class masculinities known as redneck and fighter.

"YOU DON'T NEED CLEAN HANDS ANYWAY, YOU'RE A REDNECK!"

Hegemonic practices of masculinity at Clayton focused on a carefree attitude toward schoolwork and the demonstration of physical toughness. Both practices of masculinity were reflected but also given new life through a popular identity at the school: redneck. The well-known term *redneck* carries implications of blue-collar labor, rebelliousness, and southern identity. More tacitly, it also strongly represents masculinity and whiteness (Hartigan 2003; Shirley 2003). The idea of *redneck* can thus serve as a popular cultural way to frame and enact white working-class masculinity.

In my research, I only heard the term *redneck* used at Clayton, always in reference to white men or boys and most often in lower-level or vocational classes, indicating that the concept was not connected to sophistication or academic interest. Indeed, in popular culture it tends to represent opposition to these ideals (Jarosz and Lawson 2002). Similarly, some teachers used the term in a whimsically derogatory way to describe certain boys as blue collar, uncouth, and brazenly macho, as in these two examples from my field notes:

> I am observing in Mr. Russell's shop class. One of the boys wearing a camouflage hat walks by us into the room and tells Mr. Russell, "You need to get some new soap—that stuff doesn't work." Mr. Russell says, joking with him, "You don't need clean hands anyway—you're a redneck!"

> I am observing in a resource [lowest-level] math class. [A boy has been castigated by the teacher, Mr. Kerr, for calling another boy "gay"]. Mr. Kerr says to the boy, "You only have one chance to make a first impression. Now he [referring to me] is gonna think you're a stupid redneck!"

In both examples, teachers used *redneck* to describe uncouth behavior that defied middle-class norms.

Although the term was (and is) largely derogatory, many people in this community, especially men, embraced it.[4] For example, several trucks proudly displayed bright red "Redneck" stickers. Preston explained: "Around here, it's like 'Yeah, I'm a redneck, what are you gonna do about it?' [He laughs]." At Clayton, *redneck* represented the masculine ideal of physical toughness and linked it to a local community identity. Harry mentioned this when I asked him to describe the school: "It's a rough school. It's, ah [he laughs], it's a redneck school!" Use of the term implied a sense of pride about living in this rough, white-working-class, rural location. By implying an opposition between toughness and elitist sophistication, it became a template for locally hegemonic notions of masculinity as well as race and class identity. In the peer culture, those who described themselves as rednecks were not necessarily separate from the preps, but use of the term lent a gritty, rebellious quality consistent with local definitions of masculinity, which an unadulterated prep image could not achieve. *Redneck*, like the working-class masculine space of the shop class, was a way to protest the squeaky-clean, elitist versions of manhood personified by preps and urbane outsiders. But like shop classes, the concept of the redneck also symbolized an anti-academic stance and connected this stance to a presumed powerful masculinity.

RUTTERS AND FIGHTERS

While *redneck* was largely a positive concept at the school, the concept of *rutter* was not embraced. Students used this word in discourse as a class-based insult, and it could even compromise perceptions of whiteness (see Morris 2009). For boys, using *rutter* as an invective often instigated fights, as the following excerpt from my field notes shows:

> [I am hanging out in an English class with Kevin and Roger.] Kevin and Roger talk about some fight that Roger almost got into recently. It was with a boy named Mike. Roger says, "He's tryin' to be somebody—he called me a rutter, so I got into it with him. . . . He's actin' like he's all somebody, though—I'll fight him. He's a pussy. I saw a fight he was in and it was like a pussy fight."

This exemplifies the simultaneous production of social class and masculinity among boys at Clayton. Mike essentially called Roger poor and unclean, and Roger interpreted the name calling to mean that Mike was trying to be "somebody"—that is, position himself as higher in the peer class and status hierarchy (see also Luttrell 1997; Tyson, Darity, and Castellino 2005). Although this example demonstrates class positioning and dynamics, it also reveals masculinity as an intertwined factor and outcome. Both boys denigrated certain types of fighting as "pussy" fighting, implying that the fights were insufficiently tough and masculine. Similarly, Roger described Mike as a "pussy," implying that Mike was weak and lower in status. Indeed, most of my interviewees told me that winning a fight was an expedient way to gain status in the boys' peer culture. Boys thus positioned masculinity as superior to femininity and certain versions of masculinity as closer to femininity and therefore lower in status. Avoiding pussy and rutter status often required boys to put themselves at physical risk through fighting.

Through fighting, boys could resist class-based inferiority that loomed in this context and simultaneously accomplish a strong, unyielding masculinity. Of course, not all fights occurred because of class-based insults, but the notion of being a fighter carried substantial weight for some boys at Clayton. It went beyond the simple physical activity of fighting to represent a broader attitude toward perceived belittlement and the restraints of authority. Travis, for example, described himself and his friends as "the fighters":

> TRAVIS: . . . And then the people that like to fight, they just dress like preps but they just don't put up with no one's crap.

E. M.: Okay, so they're kinda like preps, but like a tougher version or something?

TRAVIS: Yeah. Like the preps—most of the preps—they try to act tough but they're not really tough. [He laughs.] And then the fighters—no one really messes with 'em. We just don't let anyone mess with us, I guess. 'Cause we'll just fight 'em.

Fighters, according to Travis, were like the preps but more admired because they refused to "put up with no one's crap." Travis, a football player from a low-income background, felt some allegiance to the preps but critiqued their lack of true toughness. He told me a story of how one football player, a star running back named James Woods, refused to fight another boy even when he was provoked. Travis explained that many football players, especially those, like James, who were from more privileged backgrounds, "wanna act tough—like fightin' or somethin'—but they're not." For Travis, playing football in itself could not achieve the true toughness of masculinity. This could only be purely conveyed through fighting, something many preps avoided.

Some of the fighters, such as Brent, separated themselves even more from preps and openly stood up to them:

I was settin' in gym and a bunch of these preppy people [were there]—I don't like 'em. Anyway, they was settin' 'ere and they was bein' really stupid and one of 'em come up to me asking if I was gonna play football. An' I told 'em, "No." And he says, "Why not?" And I says, "Because I can't stand you eff-in' preps!" And that started a fight.

Brent reacted against what he perceived as the school's unfair favoring of preps. As he put it, preps "act like they run the school." Such favoritism had deeper community economic roots because the preps tended to come from wealthier, respected families. The fighters protested this system viscerally and, as Brent put it, were "not afraid to speak what's on your mind." Brent thought this differentiated fighters not only from preps but also from "low class" people such as rutters, whom Brent saw as afraid or unable to "speak out." The fighter attitude showed some laudable critiques of the unfair class system present at Clayton and additionally demonstrated manly toughness. But as I discuss more in chapter 8, fighting resulted in school suspensions and negative assessments from teachers, further detaching these already vulnerable boys from education.

ALTERNATIVE MASCULINITY

Not all boys at Clayton portrayed a stoic or aggressive masculinity. Some followed alternative paths, often openly or subtly critiquing the practices of masculinity deemed to be hegemonic at the school. One vivid example was

Sam, a transgendered student who was listed in school records as male but dressed like the girls and hung out with them.[5] S/he rarely even talked to boys. I first met Sam while I was observing a ninth-grade history class: s/he entered wearing flip-flops, dangly gold earrings, and nail polish and carrying a bright blue purse. Sometimes s/he also wore black high heels. Sam's display of locally typical feminine dress was tempered only by a short boyish haircut. Students and teachers later told me that s/he had been dressing this way daily since middle school and that most students had gotten used to it.

Even though students appeared to ignore Sam's gender bending, he/r uniqueness must have been difficult to endure in school, and many teachers did not appear to help the situation. Mr. Wolf described Sam as "the boy that can't decide if he's a guy or a girl." Other teachers seemed to ignore Sam in class; and happy to be overlooked, s/he slept through many classes. I asked Sam for an interview, but s/he politely declined. Yet I did learn from talking to he/r and others that s/he struggled in school.

One day I hung out with Sam in the library, where I was helping the librarian put stickers on some of the new books. Sam was in the library that day along with a few other tenth graders because they had not passed the Ohio Graduation Test (OGT) so could not go on the field trip that the school had organized for all those who had passed. I asked Sam why s/he could not go, and s/he responded, in a light whisper, "I failed too many classes last year so I couldn't take the OGT."

I mentioned that freshman year is tough. Sam said, "Yeah, you're getting used to everything being new and different," and added that s/he was trying to do better this year. From what I saw at the end of the school year, Sam did appear to be more engaged academically. Ms. Collins later told me that Sam had fallen behind partly because s/he had dropped out of school for a while and had tried to take classes online. The reason, according to Ms. Collins, was that s/he was tired of being the target of students' jokes. Indeed, although I did not observe any students directly criticizing Sam, my interviews revealed that many students did make fun of he/r:

> ROBERT: [Sam] is the dude who dresses like a chick. [He laughs.]
>
> E. M.: Oh, okay. What do people think about that?
>
> ROBERT: Most people this year don't really care. Last year, though, it got bad. He was made fun of all the time. It was really bad. My sister actually stood up for him and taught him how to talk back to people. Because he would just sit there and take it. But now he talks back and can stand up for himself, so people don't really pick on him that much.

Travis indicated that students, especially boys, criticized Sam primarily because s/he transgressed the boundaries of masculinity:

TRAVIS: In this school, if you was a lesbian it would be cool, to guys. But if you was gay, you gonna get picked on 24/7. [He laughs]. It's like that.

E. M.: So why is that?

TRAVIS: 'Cause I guess guys think lesbians are cool. And if you're gay, they think that's gay. They don't want to talk to you or nothing. We have a couple of gay people in our school, and they get picked on 24/7. But they deserve to get picked on. Who wears dresses and stuff to school as a guy?

Of course, Travis's perception that "lesbians are cool" probably stems at least partly from culturally eroticized lesbian images (see also Pascoe 2007). But he also made it clear that flouting conventions of masculinity is particularly egregious. Sam suffered for challenging the hegemonic ideal of masculinity at Clayton. Interestingly, several students told me that s/he had begun getting into physical fights to stand up against peer criticism. Ironically, Sam had to employ a physically tough, recognizably masculine practice to defend the right to defy masculine gender norms.

This tension between prevailing definitions of appropriate and revered masculinity and some boys' unconventional paths of action could also be seen academically. Sam, perhaps because s/he was a unique case, performed poorly academically. But as I have mentioned, because masculinity was defined as inconsistent with academic behavior, boys who showed interest in school and did not compete in athletics risked having their masculinity questioned, which meant that these boys had to navigate school carefully. One example was Preston, a lanky boy with light brown, spiked-up hair whom I have already introduced. Several people, both teachers and students, described him as the "smartest person in the school." Indeed, he appeared to be quite bright, both in classes and in my interview with him. But this academic potential, along with the fact that he, like Tom Jackson, did not participate in sports and played in the school band, made his masculinity suspect. For instance, I heard several boys call Preston a "fag" during class. Robert, in our interview, insisted that Preston was "actually gay." As I have mentioned, Preston's grades were not impressive. He actively participated in strategies of contrived carelessness to assuage suspicion of academic diligence.

When I asked him why he did not perform better in school, he explained, "I guess it's probably laziness. I'm well known for my not studying and my laziness. I would sooner starve than make myself a sandwich." He did, however, have ambitious career goals, with plans to go to college and eventually become a radiologist; and he intended to offset his relatively low grades with high college admission test scores. His answers to several of my interview questions differed from those of other boys I interviewed at Clayton. For example, he did not think the man should be the main provider for the family, saying, like the girls I interviewed, that men and women should be equal wage earners. This response indicated that, unlike other boys, he did not associate masculinity with familial power. He also expressed more reverence for book smarts than other boys did, saying, "I mean, you gotta be pretty book smart if you're going to go into science." Finally, when I asked other boys who their role models were, most claimed not to have one, although a few listed macho men in their family, community, or popular culture, such as Chuck Norris. Preston, on the other hand, said that his mother, a single parent, was his role model:

> I suppose my mom would be the closest thing. Because like six months ago she lost her job in [a nearby town] due to downsizing. They eliminated her position because she was co-manager with someone of a department—they terminated that position. So then she got the severance pay and she took the six months off, and now she is very sad because she's working again and she's working twelve-hour shifts so she's really thrown off by it. But she's made it through all sorts of hard times.

Here again, Preston diverged from the local scripts for hegemonic masculinity by poignantly identifying with a strong woman—his mother.

Because of local prescriptions for enacting masculinity, however, Preston had to conceal some of his more "feminine" inclinations, including academic diligence. He accomplished this, as I have mentioned, through a projection of laziness, although he often did do more schoolwork than other boys did. Another strategy he used was to project an image of being crazy, which appeared to deflect aspersions about his masculinity in ways similar to the stigma-management strategy known as *covering*, in which a person attempts to reduce attention from his or her stigma through diversion (Anderson and Snow 2001; Goffman 1971). For instance, when writing poetry in English class, other boys often resisted the task entirely. Preston would finish his poem, but he would insert what he called "dark" or "insane" imagery. For example, he wrote a poem about the plague that included graphically macabre depictions, which had the double benefit of completing the assignment and receiving interest and limited approval from other boys in the class.

Such alternative paths to constituting masculinity indicate the limits of biological or socialization approaches in explaining the gender gap. Not all boys at Clayton followed a prescribed path based on their sex category. Instead, boys such as Sam, even when painfully ridiculed, bravely adhered to gender nonconformity. And boys such as Preston (as well as high performers such as Zack and Tom) developed unique perceptions of gender, community context, and life trajectory that propelled them in an academic direction. Yet all these boys crafted alternative masculine practices under the purview of locally hegemonic versions of manhood that were not consistent with high achievement and school-focused behavior. Their examples reveal the strength of this discourse of masculinity at Clayton even as they provide possibilities for new, progressive, and academically conscientious ways of becoming a man in this rural community.

Conclusion

The best way to understand boys' underachievement is to understand the production of masculinity. Hegemonic masculinity—a set of practices defined as different from and superior to femininity—profoundly shapes the way in which boys and girls experience education; but it is not immutable and must be situated in context, including within the local community, for one to extract its full meaning. At Clayton, hegemonic masculinity has historically coalesced around the demonstration of physical labor power. Local perceptions of hard, honest, tangible labor, symbolized especially by coal extraction, gave manhood an aura of reverence and power and linked it to a stable working-class rural identity.

In the 1980s the mechanization and downsizing of the local coal company challenged the idea of respectability, creating anxiety and disrupting the established parameters for social class and masculinity. Although the change also charged the formation of class and gender identity at Clayton High School, concepts of physical vitality, utility, and practical know-how associated with masculinity continued to thrive. Class-inflected scripts offered means through which boys could produce this masculinity. The concept of the prep, for example, offered a middle-class and school-attached masculinity that still adhered to physical toughness through sports such as football. However, most other paths to masculinity diverged from academic achievement, and even preps cultivated a carefree academic attitude. Values such as working with one's hands and common sense rather than book smarts rooted masculinity in manual labor, not academic behaviors such as studying. Like sports, these practices of masculinity held power partially through their association with community pride and identity. For a redneck community, tough, gritty, hardworking, rural manhood represented not only the power of masculinity but also a sense of "this is who we are" in resistance to encroaching modernizing forces associated with condescending outsiders and academic demands. Boys thus simultaneously crafted gender, class, and place-based identities; and the paths that facilitated synthesis of these identities often led them away from studying, reading, homework, and other academic pursuits.

The class-inflected scripts of masculinity at Clayton should not be seen as a rigid typology (see Pascoe 2007) but a series of relatively distinct practices that boys engaged in variably and situationally. However, the school institution did tacitly organize such practices into a hierarchical gender regime (Connell 1996), with athletic boys commanding preeminence over other versions of masculinity and femininity. Analyses of sports such as football and the construction of hegemonic masculinity in schools are, of course, not new (Eder et al. 1997; see Connell and Messerschmidt 2005). But in my study this particular gender regime was interwoven with class, place, and academic outcomes. The school appeared to balance the countervailing influences of physical masculinity rooted in local history with state-mandated insistence on meeting certain academic standards of achievement and graduation by emphasizing sports as a primary route to masculinity. School and peer-group endorsement of preps allowed these boys to maintain masculinity even with academic success, but the option of balancing achievement with tough masculinity was reserved for a few select boys. Reasserting a division between school and manliness, some boys from more disadvantaged backgrounds questioned the presumed toughness of the preps, framing "true" masculinity as something that must be proven by fighting and resisting school authority. Those who were not athletically inclined risked being labeled as *gay* or a *pussy*, especially if they performed well in school.

Contrived carelessness was the primary method that boys from various social locations and with various aspirations used to maintain masculinity, and contextual and organizational parameters allowed it to flourish. School and peer endorsements of hegemonic masculinity as inconsistent with academic behavior promoted a strategy of academic nonchalance, distancing masculinity (and most boys) from achievement. As I will show, I saw a similar outcome at Woodrow Wilson but in a context in which race served as a more salient form of identity and disadvantage.

Chapter 6   Clownin' and Riffin'

Urban Masculinity and
the Complexity of Race

ECONOMIC RESTRUCTURING in the rural community of Clayton created a sense of class uncertainty, which impelled boys to demonstrate the strength of masculinity through hegemonic ideals of physical power and toughness. In crafting masculinities, these boys also crafted social class identities, following certain class-inflected guidelines for masculinity. Socially esteemed masculinities tended to diverge from, and occasionally directly inhibit, academic success. At Woodrow Wilson, the ongoing achievement of masculinity also detracted from academic achievement; but race and racial inequality played significant roles in shaping and motivating the production of masculinity. I do not mean to imply that race was unimportant at Clayton or that class was unimportant at Woodrow Wilson. As my previous research has shown, the idea of whiteness can be important to poor and working-class white youth (Morris 2006); and several prominent studies have examined the role of class differences among African Americans (for example, Lacy 2007; Patillo-McCoy 1999). However, I emphasize race here because it overtly marked the experiences and identities of students at Woodrow Wilson. Moreover, urban racial inequality added an additional layer to students' composition of masculinity.

This complexity of race and masculinity was evident in typical interactions at the school. For example, one day as I was hanging out in the hallway with a group of boys, a figure came jauntily bounding toward us. It was Wesley, a boy I had met before. Today he throatily greeted each boy he saw with an enthusiastic "Whazzup, my nigga?" and unctuously greeted each girl he saw with

"How you doin', baby?" He continued these gender-specific salutations as he made his way down the hall, eventually stopping next to me. Boys and girls giggled at his antics, which seemed especially funny when he continued them while standing beside a white man.

I just smiled as I looked over at Wesley, a slight, long-legged boy whose pants were impossibly tight and short compared to the loose fashions of Woodrow Wilson. But one girl standing across the hall from us eventually grew tired of his frequent use of the n word. She said, "Don't use that word; we are African American."

A girl named Angela, standing on my side of the hall, said, "Yeah, Wesley," and furtively pointed to me while giving him a sideways look.

Wesley replied, "He don't care—we down!" and then to emphasize his point, slapped my hand and said, "Whazzup, my nigga?"

"You are so-o-o childish!" Angela told him, giggling.

I describe this instance of Wesley's use of the n word not for its shock value but to underscore how racial inequality and identity appeared overtly in the daily rhythms of Woodrow Wilson. According to journalist Jarvis DeBerry, no other racial term may be quite as "capable of expressing so many contradictory emotions" (quoted in Kennedy 2003, 30). The politics and debates surrounding the n word, especially African American youths' recent appropriation and redefinition of it, are well known (see Kelley [1994] 1996; Kennedy 2003). At Woodrow Wilson I heard the word almost every day, typically as a term of endearment, as Wesley used it. Yet as a white person, I was uncomfortable and nervous about hearing it. I wondered what to do. Should I correct the boys and inform them that it is not a "nice" word, as many white teachers did? Should I laugh and indirectly encourage its use among students? Should I attempt to ignore it? When writing this book, I even grappled with the idea of excluding vignettes in which students used the word, out of concern that it might promote racial stereotypes. But as I reflected, I realized that my discomfort was precisely the point. At Woodrow Wilson the n word, along with other social mechanisms, defined boundaries and provided pathways for the localized construction of race. In addition to expressing racial solidarity, it was meant to make white people feel uncomfortable. African American students could use the word, but no one else could. Thus, it inscribed racial boundaries into everyday interactions and instilled students with a sense of identity, pride, and playful resistance to both white-dominated norms and racism.

But the n word and other vehicles of identity construction and resistance held not only racialized but also gendered connotations. As in Wesley's example, boys most often used the word, and it tended to be directed at other boys.

Girls more often discouraged its use, especially around white adults. The n word imbued both sender and receiver with an aura of defiant, unyielding masculinity. Randall Kennedy (2003) has made similar observations: "[The term] meant a black man without pretensions who was unafraid to enjoy himself openly and loudly despite the objections of condescending whites or insecure blacks" (xvii).

The n word was just one example of a larger project of masculinity at Woodrow Wilson, where boys sought to establish respect and notoriety in the face of economic and racial inequality. Hegemonic masculinity at the school, as at Clayton, emphasized power and toughness. At Woodrow Wilson, however, those attributes could be demonstrated through verbal acuity (riffin' and clownin') in addition to physicality. Further, masculinity sought expression through differently racialized scripts—for instance, through personas known as *ballers* and *gangstas*. Such actions represented not just the achievement of masculinity as distinct from femininity but also the achievement of blackness as distinct from whiteness. Wesley's use of the n word in his comments to boys, his amorous advances toward girls, and his clown persona are good representations of such race-gender tensions and responses. These pathways of masculinity emerged within a context that, like Clayton, was economically disadvantaged but that had very different racial and community dynamics from those at the rural high school.

Book Smarts and Breadwinners: Perceptions of Masculinity and Occupational Roles

Because of variations in context, Woodrow Wilson and Clayton had somewhat divergent interpretations of masculinity. While boys at Clayton dismissed the importance of book smarts, preferring qualities that were tied to manual labor and associating masculinity with economic power in the family, all of the boys I interviewed at Woodrow Wilson agreed that book smarts were important to success. Three of them qualified their comments by saying that street smarts were also important, but even they did not claim that book smarts were less important, as Clayton boys did. I asked LaMarcus, a lineman on the school's football team, whether book smarts were important.

> LAMARCUS: Yeah. Like you get a lotta stuff from books. You think about
> it, like you learn a lot of stuff. Like when people talk about
> something, it's good if you read a book you figure it out—and people
> ask you about it and you say, "Yeah, I read that out of a book." And
> then the point is if you give them the right answer then you feel
> good about that. People who read do that.

E. M.: Okay, so you think that that's something that people need?
LAMARCUS: Yeah. In a way—to be successful.

Contrast LaMarcus's positive view of book smarts with the views of my interviewees at Clayton, who claimed that book smarts were less significant than a more tactile and pragmatic "knowing what you're doing." LaMarcus was a good but not outstanding student, with a 2.9 grade-point average (GPA) at the time of the interview. But at Woodrow Wilson even low-performing boys such as David, who had a 1.7 GPA, admired book smarts. He said, "Yeah. 'Cause once you get book smart, a lot of jobs want you. And a lot of girls want you too!" David saw book smarts as a route to not only a good job but also an admired heterosexual masculinity, an indication that such skills and interests were not in themselves anathema to hegemonic masculinity at the school.

My Woodrow Wilson respondents also differed in their perceptions of family roles. Recall that boys I interviewed at Clayton thought the man should be the main provider for the family. All but one boy at Woodrow Wilson (Quentin, who aspired to a lucrative career in the National Football League) thought men and women should contribute equally to family income. Kalvin, a diminutive boy with a broad smile, had a practical explanation.

KALVIN: 'Cause if it's just the man, then you might get less stuff. Like
    if your girlfriend didn't work or somethin', but if she did you would
    be able to get more and provide for your kids a little better.
E. M.: So it's better for both to be bringing home equal amounts?
KALVIN: Yeah.

One reason for the greater acceptance of egalitarian family roles could have been the high historical and local percentage of African American women who worked in the paid labor force and led mother-headed families.[1] Many scholars argue that the male breadwinner/female homemaker model stems from an upper-middle-class white perspective, which does not necessarily match the reality of black communities (Collins 1990). In the community around Woodrow Wilson, factors of race and place created a context that influenced conceptions of masculinity. The area's economy had been more diversified for a longer period of time than it had at Clayton; and because African American women have historically worked in the paid labor force, manual labor and breadwinning had less purchase as symbols of masculine power.

Other interesting variations on masculinity at Woodrow Wilson occurred at the school organizational level. Although the gender regime (Connell 1996) of the school still centralized male athletics, it also offered more diverse outlets for school-associated masculinity than Clayton did. For example, the school had a small but active drama department that produced a school play. Clayton did not offer a drama class or put on any dramatic productions. Woodrow Wilson also had a show choir that some boys participated in without, to my knowledge, being derogated by peers. And the school band, considered to be "gay" at Clayton, was a popular, even somewhat manly activity for boys at Woodrow Wilson. In an interview, David claimed he even gave up playing football so he could play drums for the band. He became infatuated with drumming, he said, after seeing the film *Drumline*, about an African American college band. Indeed, at football games the Woodrow Wilson band commanded far more respect and interest than Clayton's band did, with spectators standing up at halftime as the band performed, clapping and cheering.

But if masculinity at Woodrow Wilson appeared so much more progressive, why did boys still underachieve in school? As at Clayton, masculinity at Wilson continued to entail a sense of power and superiority, and boys still sought outlets to represent this power in ways that diverged from academics. At Woodrow Wilson this process was simply shaped differently because of a different place-based context.

Race, Gender, and Crime in the Community

Woodrow Wilson was located in a large city with a high crime rate. In 2007, the violent crime rate for this city was 851.8 while the property crime rate was 6,996.2, both per 100,000 people (U.S. Bureau of Justice Statistics 2007). These rates were approximately twice the average for the United States as a whole in 2007, where the violent crime rate was 466.9 while the property crime rate was 3,263.5, both per 100,000 people (U.S. Bureau of Labor Statistics 2007). The neighborhood surrounding Woodrow Wilson had a local reputation for crime. As I mentioned in chapter 2, it was located in what had once been a predominately white, middle-class area (although always within the city limits) that had rapidly become largely African American and low-income. These historical factors cast a shadow of neighborhood decline and disorganization that were linked to race. Corie, a thoughtful African American boy with long braided hair whom I introduced in chapter 4, described these changes:

> Now, we're being considered a gang area. For gang activity and stuff
> like that. Because of all the recent activity that's taken place there.
> But before, it could've been considered, you know, maybe the suburbs
> or like maybe one of the little suburbs out in [a town just beyond the
> city limits]. You know, it was a nice place with new houses. The

people there were, the majority there was Caucasian, you know, it was
a nice place. But taxes started being raised on the houses and people
just started movin' out, like not caring about payments, rent, all that,
they just moved out, and so. . . . The majority now is black people, or
African American, because the houses have become HUD [Housing
and Urban Development] houses since and, they're affordable . . . and
most of the people who live out in those houses probably have some
affiliation with drugs, or some other type of, you know, illegal activity
that brings in enough money for them to live in a house like that.
And so, with drugs comes gangs, violence, and so forth and so on,
which is, basically our neighborhood today.

Corie linked the advent of drugs, gangs, and crime in the community to
class-based changes (by his mention of "HUD houses") but also to racial
changes. Other students gave similar responses. One of the more interesting
came from Shawn, one of the few white students at the school, who recounted
his white neighbor's decision to transfer to another high school.

E. M.: So who says [Woodrow Wilson] is a bad school?
SHAWN: Like if you go out, like my [white] friend Jeff, he goes to [a
    predominately white suburban school], he doesn't go here because—
    like he's been around black people all his life, but he just doesn't
    want to be around them anymore, he's just kind of tired of it. Like
    everyone from other districts think this school is bad. That's what
    I hear like all the other, like the good districts think it's bad.

According to Shawn, his friend and people in the suburbs believed
that Woodrow Wilson was rife with fighting and violence, and they associated such deviance with African Americans. Such perceptions circulated
generally as well as locally. For example, when I asked my respondents at
Clayton what came to mind when they thought about black people and black
behaviors, many mentioned gangs and gang-related violence such as drive-by
shootings.

Connections among crime, violence, and race dominated Woodrow
Wilson and its community. As I mentioned in chapter 2, both the school
environment and school policies reflected concern about crime and violence.
At the entrance was a sign warning, "This is a Drug Free and Weapons Free
Area." The school had installed security cameras outside and inside the building and had a uniformed police officer, known as a school resource officer
(SRO), stationed there full time. Along with a bevy of monitors and assistant
principals carrying walkie-talkies and strict restrictions on gang colors, these
precautions spread a net of surveillance and suspicion over the school.

Several researchers argue that urban schools have increasingly come under the purview of the criminal justice system and have adopted many of law enforcement's policies, techniques, and personnel (Hirschfield 2008; Kupchik and Monahan 2006). The atmosphere at Woodrow Wilson certainly supported this view. Law enforcement was a constant presence at the school. I regularly arrived to see police cruisers parked in front of the building and, on numerous occasions, saw students being led out in handcuffs. When I first met with Mr. Shultz, the school's data coordinator, I asked him if I needed to wear a visitor badge when entering the school. He chuckled, saying they did not really monitor adults because most would be scared to come inside in the first place. He added, "We're usually trying to keep [the students] in—making sure they don't get out and go rob a house or something—rather than the other way around."

Research in criminology has shown that stereotypes of community crime tend to be related to race as well as to gender; black males in particular bear the stigma of potential crime and violence (Anderson 1990, 1999; Quillian and Pager 2001). As Lincoln Quillian and Devah Pager (2001) demonstrate, this stereotype is so powerful that it even trumps measured crime rates. The researchers found that the percentage of young black males in a neighborhood was a more robust predictor of *perceptions* of neighborhood crime than the actual crime rate. Moreover, incarceration rates for young black men have soared (Western 2006). In 2004, 8.4 percent of black males between the ages of twenty-five and twenty-nine were in prison, compared to 2.5 percent of Latino males and 1.2 percent of white males (American Sociological Association 2007). The looming specter of the criminal justice system increasingly defines the lives of young black men, especially those growing up in high-crime urban areas. This specter also extends into schools, where black boys are often viewed as especially troublesome and have the highest suspension and expulsion rates of any race-gender group (Noguera 2003; Skiba, Michael, Nardo, and Peterson, 2002).

African American boys at Woodrow Wilson constructed their masculinity within this fraught context. While they sensed the power and intimidation of enacting a hard, streetwise masculinity (Anderson 1990; Carter 2005; Majors and Billson 1992), they also knew the likely repercussions. I was shocked to learn that Corie, an amiable, seemingly placid kid, had appeared in juvenile court because of physical assault (fighting). He described the experience.

> When you fight, you have to go to court. A girl can go in there in this nice little skirt, you know, and nice dress, button-up shirt, and talk politely, even though she just like beat someone down with a bat [he

laughs], and I'd say the most she get is maybe community service, or a fine. But, you know, a guy—a guy is a guy. I can change my clothes, but I can't change my face [he points to his face], I can't change what my body has been through. I can't change a tattoo or a scar. And so they can kinda see what I've been through and so they can kinda see, oh, he must be fighting a lot, or he must be in a gang 'cause he has a tattoo or, you know, something like that, and just kinda make assumptions on us, and base our punishments on what they assume we've been through. Like, okay, to teach him not to be in a gang, I'm gonna send him to the county jail, because I don't think you can go to prison. They read me a whole lotta stuff when I went, but I can't remember everything.

Corie and other boys interpreted masculinity as a potential liability during encounters with institutional authority. As he poignantly explained, "I can change my clothes, but I can't change my face."

Consistent with the view that strict punishments and race-gender disparities apparent in the criminal justice system are reflected in education, students at Woodrow Wilson reported bias within school. Yet in contrast to notions that African Americans tend to play the race card—that is, blame personal difficulties on racism—virtually all students I interviewed downplayed the significance of racism and discrimination in their lives. However, I did notice some distrust of institutional authority. For example, students in a U.S. history class created posters depicting their perceptions of America. While most comments on these posters were overwhelmingly positive, some cynical comments appeared as well, such as "America would be a better place without racism" and "The justice system in this country sucks." Interestingly, when my interviewees did broach racial bias, they always described boys as the victims. Quentin, for instance, told me that his parents had moved to this neighborhood from another town because they had perceived racism there, which had affected him in school.

> QUENTIN: It was a lot like a white people town. And they wouldn't like—I don't know how to say it—like if you gave anybody a look down there and you was black you was gonna get in trouble, because it was like a predominately white area, so—I mean I was gettin' in trouble at my school.
> E. M.: So people were kinda racist, is that what you're saying?
> QUENTIN: Yeah.

Students also specifically described how suspensions or expulsions hindered African Americans boys' academic progress. As I noted in chapter 4, disciplinary rates for boys at Woodrow Wilson far outpaced those for girls, mirroring national trends. For example, I interviewed a girl named Ivory, a vivacious, impressive young woman who had the highest GPA in the sophomore class. Yet like many high-performing girls at both Woodrow Wilson and Clayton, Ivory had a brother who performed surprisingly poorly in school. She said at the time of our interview that he was failing most classes and would need to go to summer school or repeat a grade. While explaining her brother's struggles, Ivory described how an earlier expulsion had disrupted her brother academically.

> IVORY: Yeah, and he got expelled from one school, but it wasn't his fault. He had brought like a keychain bullet from Disney World. And he had left it on the counter at school, like at the front of the school and they found it and he said, "Oh, that's mine." And they ended up calling the police and everything so they asked him to leave. And my mom was supposed to take it but she forgot and left it there while she was signing him out and she forgot to pick it up and leave, so he ended up getting expelled over that.
>
> E. M.: And it was just like a fake bullet?
>
> IVORY: Yeah, it wasn't real, it was just like one of those key chains that we got from like one of those old western shops in Disney World.

This incident undoubtedly stemmed from a myopic zero-tolerance policy for weapons. While such policies are ostensibly neutral, studies indicate that African American students, particularly males, bear a disproportionate share of the suspensions and expulsions resulting from them (Kupchik and Ellis 2008; Skiba and Peterson 1999). Darius, an exceedingly affable boy, described being suspended for a minor infraction after he got into a fight (not started by him) at a predominately white school.

> DARIUS: I was outside—'cause it was gym—and I think the principal was kind of racist—not to be mean or anything, but he kind of was. 'Cause I was the only African American outside and we was standing near a flagpole. And I had leaned up against it like this [he leans against a table] and when he came outside he said I had bent it! It was already bent when we went outside! [He sounds agitated.] And I got suspended for two weeks! And I think he suspended me for that 'cause he couldn't suspend me for the fight. And I got suspended for two weeks for bending a flagpole.
>
> E. M: So you think he was like looking for an excuse—
>
> DARIUS: Yeah, anything to suspend me.

The incident took place when Darius was in the ninth grade. Afterward, he left the school and transferred between two different schools. Research shows that a ninth grader's transition to high school is critical for subsequent academic progress (Langenkamp 2010). Darius told me that, partly because of his suspension and his movement between schools, he struggled academically, especially in math (a very sequential subject area), which affected his GPA (2.0 at the time of the interview).

There is no way of measuring the possible racism of this particular principal. The larger meaning lay in Darius's perception of racially motivated school discipline, which, according to my interviews, characterized the experiences of boys more than of girls. These real and perceived constraints of race molded the masculinity of boys at Woodrow Wilson, prompting various responses.

Gangstas, Ballers, and Clowns: Race and Masculinity in the Peer Culture

BEING KNOWN AND GAINING RESPECT

As I discussed in chapter 2, achieving respect and notoriety among peers was paramount at Woodrow Wilson. Both girls and boys strove to be known, but boys tended to interpret gaining respect as particularly important and pursued various pathways to achieve this goal. For boys, achieving respect involved a pronounced project of standing up for oneself. This attitude connoted a strong, unyielding, competitive presentation of self (Goffman 1959), which boys claimed they needed to achieve when they first arrived at the school. According to David, "it matters who you're with, like personality, and how you put yourself out there. Like if you come here your freshman year and you show everybody that you'll get respect and stuff like that—you don't have to do anything bad to get respect, you just have to basically give respect to get it."

Gaining respect meant that a person became known in the peer culture. This could be achieved through several possible avenues, and Darius described their variability:

> 'Cause you want to be known. And some people want to be known for
> doing intelligent things. But others want to be known for anything, it
> don't matter. And they get in trouble a lot for that. Because the
> people that try to make big names for themselves get caught up in
> that trouble, and it's kind of stressful 'cause you don't never want to
> get caught up in it.

As Darius suggested, making good grades could be one avenue to being known. Theoretically, this was true for both girls and boys at Woodrow

Wilson; yet in practice, pathways to being known differed according to gender and carried different academic implications. In constituting urban black masculinity, boys followed scripts that tended to put them at odds with school-oriented rules and behaviors. These scripts emerged from a discursive tension between the powerful but dangerous urban symbol of the thug or gangsta and the local concept of the feeble, submissive lame.

GANGSTAS AND LAMES

As I mentioned in chapter 2, the lames (like the rutters at Clayton) were more of a concept to repudiate than an actual group of people. At Clayton, the rutter symbolized a backwardness that was linked to but not necessarily directly caused by poverty. At Woodrow Wilson, the word *lame* functioned in a similar manner, ostensibly indicating those who did not dress stylishly but also implying a submission to poverty. According to Quentin, "if you ain't got money people talk about you too. They say you lame or stuff like that. I mean you ain't gotta have no clothes. But you could be positive with it and people ain't gonna say nothing. But if you ain't got no friends and got nothing, people gonna crack jokes on you." Thus, to compensate for poverty and avoid a lame moniker, one needed to be outgoing and establish oneself in the peer culture. While lames held the lowest status in the Woodrow Wilson peer culture, only a few of my interviewees depicted them as having less money than other students, and no one depicted lames as lazy and depraved, as rutters were at Clayton. Instead, being lame largely implied an inability or an unwillingness to attain respect and notoriety among peers. As David stated, "some people they don't have a chance to get respect. And all of a sudden they just see that person and they just say, 'Oh, let's go pick on him because he looks lame.' And that's how it works."

The concept of lame was more amorphous than the concept of rutter at Clayton and could apply simply to people who were quiet and compliant. Although those who made good grades were considered known and thus not lame, being lame could relate to school behaviors, as Darius explained.

> DARIUS: Well I guess they call them lame 'cause they don't have like
> the latest clothes or shoes, or they don't do like things that
> everybody else do. Like if somebody throw a paper ball like they
> won't throw it back. Like they'll take it and throw it in the trashcan.
> And if the class is loud and they tell them to be quiet, it's like "Oh,
> you're lame" for that. Or like if you try to stick up for somebody and
> everybody else is trying to put them down, then you lame for that
> too, 'cause you ain't joining in on the fun. It's stupid. . . . You can be

called lame for anything! You turn in your homework, you're lame
for turning in your homework. You're lame for bringing your book to
class. Stupid stuff!

E. M.: So if you're following rules then you can be called lame?

DARIUS: Um-hum.

E. M.: Turning in your homework, paying attention to the rules of the
classroom, and stuff like that, then that's lame?

DARIUS: Yeah, like in Ms. Williams's class when they all be loud and
stuff like that, they be callin' Michael and Teesha lame 'cause they
just sit there and do their work.

In the class Darius mentioned, which I observed many times, boys were most
often loud and disruptive, which included riffin' on people for being lame
(discussed later in the chapter). As I analyzed in chapter 4, masculinity at
both schools involved demonstrating uninterest in rules, including school
and classroom rules. For boys in particular, those who did not "join the fun" or
display contrived carelessness risked being cast as lame.

At the opposite end of the spectrum, the image of the gangsta represented
unabashed rule defiance along with a powerful masculinity. This image
responded to stereotypes of black male criminality by embracing the threat
and strength that such stereotypes can convey (see also Anderson 1990;
Patillo-McCoy 1999). While lames meekly complied with school rules,
gangstas flouted them or only complied when convenient. Gangstas, especially in specific gangs affiliated with the Bloods or the Crips and linked to
neighborhood location, composed a more recognizable group at the school
than the lames did. But this concept also had some fluidity; and whether or
not they were specifically gang-affiliated, boys in particular felt a pull to enact
this hard streetwise image.

Although not all gangstas were boys, the concept evoked a powerful sense
of masculinity. As Jody Miller (2001, 197) finds in her influential study of girls
in gangs, young women's entrance and persistence in gang life "meant inter-
nalizing and accepting masculine constructs of gang values." In chapter 8,
I will analyze the contradictions of how girls at both schools enacted stereotypical masculine practices such as physical fighting, but for now I want to
emphasize that the gangster-thug image, despite some enactment by girls, continued to demonstrate values and practices consistent with masculinity. Ivory
clarified this: "There's a couple of girls here like they're kind of thuggish and
whatever. Like most of the guys, you mostly see the guys who are thuggish and
gangsterish like wanting to be known, but there are some girls like that here
too." The gangsta concept was more consistent with prevailing norms for

masculinity—in particular, strength, potential for violence, and rule defiance (Schrock and Schwalbe 2009). These qualities endowed gangstas with a profound sense of power. Donte, whom I introduced in chapter 4, described how he had once felt the lure of gangs:

> DONTE: Like there's some people at this school that try to be so gangsta! You know what I'm sayin', try to be hard. But it doesn't work. I can see, some people can be hard 'cause, you know what I'm sayin', some people don't have their dad in their life and stuff like that, I understand that. But when you know, you acting a way, you tryin' to be like somebody else, that's not cool. . . . I'm not gonna lie. There was one time I was tryin' to be a gang banger and stuff like that. But, you know what I'm sayin', but—
>
> E. M.: So you were trying to go that direction?
>
> DONTE: Yeah, trying to go that direction. You been brought up in a way, you know, you look at yourself, like wow, this doesn't seem right. So those people I used to hang with I broke up with 'em. I was like, you know what, I'm goin' my own way. Now we cool to play basketball with or whatever. But other than that, I really don't do no more stuff like that.
>
> E. M.: What was the appeal of that for you? Like when you were thinking about going that direction, what was it that sort of attracted you to that?
>
> DONTE: I mean you walkin' with—I mean last year, we had at least twenty deep. Twenty deep. I'm talkin' about this right here full [he motions around the room], this part of the table back was full of people. We hang with 'em every day. We walk in the hallways [he speaks with pride and puffs out his chest] and I'm in the front with my dude Jamar, and it's like everybody's like this. [He crumbles a candy wrapper] We basically, we had the school on lockdown. You know one time we all got suspended for like five days.

Donte went on to describe the appeal of this power:

> Once you get like that little ounce of power, you feel like you can go all the way, like I can run anybody in this school. That's how most of the people's heads get—these gang bangers—your head gets big. That's the main thing, it's about power. Money, power, respect. It comes through in the school. You got hustlers in this school, you got people that's makin' money on the side, but you know what I'm sayin'.

For Donte, the gang promised a sense of brotherhood, respect, and even monetary potential. All these pursuits were consistent with a powerful masculinity, reflecting hegemonic ideals of masculinity but enlisting alternative routes to achieve such ideals. This is reminiscent of Albert Cohen's (1955) classic analysis of delinquent boys in gangs: "The delinquent is the rogue male. His conduct may be viewed not only negatively, as a device for attacking and derogating the respectable culture; positively it may be viewed as the exploitation of modes of behavior which are traditionally symbolic of untrammeled masculinity, which are renounced by middle-class culture because incompatible with its ends, but which are not without a certain aura of glamour and romance" (140).

The wide circulation of the gangsta image in popular culture intoxicated boys, promising the "glamour and romance" of unapologetic black masculinity. One of the most popular musicians among students at the time of my fieldwork was the rapper Lil Wayne, who flaunted a gangsta persona and was later imprisoned on drug and weapons charges. Boys were also swayed by a popular gangsta style of dress. As Alicia said, "I think it's easier for girls [in school] just 'cause all boys want to wear is red and blue [gang colors]—Like the gangster boys they wanna dress like the people they see in the videos." Boys did not necessarily follow the style of the gangsta persona in order to actually become gangsters, something that is often misinterpreted (Morris 2006; Patillo-McCoy 1999). However, they did follow these styles to project a powerful, esteemed masculinity. Whether intentional or not, such a projection placed boys at odds with school rules and prescriptions. As Nilda Flores-Gonzalez (2002) demonstrates in her extensive analysis of street and school identities among urban students, "trying out" gang associations quickly leads to school disconnection and often results in high school dropout (127).

ATHLETES AND BALLERS

Sports were one of the most useful means for achieving popularity and demonstrating masculinity while still remaining attached to school. Like Clayton, Woodrow Wilson venerated sports, especially for boys. At Woodrow Wilson, however, the sports emphasis revolved around individual sporting achievements more than community-level pride and solidarity. Turnout for sports, even popular ones such as football and boys' basketball, was recognizably sparser at Woodrow Wilson. The school's framing of sports also appeared to be more individualistic. For instance, directly across from the main entrance, a case displayed sports trophies, as at Clayton. However, Woodrow Wilson's trophy case actually included memorabilia from former students who had gone on to play college sports and even professionally in the National Basketball

Association (NBA) and National Football League (NFL). Both students and teachers pointed proudly to such sporting achievements, often using them as evidence that countered the bad image of the school.

This individualization reflected sports' slightly different and more instrumental role at Woodrow Wilson: they were a potential career. Boys saw sports as a vehicle not only to masculinity but also to a better life. Recent ethnographic studies by Scott Brooks (2009) and Reuben Buford May (2008) depict and explain the centrality of sports, especially basketball, in the life of African American boys. Particularly in poor, crime-ridden inner cities, basketball offers them a unique opportunity to become known and respected among peers as well as the potential to attain financial success through legitimate means. The achievement of masculinity—by way of both the immediate physical activity and the promise of financial security—explains why so many young black men are focused on becoming ballers. According to Brooks (2009), "[they] learn early that their community values basketball, respects superior performance, and considers this integral to their masculinity" (15). This mentality characterized Woodrow Wilson, where students claimed that, while male gangstas were respected, male athletes were revered.

Indeed, like Cole Watson at Clayton, athletes at Woodrow Wilson enjoyed privileged status. Basketball players in particular, with their imposing height, graceful movements across the court, and profound street respect, held prominence at the school. The principal, Mr. Whitman, unabashedly adored basketball: his office was littered with the school's and other teams' memorabilia. Boys who were basketball players dressed up for game days, wearing ties, button-down shirts, and slacks to signal their elite status. Other sports, including girls' basketball, required players to wear uniforms to school but not the formal dress that distinguished high-status boys' basketball. Teachers and administrators also treated boy sports stars in both football and basketball with a certain admiration, which makes sense because many of these boys were actually being recruited by top collegiate athletic programs.

Girls in my interviews confirmed the popularity (and favoritism) reserved for athletic boys. Alicia said:

> The jocks and the cheerleaders you would call more high status. Because like everybody wants to be them. 'Cause they have all the friends, so everybody like tries to cater to their every need. Like, Dre Knight, Antwan, Ray [all senior male basketball or football players]—everybody know them—everybody. So like the higher people—they're known and they're popular, they play on a team or something like that.

Like Alicia, other girls I interviewed appeared to be both enamored with male athletes at the school while also recognizing a double standard that allowed for favoritism. Candace, for example, was one of the few girls I interviewed at either school who did not want a career of her own. She said she wanted a college degree as a "backup plan," but her main goal, which she appeared to be sincere about, involved marrying a successful professional athlete: "I wanna be married to a basketball player. I wanna be a housewife that drives a Benz and stays at the spa all day." Yet even as she reinforced the hegemonic notion of a male career, seemingly best achieved in this milieu through basketball, she critiqued special treatment of male athletes at the school:

> I think boys have more opportunity than girls. Because there's a lot of sports that boys do play, so girls don't get as many opportunities as boys. And then when you play sports you have to keep your grades up in order to play, so they have it easy. And some coaches are teachers, so they show more favoritism to their players, so—but girls don't really get a big opportunity.

School officials, girls, and often parents helped promulgate athletics as the hegemonic pathway to masculinity for black boys, further revealing how race and place were shaping masculinity. At Clayton, none of the boys I interviewed wanted to pursue sports as a potential career, even though all but two played high school sports. At Woodrow Wilson, three boys I interviewed seriously believed they would have careers as professional athletes. Some, such as LaMarcus, may have had reason for such a belief. Woodrow Wilson had produced several college and professional athletes, so the school did show up on many recruiters' radar. College football programs such as Miami of Ohio, Xavier, and the University of Southern California had expressed interest in LaMarcus. However, another boy I interviewed, Kalvin, said that he intended to play in the NBA despite the fact that he did not even play for the varsity team at Woodrow Wilson. Instead, he played in a recreation league, where he worked on improving his skills to fulfill his dream of playing professionally.

> E. M.: Now is [playing in the NBA] something where like if it works out I'll do it, or is that something you're really working on?
> KALVIN: No, I'm really working on it.

Kalvin stood just five feet, three inches tall at the time of the interview. His slight stature did not preclude his ability to play professionally: a handful of players of that height have actually played in the NBA. But it certainly increased the likelihood that Kalvin would be among the hundreds of thousands of black boys currently playing high school basketball who will see their hoop dreams thwarted.[2] Yet he remained undeterred.

E. M.: Who are your role models?

KALVIN: [quickly] Allen Iverson.

E. M.: Okay, and why is that?

KALVIN: Because he's short and he plays in the NBA. He's one of the best players even though he's that little. And if he can do it than I think I can.

Because several other in-depth studies analyze the complicated relationship among basketball, African American boys, and the American dream of upward mobility (Brooks 2009; Edwards 1973; May 2008), I will not dwell on it here. But I will underscore the link between sports and masculinity, especially for young African American men. The enticing carrot of athletics as career proliferates among black boys such as Kalvin, despite daunting odds, because it promises an unparalleled way to enact hegemonic masculinity: to gain a known and respected toughness among peers and find a legitimate route to financial success. Because of constraining, contradictory expectations—such as stereotypes of dangerous black masculinity; peer emphasis on achieving known, respect-worthy status; skyrocketing incarceration rates; and highly concentrated poverty—few other routes could lead to such a compromise. Yet this route, while school-attached, was not centered on high academic achievement as a precursor to a future career.

CLOWNIN' AND RIFFIN'

Few boys at Woodrow Wilson had the ability to play varsity sports and to therefore achieve this compromise between respect and financial security. But boys at the school were nothing if not inventive. Many non-athletes crafted less revered but equally shrewd practices of black masculinity through their clown or hustler performances. One of the intriguing differences in masculinity between Woodrow Wilson and Clayton concerned boys' use of humor and verbal acuity. As I described in chapter 5, the Clayton boys valued being plainspoken as representative of a stoic, no-nonsense manliness. No "strong, silent" mentality existed at Woodrow Wilson, however, where verbal skills were virtually required for boys' survival among peers. And while Clayton, like any school, had its share of class-clown boys, several boys at Woodrow Wilson took clownin', as they called it, to another level.

Clownin' at Woodrow Wilson represented the interwoven constraints and production of race, place, and masculinity; and Donte was a prime example of its endless richness. When I first met Donte in a ninth-grade English class, he was wearing brown-tinted sunglasses and he introduced himself to me as Jay-Z, a popular hip hop artist at the time of my fieldwork. Shaking my hand firmly, he said in a mockingly formal, low voice, "Let me welcome you to our fine class, sir. We hope you enjoy your time here."

The class was listening to portions of an audio recording of Shakespeare's *Romeo and Juliet*, which most students found soporific. Donte, however, sought to energize them through regular joking commentary. The teacher, Mr. McConnell, began the class by asking what had happened in the play during their previous listening segment. An outgoing boy named Nick answered, "He asked for Juliet's hand in marriage."

In response, Donte shouted, in a tone similar to the one he had used when introducing himself to me, "Well said!" Throughout the remainder of the class, he frantically waved his hand in the air to answer almost every question; but when called upon, he often did not know the answer or made up a joke. He also interjected impromptu raps at various points. For example, Donte was amused when one of the *Romeo and Juliet* scenes was described as taking place "on the street," so he began rapping, "Street talkers, street walkers," while pounding beats on his desk.

Donte's energetic clownin' did not abate in any of the ninth- through tenth-grade classes I observed. Although his behavior rarely appeared to be rude, he certainly skated on the rule line, often getting into trouble and sometimes, as he admitted, suffering more serious punishments such as an out-of-school suspension. When I mentioned Donte to Mr. Blandford, a math teacher, he said, "Oh, you could write a whole series of books about Donte! You could call it *High School: The Best Six Years of My Life!*" But some teachers, such as Ms. Scott, grew weary of his antics, as this example from my field notes shows:

Donte comes in the classroom, sees me, and immediately starts talking to me. He tells me everyone in the class is famous. He says a boy named Kevin is Kevin Garnett, an NBA player, and calls the one white girl in the class "Buckwild," who was a white woman on a reality television show with the rapper Flava Flav.

Someone shouts, "Then where is Flava Flav?"

Donte says, "I am!" Donte then decides that I'm someone famous, too, and names me Steve Nash, a white basketball player in the NBA. "You gotta show me some of your moves, Steve," he says.

[When Ms. Scott begins the class] Donte continues talking. As she dims the lights for the overhead projector, he sings, "When the lights go down in the cit-ehhh."

Ms. Scott starts reviewing isosceles triangles. Donte quickly interrupts her: "Ms. ahhh, Scott—what do you have?" [She had been out sick the day before.] She seems confused by Donte's question. Donte continues, "I mean, because, maybe you should get it checked out or something, you know, because I'm concerned—"

Ms. Scott replies, "Thanks for your concern, Donte," and continues teaching.

Alicia [whom I later interviewed] answers Ms. Scott's first question about the triangles. She answers the next question as well, along with a girl in the front. Alicia answers again, and this time Donte chimes in and repeats what she said in an exaggerated formal voice, trying to appear attentive.

Donte then starts talking about shapes and triangles and sarcastically adds that he is glad this isn't more confusing. Alicia says "Shut up," laughing.

Ms. Scott, seemingly perturbed, says, "Thank you, Donte." Donte then starts talking to Alicia.

. . . Donte blurts out something about Jimmy Dean sausage. One of the boys across the room says, "That nigga just say anything that comes to his head."

Alicia and the girl in front of me have been laughing at him, even though this time Alicia turns to him, laughing, and says, "Shut up— you're childish!"

Ms. Scott hands out the worksheets. She asks if I want one and Donte informs her, "Do you know who that is? That's Steve Nash!"

I shrug my shoulders and say, "Apparently today I'm Steve Nash."

Ms. Scott looks at me knowingly and says in a weary voice, "*Every day* it's like this."

Donte was unique in his clownin' acumen but not unique in the interest and constancy he showed in such verbal gaming. All boys at Woodrow Wilson, including gangstas and athletes, had to play such games and play them well or risk the dreaded label of *lame*. Girls made jokes in classes, too, but did not command the spotlight as boys such as Donte consistently did. This project was especially important to boys and representations of masculinity because it tacitly and cleverly expressed a superior position above pedantic classroom rules and requirements. Such verbal agility also expressed itself interpersonally among boys. It evolved into an ongoing competition of gamesmanship and ritualized insults known as *riffin'*.[3] In my observations, while most girls could certainly hold their own in riffin', it featured much more prominently in the interactions of boys.

For example, early in my fieldwork at Woodrow Wilson I observed a ninth-grade science class in which two guidance counselors led a lesson on bullying. After discussing bullying, the counselors organized students into groups to create skits depicting an instance of bullying and how to respond to it. A group I observed included four earnest students: two boys named Malik and Tayshaun and two girls named Claire and Jamilla. Tayshaun suggested that their topic should relate to riffin', but Malik claimed that riffin' was not necessarily bullying. Tayshaun disagreed, saying "But riffin' is violent!"

Malik suggested that bullying over grades would be a good topic, but Claire said, "Nobody bullies over grades." Jamilla agreed, and the girls suggested that the skit involve bullying over clothes.

Tayshaun then suggested that the group "talk about riffin' on people trying to be smart." Malik seemed to agree, but the girls did not. Tayshaun pleaded his case, "But people do make fun of people because they're smart." The girls, however, continued to refuse, and the group eventually decided on the topic of bullying over clothes.

This example shows not only boys' interest in and knowledge of riffin' but also gendered interpretations of bullying, with girls relating it to clothing and appearance and boys relating it to grades and "trying to be smart." In truth, I did not observe boys actually making fun of each other because of good grades, but they could certainly get riffed on for nerdy, academically focused behavior deemed to be lame. Boys in particular were expected to joke around and defend themselves through riffin' to garner respect. Donte, in fact, claimed that he saw this behavior as more important than focusing on academic performance in school, especially in establishing a reputation in ninth grade.

> DONTE: Like last year we had this thing where, um, you're gaining, let's see, respect. Riffin' is when you actually battlin'. We don't say it as like a putdown, it's like a comedy thing you do, like usually we, like who you battle against, it's fun. You know MarShawn?
>
> E. M.: Yes.
>
> DONTE: Me and him we usually go at it sometimes, riffin'. . . . Man, me and MarShawn, we like the coolest dudes! We play—me and him take so many people's money playin' basketball together, so—me and him we always been cool.

Donte regularly got into trouble for riffin' and clownin' in classes. As he said, "well, I'm a keep it real here. Last year my record for [disciplinary write-ups] was at least, man, I'd say a good twenty." In his eyes, however, the very behavior that got him into trouble also made him the "coolest dude," so he had difficulty curbing it. He also hinted at another popular behavior linked to clownin' and riffin' at Woodrow Wilson: hustling. Many boys engaged in gambling and inventive entrepreneurial activity. One boy at the school, a very clever AP student named Kyle, actually carried around a small cache of candy in his backpack, which he sold surreptitiously (this was against school rules) between classes. He even sold his own variety packs of assorted candies he had industriously sorted into plastic baggies. I asked him one day how much money he made from his business, and he replied confidently, "On a good day, thirty-five to forty [dollars]. On a bad day, around twenty."

For boys such activities held multiple meanings and purposes. As several authors have adeptly explained, they parallel a central feature of the historical construction of black masculinity, where "ability with words is as highly valued as physical strength" (Majors and Billson 1992, 99). This performance of black masculinity through the trickster or hustler script may have origins in historical discrimination against black men. Blocked from hegemonic paths to masculinity through a career, many black men crafted a clever, veiled critique of inequality along with the pursuit of alternative methods of income (Kelley [1994] 1996; Majors and Billson 1992; Scott 1990). Such pursuits, similar to the actions of many class-clown and hustler boys I observed at Woodrow Wilson, stop short of open defiance and disguise their challenge of conventions through humor. As with Wesley's use of the n word, which opened this chapter, clownin' also critiques and distances itself from whiteness. According to Majors and Billson (1992), "black humor [is] the vehicle for mocking white pretension and hypocrisy" (63). The clownin' I observed at Woodrow Wilson partook in this mockery: boys would use an exaggeratedly formal voice to represent "proper" white speech and conventions.[4] Donte used this voice when introducing himself to me, and I also observed boys using it when asking another classmate for learning materials ("Please, sir, may I borrow a writing utensil?") or when other students violated rules ("Brittany, you are talking and you are not paying attention. This is going to affect your grade.").

Like Donte, Wesley excelled in formal mockery and other customs of the clownin' idiom, which he used to compensate for his otherwise nerdy exterior. For example, Ms. Williams often closed the door once class had begun, and it locked automatically. When late-arriving students knocked to come in, Wesley would say in exaggeratedly formal tones, "Why are these people continually coming in late and disrupting our class?" He often used the n word, as we have seen; but when someone else used it in class, I heard him respond in his formal voice, "Hey, stop the use of profanity in here at once!"

Although Wesley satirically introduced himself to me as a "member of the East Elm Crips," he lacked the toughness and bravado necessary to represent a gangsta persona. He also lacked the athletic skills necessary to play sports. Such restraints compromised his performance of manliness, and I did record instances in which tougher boys called him "gay." But through his endearing humor, Wesley was able to deflect many of these aspersions and achieve known status. Donte explained the situation.

> E. M.: Okay, are there like nerds here? 'Cause thinking back to my high school days, there were kind of like jocks and preps and nerds and stuff. Does that happen here?
>
> DONTE: There's this dude named Wesley. He's like my, he's my dog, man!
>
> E. M.: He's funny—
>
> DONTE: Yeah, he's funny, right, you know what I'm sayin'. So it's like this dude could be a geek, but the way he acts just makes him change his whole—like you can't call him a geek, 'cause he's really funny, you know. 'Cause me and him, we're like FBI agents, we play like FBI agents and stuff. So—he's a cool person. 'Cause everybody knows him 'cause it's just like Wesley! Wesley, you know who Wesley is 'cause he's like a clown.

For boys such as Donte and Wesley, who failed, by either choice or ability, to exude a tough, hard front, clownin' and the demonstration of "verbal adroitness" (Delpit 2006, 57) could protect them from lame or gay status. As a standard of black masculinity, such practices also allowed boys to demonstrate African American manhood through playful impudence and humor at the expense of white middle-class decorum. For some of these boys, such as Kamani described in chapter 4, clownin' cleverly allowed them to demonstrate classroom centrality and rule defiance that bolstered masculinity while not necessarily mitigating high achievement. But among many teachers, especially in non-advanced classes, such playfulness could be misinterpreted or was simply annoying, as it was for beleaguered Ms. Scott. This strained the relationships of boys such as Donte and Wesley (neither of whom performed well in school) with teachers, resulting in disciplinary actions and social distancing from academics.

"It's Not Something You See Boys Doing": Masculinity and Academic Behavior

The practices of gangstas, ballers, and clowns produced certain variants of black masculinity at Woodrow Wilson. Yet as I have mentioned, none aligned neatly with school and some, especially gang banging and clownin', based themselves explicitly on indifference to school rules. To be sure, many boys did take school seriously and desired good grades. For example, LaMarcus aspired to a career in the NFL but also insisted he would complete a college degree and even participated in the school's science club. However, as at Clayton, the achievement of masculinity at Woodrow Wilson often hindered such achievements in the classroom. LaMarcus's commanding size and known athletic ability protected his masculinity, allowing him to more openly express academic interests. A girl I interviewed named Courtney, for example, appeared quite impressed with him, saying, "He is the baddest motherfucker. But when it come down to learn about stuff, he know it. He just don't show it." To represent the strong masculinity that heterosexual girls admired, boys could be smart but needed to avoid showing their efforts to follow classroom lessons and mandates, an attitude that reinforced contrived carelessness.

Such mandates included studying and doing homework, two things boys almost universally denied doing much of. Boys indicated that many behaviors required for schoolwork—sitting still, reading, finishing worksheets and homework—simply matched the natural tendencies of girls better than of boys. (Girls, as I will show in chapter 7, did not evince such a view.) At first glance, this belief appears to support biologically based arguments for boys' underachievement—that the biological composition of boys puts them at a disadvantage in following classroom requirements. Donte, for example, stated, "Boys—we just so energized, we just can't stay still in one place! Just look at somethin' in a book like this [he stares down at the table], we be like just 'Man, I'm out.' And then you just get up, play basketball, or somethin'." David said, "[Girls'] concentration level is higher. I don't know, I guess that's just how God made it!" Yet as I found at Clayton, such behavior at Woodrow Wilson stemmed more from boys' contrived carelessness than from inescapable natural forces.

For example, girls at both schools were more likely than boys not only to complete assigned schoolwork but also to admit to academic effort and preparation. When I asked students why, they tended to frame their explanations in gendered terms. David, for example, had a twin sister who performed much better than he did in school. Like other boys, he claimed that he did not need to study ("I just don't need to study, I just remember how to do it"), despite his low GPA. Yet he said his sister studied regularly.

E. M.: Are there people that study all the time?

DAVID: Yeah, like my sister! She gonna stress me out with her studying! 'Cause she want to be a doctor. She's all serious about that. She's like trying to get me to study, she'll be like "What's so hard about it?" I'm just like "I just don't like studying!"

Elsewhere in the interview, David explained that it was easier for girls such as his sister to study and do schoolwork:

> E. M.: Do you think it's easier for girls in school, or is it easier for boys in school?
>
> DAVID: Girls! Way easier!
>
> E. M.: Why is that?
>
> DAVID: Like girls are more mature, they understand that—for some reason they just understand that they have to get their work together. And they're more strict about getting their work. Boys, we're worried about the girls. We're falling behind because girls, they're trying to get their A and we're trying to get them! So we get distracted. But like girls, they just, they have their—I don't know, there's something weird about that! How they know they gotta get their grades. Most of the girls get their grades and the boys don't. So the boys just trying to do too much, I guess. Tryin' to be too much. Be in gangs and stuff.

According to David, girls were more likely to "get their grades" because they had fewer distractions than boys did. What he described as drawing boys away from an achievement focus were the very behaviors that constituted masculinity: impressing girls in classrooms and acting like tough, hardened gangstas. Girls, as David insightfully revealed, could focus on achievement because the production of femininity did not require them to "try to be too much" and demonstrate identities that superseded and often directly detracted from schooling.

Like boys at Clayton, boys at Woodrow Wilson expressed a somewhat imperious attitude toward girls and studying. Most, as David implied, saw schoolwork, especially done at home, as a needless waste of time. When I asked Kalvin about studying, he said, "It's just not—it's not on my mind to study. I don't go home and study—I go outside or something." When I asked him about gender and studying, he stated that girls study more than boys do; and when I asked him why, he explained, "It's not something you see boys doing." Boys avoided homework and studying because they interpreted such activities as less manly and significant than pursuits such as going outside or playing sports. Quentin explained that he was often too tired to do his homework because of football.

> QUENTIN: 'Cause homework, really that's half your grade in some classes, just homework.
>
> E. M.: So if you get the homework turned in, you're okay. Is that hard to do sometimes though?

QUENTIN: Yeah. Like I got football conditioning after school now. And
like I be tired when I get home. And sometimes I won't do it. Then
it builds up, then you got all this missin' work. And then sometimes
the teachers won't give it to you, like your missin' work, and it'll just
be zeros and that's it.

Yet Quentin could not fathom cutting back on football conditioning simply
to do homework because football not only represented a strongly masculine
pursuit but in his mind promised a profitable professional career and a breadwinner role. (Recall that Quentin was one of the only boys to think that the
man should be the main provider for the family.) Performing masculinity was
more important to many boys than performing academically was.

As at Clayton, boys at Woodrow Wilson who did perform well academically had to cover up any suspicion of planning and effort. Darius said, "Some
of them act like they don't [study], but then you see their test results and you
be like 'I know you studied for that test!'" Vanessa, a deliberate, soft-spoken
girl, described how boys finished schoolwork clandestinely:

E. M.: Is it easier for girls in school or for boys in school?
VANESSA: I'm gonna say girls.
E. M.: Do you think that girls are more likely to do their work than
boys?
VANESSA: Yeah.
E. M.: I've noticed that a little bit. Why do you think that is?
VANESSA: I don't know because the boys, like there was one boy last
year that the teacher said he wasn't doing his work, like he would
just talk during class but then at the end of class he would just hurry
up and get his work done and then turn it in when nobody was
there, so I don't know what the point was of that. Like I don't know
why they do that.

As at Clayton, boys here hid their interest in completing schoolwork to
protect their masculinity. They could gain respect for achieving very high
grades; but as I showed in chapter 4, they had to achieve those grades without
exhibiting any conscientious focus on schoolwork. Finishing schoolwork, of
course, did not directly constitute femininity for girls. But the behaviors
required for completing schoolwork and the conciliatory, rule-adhering
standpoint this symbolized did not compromise femininity as it did masculinity. Beset by grave, pervasive inequalities of racism, poverty, crime, and
incarceration, boys at Woodrow Wilson turned to local scripts of manhood to
gain a sense of control and respect. Unfortunately, this powerful manhood

could not be achieved through academic behaviors, which simply were "not something you see boys doing."

Conclusion

Masculinity at Woodrow Wilson showed interesting and salient distinctions from masculinity at Clayton. Woodrow Wilson boys were more receptive to the importance of book smarts and the possibility of men not being the primary family breadwinners. The school also endorsed more nonathletic avenues for boys' recognition, such as drama and band. Yet Woodrow Wilson, like many predominately minority urban schools, still had a distinct academic gender gap favoring girls. Such underachievement stemmed from intersecting influences of race- and place-based inequality. At Woodrow Wilson, these influences created circumstances that challenged boys' sense of power and superiority, prompting them to seek out and enact locally available scripts of masculinity. These scripts, especially those for gangstas and clowns, reinforced the assertion of black masculinity through clever or open defiance of the rules and norms of white-dominated institutions such as schools. Boys also negotiated the looming shadow of crime, incarceration, and stereotypes of black male violence that infiltrated Woodrow Wilson. This is not to say that boys resisted education; in fact, as their interest in book smarts showed, they clearly valued educational pursuits. However, they did resist, often in a veiled way (Dickar 2008; Scott 1990), particular processes and requirements of schooling that they perceived as infringing upon or inconsistent with masculinity.

My comparative analysis of Clayton and Woodrow Wilson demonstrates how intersecting differences of race, class, and place alter gender and, in turn, how gender alters the interpretation and enactment of these differences. It also shows how central features of hegemonic masculinity endure across contexts. The doing of masculinity and the particular definitions of hegemonic masculine practice differed between the rural and the urban school, underscoring such processes as contextually situated (Connell and Messerschmidt 2005). However, the signal accomplishment of masculinity as different from and superior to femininity guided the construction of gender at both schools. Although being a man at Woodrow Wilson did, progressively, allow for book smarts and shared family roles, it still subordinated public academic behavior such as rigorous study or model classroom deportment. Although less emphatic about physical toughness and pain endurance than it was at Clayton, local hegemonic masculinity at Woodrow Wilson was still achieved through power, superiority, and competition. Ultimately, in both locations, boys' constructions of manhood hampered their academically focused behavior.

Chapter 7	"Girls Just Care about It More"

*Femininity and Achievement
As Resistance*

COURTNEY, A CONFIDENT, perceptive girl at Woodrow Wilson, did not hesitate to disagree when I asked her if the man should be a family's main provider. Courtney had been through a lot in her seventeen years. Her parents had both dropped out of high school, and she lived with her father, who worked in lawn care. She had spent most of her childhood in Mississippi, but the onslaught of Hurricane Katrina severely disrupted her family and community. After the storm, her school became dangerous and chaotic.

Courtney struggled academically and eventually had to repeat ninth grade. But she reached a turning point after moving with her father to a neighborhood near Woodrow Wilson. Here, she realized that better academic performance was imperative if she wanted to fulfill her goal of becoming a nurse, so she put far greater effort into her grades, proudly telling me that she was now making the honor roll. She viewed her career plan as a means of freedom from economic disadvantage and dependence on men. Courtney gave a direct rationale for her refusal to rely on a male provider: "You can have your own money; you ain't gotta depend on nobody else. Some people be acting stingy with they stuff. So you can be like, 'Well, I got my own stuff, I can buy whatever I want with my own money!'"[1]

Girls at both Clayton and Woodrow Wilson strove for independence in the face of myriad disadvantages. Much of the focus on the "trouble with boys in school" leaves girls on the sidelines; yet the social production of gender is relational, and studies should not merely describe what male bodies do. Girls and femininity are critical pieces of the puzzle explaining masculinity and schooling. By concentrating on disadvantaged boys as troubled and troublesome, one might be left with the impression that girls are sitting quietly at their desks, hands clasped, papers neatly organized, conscientiously listening and obeying. Girls in my research, however, exhibited a complex, multifaceted connection to local parameters of femininity and masculinity. Their achievement stemmed not from learned compliance or natural carefulness but from their own rebuttal of gender inequality and, as Courtney asserted, their quest for independence.

Girls' interest in self-determination intertwined with local definitions of femininity, often under a veneer of *emphasized femininity*—that is, the idealized features of femininity that bolster male dominance (Connell 1987; see also Grindstaff and West 2006; Schippers 2007). Compared to boys, girls, as I have already shown, were more interested in following school rules, finishing homework, studying, and doing other activities related to high achievement. Although it might be easy to chalk up such actions to internalized docility, I argue that girls' school-oriented behaviors were far from passively compliant. Rather, they constituted a veiled form of resistance—what I call *conscientious resistance*.

For many people, the terms *resistance* and *opposition* connote public, open, and often physical acts of defiance—for example, the way in which the boys I studied refused to follow school rules. Yet as James Scott (1990) convincingly shows, resistance can occur through many hidden actions that are purposely difficult to discern from a dominant standpoint. Drawing from this insight, I suggest that girls' resistance in school can be difficult to identify, perhaps because observers tacitly view their school behaviors from a male-centered standpoint. For example, resistance in education has been viewed as not only open defiance but also a reaction to race or class inequality (Bourdieu and Passeron 1977; MacLeod 1995; Ogbu 2004). Although such a perspective highlights race or class as a dominant mode of disadvantage, scholarship on intersectionality (discussed in chapter 1) suggests that one must observe how multiple areas intersect. This perspective, while complex, better fits social reality, as the gender gap in education illustrates. Here, focusing solely on race and class does not offer insight into why disadvantaged girls tend to outperform disadvantaged boys. I believe that, for some girls, gender can be a starting point for educational resistance; but instead of openly defying schooling, they may resist gender subordination through school rather than against it. Like "hidden transcripts" of resistance (Scott 1990), girls' rebellion may not be immediately apparent—unless one re-characterizes the idea of resistance. As I learned in my research at Clayton and Woodrow Wilson, girls' opposition to gender inequality in school can be hidden in plain sight: their ostensible adherence to rules, regulations, and requirements are unapologetically aimed at achieving recognition and independence in a male-dominated society.

Gender and Resistance: The Example of Religion

Literature on gender and religious observance offers a conceptual template for understanding conscientious resistance. Several scholars have mused over a paradox of women's religious observance: women of virtually every religious affiliation tend to be more religious than men, even though religious principles are often overtly patriarchal (Avishai 2008; Daly 1973; de Vaus and McAllister 1987). Although early analyses of this paradox proposed that women had been socialized into acceptance of patriarchal religious principles (Daly 1973), subsequent studies disputed this "doormat" perspective, claiming that devout women negotiate religious principles, often strategically, for their own empowerment (Bartkowski and Read 2003; Davidman 1991; Pevey, Williams, and Ellison 1996). John Bartkowski and Jen'nan Ghazal Read (2003), for example, show that many Muslim women who wear the veil interpret it as liberating, not repressive. These women argue that the veil actually allows them more freedom to navigate the public sphere because men interact with them based on what they do rather than how they look. These women have thus transformed what appears to be a signal of patriarchal oppression into a means of freedom and independence. In this sense, women who comply with such conservative religious precepts may ironically use their compliance as a means of opposition to gender inequality. Their interpretation of the veil is not a submission to male power but a form of resistance to an objectifying male gaze.

These findings echo Scott's (1990) contention that resistance and compliance are not always what they appear to be. In fact, we may sometimes mistake one for the other, depending on how we interpret the intent and direction of such behavior within the context of intersecting modes of inequality. As I have shown, many boys at Clayton and Woodrow Wilson rebelled against school rules; but such rebellion is actually a means of complying with norms of risk-taking masculinity. In contrast, girls at Woodrow Wilson and Clayton who followed school rules actually used this institutional compliance as a means of resisting gender inequality.

Doing Femininity in School

As I mentioned in chapter 1, most analyses of gender in the U.S. sociology of education have relied on a sex-role socialization approach, which suggests that girls accept an acquiescent, sociable gender role. In school, this encourages them to be "good girls" who listen to the teacher, avoid getting into trouble, complete assignments, and so on (see Mickelson 1989). However, especially in adolescence, their non-independent role can devolve into a focus on bodily appearance and loss of self-confidence, making girls passive and insecure (AAUW 1992; Gilligan 1982; Orenstein 1994; Sadker and Sadker 1994). I agree with the core assertion of socialization theory that gendered behaviors are learned rather than biologically ingrained. However, sex-role socialization tends to downplay inequality and power in gender dynamics and does not account well for variations in how boys and girls enact gender.

As I will show, girls in my study differed in how they represented gender. First, different understandings of femininity guided gender production at each school, demonstrating that gender is not a singular role but one shaped by race and place. Second, girls' academic behaviors were influenced by systems of power related to gender as well as to race, class, and place. While girls often seemed to exhibit compliant personae and girls at Clayton appeared to suffer from low self-esteem, a deeper analysis reveals that they used such behaviors to gain recognition and empowerment.

For these reasons, understanding how girls do femininity is a necessary component of understanding why their academic achievement is higher than that of boys. Acting within the established gendered expectations and hierarchies of their respective schools and communities, girls at Clayton and Woodrow Wilson strategically reproduced and modified gender. This does not mean that gender was always salient in their actions. They did not complete their homework because they thought the action would make them feminine. Instead, they tended to act in accordance with normative parameters of masculinity and femininity, which preserved gendered ideals, even if the girls did not necessarily produce these acts in a conscious effort to represent gender (Risman 2004). Further, girls worked within intersecting normative and structural constraints that funneled but also stretched notions of femininity (Jones 2009). How they performed gender depended largely on strategies for empowerment in their disadvantaged environments and had important effects on achievement.

"Girls Get Their Work Done": Perceptions of Femininity and School Compliance

Teachers at both Woodrow Wilson and Clayton regularly described girls as compliant and conscientious, especially in relation to presumably indolent and recalcitrant boys. At Clayton, as I have mentioned, teachers appeared to be somewhat surprised by the higher achievement of girls because many described men and boys as wielding more power locally. A science teacher named Mr. Deering said, "I think the girls are more conscientious. They will work more, do more of what you ask them." He contrasted this opinion with a description of two boys I sat next to in his class: "They're smart, but they don't do a whole lot." Descriptions of girls as hardworking peppered my field notes. When I asked Mr. Wolf about Rebecca, a student I had interviewed, he explained, "She is a C student, but she works very hard," adding, "The girls try much harder. They do all the work and put in more effort." Teachers also described girls as better behaved. A veteran ninth-grade teacher named Ms. Jacobs said, "At this age it seems like the girls are nicer. Girls can be hateful when they want to be, but boys cause more trouble." Teachers at Clayton thus agreed with the "good girl" image which many people say is responsible for girls' high achievement.

At Woodrow Wilson, teachers also described girls as more conscientious than boys. Mr. Terry asked students in his history class to keep binders containing all of their class assignments, handouts, and notes. He explained that this requirement highlighted gender differences, saying, "The girls are definitely more organized. Like this binder. They'll have everything done and in order. You don't have to tell them over and over." He added that boys often complained about the binder, whereas girls would "listen to what you say and don't try to get around it—they just do it." Teachers at Woodrow Wilson also highlighted girls' tendency to do their work. Mr. McConnell said, "The girls are more concerned about grades. They will do their homework, but a lot of the boys won't. That's one of the reasons I do homework more in class."

At Woodrow Wilson race had a salient influence on perceptions of girls and gender differences. As I have mentioned, many teachers used race and the concept of African American culture as a curious explanation for gender differences in achievement. For example, when I asked Ms. Jones, a young and energetic African American ninth-grade teacher, about two boys in her class who participated regularly and appeared to be engaged, she surprisingly informed me, "They are not my best students—they are smart if they apply themselves, but they don't do the work." She continued, "Mostly it's the girls that are real quiet, but they'll pay attention more and get their work done. Boys don't finish homework." This sounded like a fairly typical explanation for gender differences, but Ms. Jones went on to comment that she thought the boys' attitude was at least partly attributable to "African American culture": "There is this idea that school is not cool. It's a stereotype about being lazy. But some just don't see education as important and don't put the effort in. That's more with the boys."

Mr. Adkins, a white ninth-grade science teacher, had a similar analysis. When I told him that I was finding a gender gap in achievement that favored girls, he vociferously agreed: "Girls in my classes are like your perfect students— most of them. They receive instruction, they do the work you ask them to do for the most part. Boys are more kinesthetic—they're always more active and they'll get easily distracted." Again, this was a fairly typical illustration of compliant girls and obstreperous boys, but Mr. Adkins explained, "I think it has something to do with African American culture. It has always been matriarchal and the women have been in charge more."

Such views of strong women in African American communities could lead to negative perceptions of black girls as too assertive. For example, I recorded more confrontations between girls and teachers at Woodrow Wilson than I did at Clayton. These findings echo previous research I conducted in Texas, where I found that black girls in general performed well academically but that teachers tended to see them as overly assertive, confrontational, and loud (Morris 2007). A similar dynamic appeared at Woodrow Wilson. Mr. Sampson, for example, struggled with an African American girl named Myranda. She was a good student but thought that he did not manage class-room behavior well or challenge students enough academically. When I first sat next to her at the beginning of class, she informed me, "We don't do noth-ing in here," with the disdain of someone who felt cheated. Myranda chal-lenged Mr. Sampson several times in class. For example, after he mentioned that many students had missed class because of "take your child to work day," Myranda replied, "No duh," which the teacher chose to ignore. Later, trying to get everyone's attention, he yelled, "Ladies in the back!" several times in the direction of Myranda and her friends. He became frustrated when they refused to respond and said loudly, "I guess Myranda doesn't know I'm talking to her because I'm using a nice word." Following discussion with the class, Mr. Sampson directed students to work quietly on an assignment. After a short time he said sharply, "Myranda—rule number two is 'don't be loud.'" After class I asked him about gender differences, and he said that girls tended to per-form better than boys but complained about their comportment: "The thing about the girls in that class is you have to tell them five times to be quiet."

Thus, a slight variation in perceptions of compliance appeared across the schools. At Woodrow Wilson, many teachers described African American girls as academically strong but socially overbearing. This corresponds to stereotypes of strong black women as emasculating matriarchs (Collins 1990). Girls, especially in urban neighborhoods, contend with such stereotypes in school, where their femininity can be perceived as coarse and aberrant (Morris 2007). Nevertheless, they form a femininity that is free from constrictive white middle-class versions of womanhood and provides them with tools for greater independence.

In general, however, teachers described girls at both schools as more conscientious and more concerned about grades than boys were. Girls "got their work done," using several academic and gender strategies to succeed at both Woodrow Wilson and Clayton. Consistent with previous research (Jones 2009; Miller 2008; Morris 2007), I found that black urban girls at Woodrow Wilson crafted strong, independent personae to navigate their rough neighborhoods and complete their schoolwork. At Clayton, I found that white rural girls operated under a deferential and self-deprecating form of emphasized femininity but still succeeded academically. In both schools, girls performed well because of an active desire to use school as a path to empowerment.

Femininity and Girls' Academic Strategies

Teachers' perceptions of girls as hard workers were reflected by the girls themselves. It is impossible for me to divine which factor occurred first: girls' hard work or teachers' perceptions of girls as good students, which influenced girls' self-concepts. What I found, however, was that underneath their compliant exterior girls crafted forceful strategies for academic success aimed at empowerment. These strategies, not simply "being organized" or "doing what they were told," facilitated girls' academic success.

"BOYS JUST DON'T CARE AND GIRLS ARE LIKE, OKAY, IT'S TIME TO BE SERIOUS"

Boys' contrived carelessness entailed an affected indifference to schoolwork, often accompanied by class-clown antics. Girls also enjoyed laughing and telling jokes, but they did not make clowning a classroom identity, as boys did. Girls at both schools appeared to recognize when to be serious about their schoolwork. For example, I conducted a group interview at Woodrow Wilson with three girls named Vanessa, Shontae, and Kenda, who all took the same biology class with Ms. Murphy. They contrasted their behavior in this class with that of a group of boys in the back, who "act like clowns," according to Shontae. Kenda added, "It's like they know the work, they just don't do it. They don't always get good grades." The girls offered a simple reason for why they themselves made better grades: they paid attention and completed assignments. According to Shontae, "All three of us sit up front and then sometimes my friend Maria will sit up front with us too and we'll do our work."

The concept of work emerged as a consistent, if simple, explanation when I asked girls about gender differences in school. For instance, Chelsie at

Clayton answered directly, "We do our work." Several girls echoed teachers' descriptions of basic gender differences in students' willingness to do academic work. Jamie at Clayton described boys as more physical and better at sports and physical education: "Boys—they have—how do I say it?—it's natural to have the natural athletic ability when girls have to try harder to be athletic, I guess." She mused that girls, by contrast, do better in academic subjects because "boys just don't care and girls are actually like, okay, it's time to get serious." Lyndsie at Clayton concurred, suggesting that boys put more energy into athletics than academics: "I think girls just put forth more effort [into academics]. I mean, I think if the guys really applied themselves they could [make good grades]." She continued, "There are smart boys—so I don't think it's easier for girls, I think girls just care about it more."

Some research consistent with a sex-role socialization approach suggests that disadvantaged girls do better in school because they stay inside more than boys do and can thus do their homework and keep off the streets (Ehrmann and Massey 2008). I believe there is some truth to this, but the framing casts girls as too passive. The girls I interviewed wanted to go outside and socialize with friends; they did not stay behind locked doors. Yet they were able to balance the need to complete homework with sports, activities, and socializing. Emily at Clayton said, "I just don't like being cooped up—sitting down. But if I'm doing homework or something, I know it has to be done." Girls, like boys, were active and fun-loving but more clearly understood the importance of completing schoolwork in addition to having a social life.

Of course, not all girls sailed through school. I interviewed several at both schools who admitted that they had struggled in ninth grade. But unlike many boys I interviewed with similar experiences, the girls used this struggle as a stimulus to redouble their academic efforts. Janna at Clayton, like Courtney at Woodrow Wilson, had floundered academically in ninth grade and had been retained, although she was making As and Bs at the time of my interview with her. Like Courtney, Janna had been through a lot in her young life. Both her parents had dropped out of high school—her mother at the age of fifteen, after she became pregnant with Janna's older sister. Janna did not live with either parent, both of whom were unemployed. She said that her mother struggled with drug addiction and that her father had moved out of state. Yet despite her turbulent family life, Janna performed remarkably well in school. She claimed to have unlocked a secret to academic success: don't goof off. Janna explained, "I spent most of my time goofin' off last year." But then she realized that "like half the colleges that I want to go to, they're expensive. And the only way you can get a scholarship is by getting straight As." Janna even claimed that she helped tutor many of her male friends who struggled in school. She explained that these boys found it difficult to take schoolwork seriously: "Mainly it's the girls that's doin' all the work and the guys are goofin' off."

In addition to goofing off in class, boys also produced contrived careless-ness by refusing to admit to studying or academic preparation. They appeared to revel in the risky bravado of taking tests without being prepared (or at least they tried to act as if they did). As I have shown, perceptions that many boys were naturally smart ironically undergirded this unwise strategy. Girls tended to use an opposite and more effective strategy of admitted academic prepara-tion. In contrast to boys I interviewed, some of whom virtually bragged about their lack of conscientiousness, Brittany at Woodrow Wilson claimed to spend considerable time on studying and schoolwork. She described an aversion to academic risk that was very different from boys'.

> BRITTANY: Like for math I don't have to study because, I mean, it's just
>   over what you're learning now, but if it's over like a huge subject
>   that you've been learning for a couple of weeks then it's always nice
>   to go back to it and make sure you have everything so when you
>   have the test you don't freeze up like "my gosh, I didn't study that,
>   I forgot about that." So I always like if it's even for five minutes or
>   like for an hour, I'll always take some time to study, depending on
>   what it is I have to study.
> E. M.: So you like to be prepared in a sense?
> BRITTANY: Yes—I mean, there are people that like if they're that smart
>   and they remember it even after all them weeks and everything from
>   the very first day then that's good. But for me, if it's been that long
>   then I'll have to study.

Brittany was clearly interested in preparing so that she could reduce her chances of freezing up on a test, in contrast to those boys who chose to rely on their "photographic memories" or simply displayed a nonchalant attitude toward academic preparation. Brittany's strategy of risk aversion must have been a major explanation for why she was in the top 10 percent of the sopho-more class. She saw studying and preparation as a way to assure recognized status through good grades.

Not all girls claimed to study and prepare as diligently as Brittany did. Ivory at Woodrow Wilson, for example, was one of the only girls I interviewed who described herself as smart. Although she ranked highest in the sopho-more class when I interviewed her, she often surreptitiously defied minor classroom rules—for instance, sending and receiving text messages on her cell phone and eating candy in class. She also admitted that she did not always study or prepare as much as her classmates and teachers thought she did.

In biology, for example, she said, "I turn all my stuff in," but admitted, "Truthfully, I don't really read the chapters!" She explained her success in the class by saying, "I guess I'm just smart." Later in the interview, however, even Ivory claimed to prepare for exams in advance. She told me, "If it's like a big exam or a big test, then I will sit down and take notes. I'll write like pages and pages of notes and then I'll go over it and over it."

The important difference between the academic behavior of girls and boys was not necessarily that all girls studied fastidiously. Even high-achieving girls such as Ivory admitted lapses and did not always personify the "good girl" image. Instead, the important difference lay in girls' greater social freedom to publicly demonstrate academic effort and interest. Girls were less fettered by peer norms to conceal school engagement. They could put effort into school without as much threat of peer chastisement for being gay or a pussy. In other words, academic engagement, while not necessarily confirming girls' femininity, did not compromise it. Jamie at Clayton, for example, participated in the school band, which for boys connoted being gay. She noted that others at the school belittled the "band geeks" but was proud to be a member of the group: "I'm kind of in that group! Enjoys doing math, science—has good grades, reads a lot for fun, is in the band. Like if you're in the band you're a nerd!" Jamie's proud nerdiness confirmed Travis's assertion in chapter 5 that students made fun of boys in the band for being gay while girl band members "ain't really said nothin' to."

GIRLS' CLASSROOM BEHAVIOR

During class, girls at both schools publicly admitted to academic preparation more often than boys did. At Clayton, for example, I often observed Mr. Tanner's ninth-grade English class. Mr. Tanner was, without question, an outstanding teacher. He had a gift for motivating interest and passionately wanted students to succeed, sometimes spontaneously offering to buy them a pizza if they showed extraordinary effort. Even lower-performing boys, such as Roger, who had repeated ninth grade, appeared to be engaged in Mr. Tanner's class. Yet despite an environment that encouraged boys to learn, girls more openly exhibited their preparation.

One day, Mr. Tanner led the class in a discussion of George Orwell's novel *Animal Farm*. As the students read and discussed it, he asked them to identify key points of meaning as well as basic mechanics of grammar such as parts of speech. He wrote a sentence from the book on the board and began to diagram it. After mentioning prepositions, he asked students to name some. A group of girls in the back began laughing and one of them, Janna, began rapidly naming several prepositions.

"Excellent!" Mr. Tanner exclaimed, "How did you know them so quickly?"

"I keep a list of the parts of speech in my wallet," Janna replied proudly, holding up a worn, folded piece of notebook paper.

Mr. Tanner's face beamed with satisfaction. "That's almost worth a pizza," he said.

At both schools girls also sought help from teachers more than boys did. Hegemonic masculinity encourages boys and men to avoid showing vulnerability or weakness. At school this meant that boys tended to try to learn material independently even if they failed to immediately grasp it. Girls had no such concerns. For example, early in my fieldwork at Woodrow Wilson, I observed an algebra class taught by Mr. Blandford. I sat next to a student named Shammond, an outgoing, dark-skinned boy who wore a diamond earring. I noticed that the class included one white student, a boy with reddish hair and a green Philadelphia Eagles jersey. The boy, whose name I later learned was Nate, remained very quiet while other students participated, including several girls who asked most of the questions. When Mr. Blandford asked students to work on problems individually, a girl named Destiny sighed loudly in frustration and begged him to come help her. She complained, "I understand when you tell me, but when I do it myself I don't get it." Mr. Blandford worked with her briefly, and Destiny asked him to put the problem on the board. After he complied, Destiny claimed that she now understood the problem and kept working. Meanwhile, Shammond finished his work quickly and then beat out a rhythm on his desk. Mr. Blandford came over to inspect his work and told him that he had done the problems wrong. Shammond frowned and began working again.

After class Mr. Blandford told me that Destiny was doing well, even though she had said she did not understand. Shammond, on the other hand, "isn't doing it right. He'll answer questions, but he doesn't really follow." Mr. Blandford suggested that the students who really struggled were those who never asked questions, such as Nate: "Like that white boy with the red hair over here, he'll never ask a question, but he doesn't have a clue. But he's well behaved and a nice kid, so I guess he's just been passed along."

Boys' reluctance to ask questions often concealed their lack of knowledge of the material. For example, although he performed poorly, Jimmy at Clayton virtually never asked a serious question in class, instead trying to make clever and amusing comments. According to Ms. Collins, "he doesn't have any idea what we're doing and so he goofs off." Jimmy's sister, a senior who was in the top 10 percent of her class, showed a greater willingness to get help from teachers to improve her academic performance. Mr. Clark explained that Jimmy, who was taking freshman-level basic math as a sophomore, had the same level of intelligence as his sister but did not use her strategies for academic success. "This [math] class is below him. He's really bright, but just doesn't do the work. The interesting thing is, his sister—his sister is a senior and she's in advanced courses—calculus, physics, going to college, everything. She's smart, too, but it is a struggle for her a little. But what she does is she comes in for extra help and tries really hard. It's interesting because Jimmy is just the opposite!" For Jimmy, hiding his lack of knowledge behind classroom humor protected a carefree, independent masculinity but resulted in lower achievement. For his sister (as for Kaycee in chapter 3), admitting difficulty and seeking help from others did not impugn her femininity and therefore served as a gender-consistent and more academically successful strategy.

Disengagement was another classroom strategy that I observed more often among boys than girls. This included sleeping in class and generally acting careless and disinterested. Yet while teachers interpreted such behavior as a lack of desire to learn or even a lack of respect, it often concealed students' ignorance of the material. The strategy served boys' sense of masculinity well because it projected contrived carelessness and avoided public admittance of vulnerability. For example, one day I observed Ms. Gerrard's geometry class at Woodrow Wilson. The class was computing the surface area of cones; and I sat next to Darius, a boy I later interviewed, and a girl named Sharelle. Although I had noticed that Darius was an attentive and polite student in other classes, today he buried his head in his arms and went to sleep almost immediately. Ms. Gerrard, a quick, no-nonsense teacher, asked him to wake up several times and seemed to grow more annoyed each time. Meanwhile, Sharelle grew frustrated with the pace of the class, asking, "Can we keep it moving please? I mean, how easy is this problem?"

Ms. Gerrard turned to her and warned, "Sharelle!" Darius glanced momentarily at Sharelle and then put his head back down on the desk. Ms. Gerrard eventually stopped trying to wake Darius up, and he slept for the remainder of the class.

When I later interviewed Darius, I discovered that his lack of engagement in geometry stemmed not from laziness but from anxiety over his grasp of the material. As I mentioned in chapter 6, Darius had changed schools several times between seventh and ninth grade. In addition, his father had died when Darius was in seventh grade; and because of these difficulties, he had academic gaps, especially in math. I asked him about his geometry class:

E. M.: Ms. Gerrard had to wake you up a couple of times when I was in [geometry] last time! What's going on there?

DARIUS: It's 'cause when I don't know how to do nothing or understand it, I'll kind of like put it to the side, or just leave it there, and then just come back to it later. 'Cause the way she teach—most of the stuff I don't understand, so I just wait until I get home and teach it to myself. And sometimes that don't help—right now, I'm failing her class.

I asked him why he did not just ask Ms. Gerrard for extra help, but he explained that she already thought he did not care because he often slept in class. He said that Ms. Gerrard thought "if I really wanted help then I would pay attention in class." But Darius purposefully chose not to pay attention because he did not want to publicly admit his lack of understanding, thus creating a cycle that lowered his grade and furthered his academic disengagement. Reluctance to show vulnerability hindered such boys; but girls actively sought help from teachers, asking questions and publicly acknowledging when they did not understand, which aided them academically.

"I MAY LOOK DUMB, BUT I CAN DO MY WORK EVERY NOW AND THEN"

At Woodrow Wilson, girls such as Sharelle and Destiny sought classroom help while still exhibiting self-confidence. At Clayton, however, a slightly different dynamic emerged. Consistent with the American Association of University Women's (1992) finding that adolescent girls experience a slide in self-esteem, Clayton girls seemed to have less self-confidence than boys did. Regretfully, I recorded many instances in which girls at the school diminished their own accomplishments and even described themselves as dumb, especially in traditionally male-dominated subjects such as math. Paradoxically, however, they maintained higher achievement than most boys did, even in math classes; and I also found that teachers typically responded to the girls' public self-deprecation with help and reassurance, as shown in this field note from my observations in a lower-level math class:

Amanda, a girl with light hair and glasses that frequently fall down her nose, calls the teacher, Mr. Kerr, over and says [in reference to a math problem], "I can't do it."
Mr. Kerr asks, "Why not?"
Amanda says, "Because I'm dumb."
Mr. Kerr says "Well, don't say that—I'm ugly and my wife still lets me go out in public!" He helps her work through the problem. Amanda then completes the remainder of her work with newfound zeal.

Meanwhile, a boy named Chase sitting next to me has finished his
problems very quickly. I ask if he had any difficulty and he replies,
"I finished in like five minutes—that stuff's easy!"

Although my previous example featured a girl in a lower-level class, I more
often observed self-deprecating girls who performed competently or even very
well in the classroom. For example, in a freshman math class, I noticed a girl
named Beth who had recently transferred to the school. She wore copious
makeup and during class spent some time combing her long straightened hair
and searching for split ends. She sat at a table with two boys who both wore
camouflage hats and talked about hunting. One of the boys turned to Beth and
asked her about hunting rifles. She replied, "I'm a girl, I don't shoot guns."
As the boys continued their conversation, however, Beth mentioned that
her father hunted and impressed the boys with her knowledge of hunting.

Mr. Clark, the teacher, was leading the class through what he called the
"box and ship" method of computing equations. After the lesson, the students
worked independently. Beth frantically waved Mr. Clark over to check if she
had done her work correctly. After looking at it, he told her that she had done
the problems perfectly. Beth replied, "See—I may look dumb, but I can do my
work every now and then."

Mr. Clark frowned at her and replied, "You are not dumb and if you paid
attention more you could do even better."

Even in the few Advanced Placement classes at Clayton I observed
this phenomenon. In a calculus class, for example, a blond, curly-haired girl
named Ashlee became frustrated and proclaimed, "I'm quitting. I suck at math
and I quit!"

Mr. Clark, who also taught this class, came over to help her and said,
"Your first statement might be true, but your second definitely is not."
Paradoxically, moments earlier Ashlee had returned from the office carrying a
certificate for making the all-A honor roll. Clearly she did not "suck at math."
But at Clayton, even high-performing girls projected an academically vulnerable image, while lower-performing boys projected a veneer of self-confidence
by way of bold statements such as "that stuff's easy!"

This paradox makes sense in light of the local operation of emphasized
femininity. In contrast to many African American communities, where
women have historically gained some economic empowerment by working
outside the home (Collins 1990), Clayton's history reflected the patriarchal
relations of the coal industry (Yarrow 1985). In most coal-dominated towns,
men worked almost exclusively in the industry while women stayed at home.
Thus, Clayton girls were just beginning to perceive new paths for femininity

beyond reliance on men, and perhaps they still associated traditional gender relations with their attachment to community and place. Several girls, for example, expressed ambivalence in their interviews about leaving the area, stating that better opportunities for employment and higher education lay elsewhere but that they thought Clayton remained a "great place to raise kids." Alternatively, girls and women in Clayton may have had a long history of crafting hidden means of resistance to patriarchy, as they have done in other Appalachian communities (Dunaway 2008). Whatever the explanation, girls still felt the need to project a self-deprecating exterior in order to negotiate with ingrained male power.

Girls' overt debasement of their ability appeared to effectively mask their resounding success. While the discourse of the girl-biased gender gap was well worn at Woodrow Wilson, teachers and administrators at Clayton appeared to be interested but surprised when I mentioned it there. Further, Clayton girls' self-deprecation actually sparked their academic efforts. Kaycee stated in chapter 3 that she thought she had to put more effort into school because she did not see herself as intellectually gifted, suggesting that girls have to study more because many subjects "come to [boys] naturally." Emily also claimed that she had to try very hard to do well in school. She contrasted her effort with that of a male friend who appeared to project contrived carelessness: "Like I know a guy, he's in our social studies class and his name is Billy, and he sleeps every single day. And one time he even missed a day and he got a test back and it was like a perfect score. I wanna know how he did it!" Although seemingly debilitating, this perceived need to try hard propelled girls' achievement. Even if they were not necessarily seen as innately smart, girls made use of behaviors and attitudes that resulted in higher grades and opened doors to further education and employment.

Conscientious Resistance

Girls succeeded because they employed strategies of preparation, questioning, and engagement, all of which were academically advantageous. Femininity guided these behaviors because gender discourses did not frame them as compromising femininity in the way in which they compromised masculinity. But if girls did not use these strategies as salient representations of gender per se, why, exactly, did they do their schoolwork so conscientiously? Arguing against the sex-role explanation that girls simply did what they were told to do, I suggest instead that they used their achievement to propel themselves toward recognition and empowerment. This was apparent in two ways at both Woodrow Wilson and Clayton: through perceptions of future family roles and in girls' negotiation of the schools' gender regimes.

"YOU AIN'T GOTTA DEPEND ON NOBODY ELSE"

Girls at both schools expressed a firm desire for future independence. Even at Clayton, a community that teachers described as traditional and patriarchal, girls did not think men should fulfill a breadwinner role in the family. Instead, girls at both schools thought income arrangements in the family should be equal, and all but one girl I interviewed firmly stated that they wanted their own careers outside the home. Girls' efforts to achieve empowerment and independence drove their perceptions of family, career, and their futures. As Courtney cogently stated in the introduction to this chapter, girls did not want to depend on anyone else. Such self-determination stands in opposition to emphasized femininity, which encourages dependence on and receptivity to men (Connell 1987). Thus, while girls typically hewed to rules in school, their efforts did not indicate docility but resistance to gender subordination.

At Woodrow Wilson, girls' views of an independent future parallels research on African American women and the family (Collins 1990). Because of longstanding discrimination against black men, black women have historically worked outside the home and learned not to rely on men economically (Fordham 1993). As I mentioned in chapter 6, even boys at Woodrow Wilson agreed with egalitarian gender roles in the family. Girls such as Ivory referenced their own mother-headed upbringing as proof that women could and should be economically independent:

> E. M.: Do you think the man should be the main provider for the family?
> IVORY: I think it should be equal because my mom is the main provider
> for my family and she's doing a pretty good job! I would rather be
> the one that's making most of the money! But I think it should be
> equal, like if you do make more money that's good, but I don't have
> in my mind it's set, like the man is the one who runs the family.

Again, this finding is consistent with previous research on African American perceptions of family roles. I was more surprised to find an identical view among girls at Clayton. Every girl I interviewed there disagreed with the idea that a man should be the main provider. (Recall that all but one Clayton boy told me the man should be the main provider.) Some girls, such as Janna, expressed a fiercely independent femininity. When I asked her about provider roles in the family, she said:

> Equal! There is no way I'll be able to stay in a house 24/7 with kids!
> Oh, no-o-o. I'm not much of a house girl—I'm not much of a girly
> girl. I like doing things outside the house. Like when we lived on a
> farm I had to be outside, and if I wasn't able to do what I had to do

inside I wasn't allowed outside for that day. And I always helped my
dad with the hay, helped him with the feeding, helped him place
gardens, and ever'thing while my sister and stepmom stayed inside.

Janna's description of herself as someone who enjoys being outside
undergirded her desire to avoid being tied to a purely domestic role.
Although most girls did not as adamantly shun domesticity, they still firmly
asserted their intentions to achieve independence through employment.
In chapter 5, for example, Lyndsie said that she "loves kids and wants kids"
but still wanted her own source of income so she would not have to depend
on anyone else.

The only girl I interviewed at either school who thought the man should
be the main provider was Candace, an African American girl at Woodrow
Wilson. However, her explanation demonstrated an interesting appraisal of
masculinity compromised by structural inequality:

My grandmother and my mom always say, when you make more
money than the man, that's when problems start coming in. Because
you make more money they feel like they're not the man of the house.
Or they not making enough money—you're providing for the family.
So you're better off to just let the man do what he has to do to be
a man.

Candace was raised in a mother-headed household, which perhaps
had shaped her views, but in some ways she contradicted them. As I mentioned in chapter 6, she told me that she wanted to marry a professional
basketball player and become a housewife. Yet despite this vision of emphasized
femininity, Candace still endeavored to succeed in school (she was making
the honor roll) and go to college to obtain a four-year degree. I asked her why
she wanted to do this, and she replied simply, "Because he [a future husband]
could always leave."

Girls at Woodrow Wilson and Clayton grew up in a context of high
male unemployment and instability. These teenagers were not surrounded
by economically powerful men, as girls in wealthier communities often
are. This structural economic disadvantage created an outlet for girls'
independence and construction of alternative femininity. The limited male
economic power in both communities created freedom for girls to craft
independence, and they used conscientious resistance in school as the key
to this liberation. As Alicia said in chapter 4 when she was contrasting
herself with a boy who refused to follow school rules, "if that's what you
want to do with your future, go ahead. It's not me. I know I'm going

somewhere in life." Girls' compliance with school precepts did not result inevitably from some core part of their being; it resulted from their clear understanding that, by following school rules now, they could enjoy a success-ful, self-reliant future.

"I WANT TO KEEP MY GRADES UP THERE AND STUFF SO I ACTUALLY LOOK HALFWAY INTELLIGENT!"

While future trajectories provided general motivation for girls' attention to school requirements, these plans were not necessarily salient in girls' day-to-day school experiences. There was a more proximate reason girls got their work done: it gave them a modicum of recognition within school gender regimes that focused squarely on boys. Whether that recognition was positive (as when boys were highlighted as athletes or naturally smart) or negative (as when boys were known to be dangerous or recalcitrant), boys tended to occupy the bulk of school and classroom attention. As Myra Sadker and David Sadker (1994) have shown in observations of primary school interaction, boys tended to monopolize teachers' attention, often because of poor behavior. In my observations of high school boys, perceptions of their behavior became stigmatizing but also notorious labels. Further, in both high schools, sports fame was reserved almost exclusively for boys. Even the winning girls' basket-ball teams at both schools tended to be dismissed. Girls attained greater popularity through cheerleading, an activity that requires impressive physical ability but is still interpreted as supportive of male athletics (see also Grindstaff and West 2006).

Many girls strove to navigate this boy-centered gender regime by empha-sizing classroom performance. To be sure, both schools had "girls who acted like boys" (Pascoe 2007, 115) by crafting a gangsta, jock, or fighter image. I will explore that issue in chapter 8, but for now I want to emphasize that girls did not have the same pathways to recognition available that boys had, even in perceptions of intellect. I recorded no instances among teachers, adminis-trators, or other students in which underachieving girls at either school were described as naturally smart. For girls, this meant that intellectual acknowl-edgment depended much more on the demonstrated achievement of good grades. For girls more so than boys, grades were badges of academic recogni-tion and intelligence.

Rebecca at Clayton, for instance, described how she struggled in school during her freshmen year but brought her grades up to As and Bs in her sophomore year by studying intently with her mother's help. She also explained, as I mentioned in chapter 4, that girls she knew took studying seriously but boys did not. Rebecca did not consider herself inherently smart;

she said she needed to study in order to compensate, and she desired to make good grades as a public representation of her competence: "Like I don't like to get Fs or Ds because they'll [other students] kind of think I'm stupid or whatever. I kind of want to keep my grades up there and stuff so I actually look halfway intelligent!"

Girls at both schools used grades as a public emblem of intellect, which fueled their dedication to schoolwork. Alicia at Woodrow Wilson, for example, said, "I'm dedicated and focused. And I like to impress people. . . . They pull out my grades and are like 'Oh, Alicia, you're smart.' Like my friend Maria—me and her will always battle on who has the better grade at the end of the grading period and I'm like always wanting to impress somebody." Contrast Alicia's focus on grades as a measure of intelligence with the discourse surrounding boys: that grades did not necessarily reflect true ability. Moreover, Alicia cast her academic success as a way to gain recognition among peers, saying "I like to impress people." Several girls mentioned that they thought their school success could "impress" or "inspire" others. Boys, by contrast, gained masculine recognition by demonstrating physical capacity and toughness through sports or street respect. The gendered school pathways available to girls channeled efforts to gain notoriety into more academic directions. Girls made the most of these pathways, viewing academics not only as a way to go to a good college or get a good job but to impress teachers and peers at school.

Girls crafted their academic identities in opposition to boys who monopolized attention either through classroom disruption or athletic preeminence. At Woodrow Wilson girls often demanded that boys behave better so they could learn. I recorded many instances of girls exhorting a rowdy class to "shut up!" or "stop acting childish!" For example, one of Ms. Williams's classes had an earnest and feisty girl named Teesha. One day, when I was observing the class, Ms. Williams led the students in reading the play *Twelve Angry Men* aloud. She asked Teesha to read first. Teesha, a good student, read her part swimmingly, even adding dramatic inflection. This caused several boys to snicker, including MarShawn and Laron, who sat in the back. Ms. Williams noticed this and asked Laron to read the next part. He was clearly not a strong reader: he read his part slowly and mispronounced several words, such as "peck-a-lar" for *peculiar*. He tried to cover this up by making jokes and losing track of his place. This caused the rest of the class to devolve into a cacophony of separate conversations, which frustrated Teesha, who cried, "Shut up! C'mon!" Ms. Williams eventually succeeded in getting the class back on track, but Laron lost his place again, prompting laughter. Exasperated, Teesha exclaimed, "Oh my God!" while looking up at the ceiling.

Girls often facilitated boys clownin' with supportive laughter. However, they also demanded access to education and became frustrated when unruly classes impeded this. Teesha did not craft a delicate good-girl image (she often butted heads with Ms. Williams), but she did stand up to disruptive students—often boys—in order to learn. I suggest that such insistence on learning not only served girls well academically but also constituted an indirect form of resistance to the greater classroom attention directed at class-clown boys.

Girls' focus on academics was also sparked by the school privilege of male athletes. As I have discussed, both schools revered athletic success, and boys' sports occupied center stage. Many girls appeared to support hegemonic athletic masculinity by attending games and adoring male sports stars, just as they supported boys' joking in class. However, they also criticized the schools' focus on sports. In chapter 6, I mentioned that Woodrow Wilson girls critiqued the emphasis on boys' sports. At Clayton, too, girls thought the school overemphasized athletics. Chelsie, for example, said, "Sometimes I think we [the people at Clayton] focus too much on sports and not on academics. Like the teachers are focusing more on the football game than teaching, and they give the football players and athletes too many breaks sometimes." No boy I interviewed, even those who did not participate in school sports, dared to criticize athletics. But girls enjoyed somewhat more freedom to do so because sports did not emblematize femininity as they did masculinity. This unexpected freedom allowed girls such as Rebecca to renounce the domination of school sports:

> I wish they would just take the football and everything out, because
> our education is low. I don't know if you've seen on the news and stuff
> about Clayton and our education. They had something in the paper
> not too long ago. And then yet you see football going like 9–0 or
> somethin', like winnin' all these things. It's our education—we should
> really be studying instead of out playing sports. Which—I ain't doin'
> track this year probably because I wanna make the A/B honor roll. Or
> get all As—that'd be awesome. I think we should be studying more.

I do not necessarily agree with Rebecca that sports and academics are mutually exclusive (I will return to the issue of school sports in chapter 9), but her point was that academic success was a more accepted feminine pathway for recognition. Girls in both schools certainly participated in and enjoyed sports; but while athletics emphatically represented hegemonic masculinity, they were not an avenue to emphasized femininity. This released girls from an overemphasis on sports or other representations of physical toughness and highlighted academic success as a valuable means for them to gain status in the school gender regime. Their academic diligence and critique of athletic overemphasis demonstrates the simultaneous compliance and opposition of conscientious resistance.

Conclusion

Many perspectives on boys' difficulties in school do not give girls much credit. Commentators, especially in the popular press, often frame girls as passive receptacles of biological or social forces. A doing gender approach, by contrast, suggests that girls have agency to make their own decisions. This perspective indicates that girls' actions are strategic but not always fully understood attempts to navigate the structuring mechanisms of gender. Gender norms serve to channel behavior, but girls and boys necessarily act within such established patterns to reproduce and occasionally subvert and redefine them. In some cases, as with religion, girls and women may act in ways that appear to accept dominant, restrictive definitions of femininity but actually provide a sense of freedom and independence. When applied to academic behavior, this suggests that girls do not perform well academically simply because of their brain circuitry or their previous socialization experience but because they *choose* to try in school. My interviewees associated this choice with independence and empowerment, not acquiescence. The concerted educational efforts I observed at both Woodrow Wilson and Clayton defied any notion of natural or socialized docility, and previous research supports these findings. For example, referring to high-achieving young women of color, Nancy Lopez (2003) observes that "women identified education as a means of securing social independence and helping their families" (170).

The concept of conscientious resistance explains how girls' forceful desires for independence and recognition drove their greater school compliance. Much of the popular literature on boys' academic struggles tends to indirectly neglect or vilify girls, casting them as teacher's pets or unfair beneficiaries of feminist educational programs. I observed neither effect at Woodrow Wilson and Clayton. Instead, I observed bright, active girls who used school effort as a means of empowerment in the face of daunting gender and economic disadvantages. I am not saying girls were perfect. Some got pregnant during my fieldwork and dropped out of school, others clashed with teachers, others got suspended from school for physical fights, and many neglected to do their work. But overall they exhibited academic strategies that proved to be more effective than those used by boys. While these strategies did not in themselves constitute femininity, how femininity and masculinity were accomplished in each school setting channeled and encouraged such efforts.

As I mentioned in chapter 1, the notion that girls are leaving boys in the academic dust (an idea that is common in the popular press) is hyperbolic. Gender gaps in achievement and attainment are nuanced, depending on the metrics and outcomes used (Buchmann, DiPrete, and McDaniel 2008). Even among low-income students, for example, math test scores on the National Assessment of Educational Progress in fourth and eighth grades do not show wide gender gaps; boys actually score slightly higher, on average (National Center of Education Statistics 2010). But girls do appear to pull away from boys, particularly in high school (Shettle et al. 2007). And perhaps because of this trend, girls eventually matriculate into and complete post-secondary programs at a higher rate than boys do (Buchmann et al. 2008).

Girls at Woodrow Wilson and Clayton revealed some of the factors underlying these trends. Both groups of girls concentrated on grades as badges of recognition and sought high educational achievement and attainment. Their minds focused on academic work, not on supposedly inherent tendencies or capacities. As I will discuss in chapter 9, such a growth-based intellectual focus tends to increase achievement enjoyment and outcomes over time (Dweck 2007). My data emphasize the gendered processes intertwined with girls' efforts. Girls enlisted prudent strategies of academic diligence such as asking questions in class, completing homework, and preparing for tests. They found such strategies not only academically useful but also means to freedom from gendered constraints—a direct yet oblique path of resistance.

Chapter 8   Friday Night Fights

W<small>HEN</small> I <small>FIRST TOLD</small> Kevin at Clayton that I was writing a book about high school student life, he responded immediately, "Well, you'll have to put a lot in there about fighting." Although his statement might appear to be flippant, I found that fighting was indeed an important part of school life at both Clayton and Woodrow Wilson. Fights occurred regularly and were popular aspects of school life—a sort of underground sport, which, perhaps even more than school-sanctioned sports, paraded and tested masculinity. Not only were the willingness and ability to defend oneself physically (and harm an opponent) enduring signals of masculine power, but fighting also brazenly defied institutional rules and decorum. Interestingly, however, boys were not the only fighters at school. Girls at both schools got into fights, some of them in ways that were indistinguishable from the boys' approaches.

Fighting, Masculinity, and School Life

Fighting provokes a flood of emotions arising from both the fight itself and from people's views about the act of fighting. Fighting also tends to vary according to social location, as evidenced by the fact that engagement in fighting is divided along class lines. Table 8.1 shows that, as income increases, the likelihood of student fighting decreases. This does not mean that lower-income students are belligerent, but the data do show that, for whatever reason, fights are more common among disadvantaged youth. Yet I do not want my analysis to feed the hysterical assumption that schools, especially low-income ones, are rife with violence (Devine 1996). Fighting certainly occurred during my fieldwork, and students certainly enjoyed talking about it,

Table 8.1
Percentage of Students Ages 12–18 Who Answered
Yes or No When Asked If They Had Been Involved in
a Physical Fight in School, 2005

Household Income	Yes	No
Less than $7,500	8.8*	91.2
$7,500–14,999	12.8	87.2
$15,000–24,999	11.5	88.5
$25,000–34,999	5.5	94.5
$35,000–49,999	4.6	95.4
$50,000 or more	3.5	96.5

SOURCE: National Center for Education Statistics, School Survey on Crime and Safety, 2007 (http://www.nces.ed.gov).

*Interpret with caution due to large standard error.`

but by no means did it control the climate of either school. Therefore, instead of documenting acts of school violence, I want to dissect the conditions that necessitated physical confrontation and examine how such confrontations affected masculinity and femininity.

Although the frequency of fighting might vary according to income, getting into a fight often serves as a visceral rite of passage for boys in any segment of our society—including myself. When I think back to my first fight, I am reminded of the pain, outrage, exhilaration, and force that can come from physical violence. I am not exactly a natural fighter. My only real physical confrontation occurred when I was in seventh grade and attending a school football game with a friend. As we were walking to a dimly lit concession stand, a group of boys from the rival school suddenly attacked us. In what must have looked like an absurd wrestling match, my attackers and I became a flurry of arms, legs, fists, grunts, and cries. Time accelerated but also seemed to stand still. At that moment the only thing that existed was the fight and the immediate imperative (in my mind) of survival. My friend and I eventually succeeded in fending off our assailants, who left as suddenly as they had emerged. And that was it. As powerfully as I had experienced the initial shock of being attacked, I now experienced the intense elation of having survived and, indeed, succeeded. My ribs and face ached, but my friend and I buoyantly recalled our surprise, bravery, and newfound physical prowess. For the first time in my life, I felt like a man.

Few other social acts so profoundly convey the raw power, aggression, and pain that seem to be fundamental to manhood. As Ann Ferguson (2000) states in her lucid analysis of fighting and school, "fighting is the emblematic ritual performance of male power" (193). Among the disadvantaged African American boys she studies, fighting promises masculine power, particularly for those who have been pushed away from school and seek to create a reputation through alternative means. Similarly, Elijah Anderson (1999) shows how street-oriented youths fight to establish respect in harsh inner-city neighborhoods: "As a means of survival, one often learns the value of having a 'name,' a reputation for being willing and able to fight. To build such a reputation is to gain respect among peers" (67). Fighting allows disadvantaged boys to simultaneously achieve recognition, protection, and manhood. But this performance creates an educational impasse: while it follows cultural norms about masculinity, such as physical prowess and aggression, it openly defies the norms of the school. Thus, boys chase the power of masculinity while slipping away from the potential of education.

"You Can't Puss Out"

Local conditions at Clayton and Woodrow Wilson allowed fighting to emerge and recur as a common mode of expression. A key antecedent was the notion that people had to stand up for themselves. Without prompting, students described both schools as rough environments in which self-reliant toughness was a necessity. Travis at Clayton said, "Don't come in here thinkin' you're gonna be hard, because you're not! Somebody will smack you around." David at Woodrow Wilson explained that, especially in his ninth grade year, fights occurred frequently: "It was like . . . war. It was like, okay, here go another fight!" In such challenging contexts, students felt the need to confront others directly and to refuse to back down, even if that meant a physical fight.

When I asked students how one could avoid a fight, most informed me that such a thing almost never happened and that it was virtually impossible to accomplish without losing face. Darius at Woodrow Wilson, for example, explained that people have to fight to "show that they ain't no wimp, and they won't take mess from nobody." Boys and to a lesser extent girls at both schools emphasized that, without the willingness to fight, a person would be dominated and belittled. Shawn at Woodrow Wilson used the analogy of the appeasement of dictators:

> SHAWN: Yeah, that's like Hitler like in the old days, when he tried to take over like . . . Poland, people tried to avoid it but that wasn't it, they got pushed too far back and had to fight him anyway.
>
> E. M.: So at a certain time you just have to confront them and work it out with them, so telling someone else isn't going to help?

SHAWN: It'll help for a little bit, but then you'll have to confront them
anyway.

Even if someone was not threatened personally but knew about or witnessed a
fight, social norms discouraged them from informing school authorities. As I
have elaborated elsewhere (Morris 2010), students at both schools believed
that relying on school officials to help them resolve conflicts was snitching,
which they vehemently derided (see also Miller 2008).

Fighting ability deflected social criticism and helped students cultivate a
tough front (Dance 2002). Quentin at Woodrow Wilson explained, "People
act like they always gotta prove something here, like they tough." David concurred: "They'll know not to mess with you no more. You can fight now." Boys
in particular perceived an exigent need to prove and defend their toughness by
not backing down from a fight, as Robert from Clayton explained.

ROBERT: Like if you can't prove that you're tough then people are going
to make fun of you. So if you can't fight, then you definitely get
lower status.
E. M.: And this is true for girls and guys—being tough?
ROBERT: Hmm. I don't really know about girls. It's probably actually
more important for guys, like some people especially, you have to
prove yourself. Or people will make fun of you.

Boys used the gendered accusation *pussy* to castigate boys who refused to
fight. I asked Roger at Clayton if telling a teacher that someone was harassing
you would be a viable way to avoid a fight. He chuckled and said, "Well, you
wouldn't want to do that. No one would do that 'cause you would get called a
pussy." Similarly, Travis explained, "You can't puss out and be like 'Naw, I
ain't gonna fight you.' Because then the rest of the year you gonna get picked
on because you just got punked by some kid."

In this way, willingness to fight composed not only a general survival
strategy in these disadvantaged contexts but also a strategy of masculinity.
Some boys derogated and feminized what they perceived to be weaker confrontations as pussy fights. When I first talked to Kevin, Warren, and Roger at
Clayton about fighting, for example, Kevin told me that there had been three
fights at the school the week before "but one was just a pussy fight." At
Woodrow Wilson, boys would call a person who did not fight or play-fight well
a "little bitch." Other boys, however, emphasized that as long as someone
bravely committed to a fight, they would gain respect, even if they lost. Brent
at Clayton explained, "The way I see it is, it's not that you win or lose the
fight, it's that you had enough heart to fight it." For many students at both
schools, then, simply subjecting oneself to a fight secured respect; and for boys

this also demonstrated the bravery and physical risk taking that secured local hegemonic masculinity. Indeed, as Robert suggested, it was more imperative for boys than for girls to prove themselves through fighting. Willingness to fight thus constituted a profound means for boys to present themselves as men.

Feel the Pain

Among boys, a deeper sentiment underlying fighting was the perception that the ability to endure physical pain was proof of a person's toughness. Physical prowess, as I have mentioned, operated as a hegemonic signal of masculinity at both schools. At Clayton especially, where the onerous and dangerous work of coal extraction had historically helped to define masculinity, boys enjoyed discussing bodily injuries. My observations aligned with other studies of rural areas, which document a strong tendency among men to take physical risks that often result in accidents and injury (Courtenay 2006; Harrell 1986).

An injured male athlete at Clayton could amass considerable respect by discussing and displaying an injury. For example, I observed a math class in which a junior basketball player who was wearing a cast regaled two sophomore boys with the story of how his ankle had "snapped" when he landed wrong, telling them he had heard a loud "pop" at the moment of the accident. Although the injury meant he could not play ball for at least the remainder of the season, the boy appeared to bask in the recognition that came from having experienced and survived such pain. Many boys at Clayton seemed to be proud of such battle scars and excitedly recounted unadulterated stories of their accidents and wounds. Roger, for example, explained to me why he couldn't play organized sports.

> ROGER [speaking with great pride]: Well, I gotta get stuff done in this knee—I got like torn ligament stuff in it. [He pulls up his jeans to show several deep scars around his knee.] But it's pretty messed up. And then my foot—I gotta go back and have it rebroken and put back in place. I did it all in a motorcycle accident. . . . Yeah. And I broke my right arm on a four-wheeler. Broke my knee on another motorcycle. . . . My dad—my dad's friend, we had two motorcycles and went down like my driveway and I was goin' pretty good and he hit me head on. He thought I was playin' chicken with 'im. And it broke this knee. And we was up riding, like riding up this hill in a four-wheeler and my buddy tried to get away so he wouldn't hit me, and I looked and this four-wheeler came like right across me and took my helmet off and the four-wheeler landed like right there and smashed my foot. Crushed it all up. And then I tried to ride the rest

of the day. Got home and took my boot off and it just went—[With his hands he mimics the swelling.]

E. M: One of those things that you just didn't notice at the time?

ROGER: Oh, no, I noticed it.

E. M.: Oh, you just ignored it?

ROGER: Yeah.

Roger's stories demonstrated two critical meanings of physical trauma and masculinity. First, they illustrated the risk taking associated with strong manhood at both schools. Boys shored up masculinity by showing they would not back down and were willing to take risks, even when such behavior (as in Roger's "playin' chicken" example) resulted in serious costs. Second, in describing graphic details of his injuries, Roger highlighted how boys chose to stoically manage physical pain. Boys could admit that something had hurt, but they could not demonstrate any emotional reaction because they associated overcoming physical agony with a sense of strength and mastery.

Indeed, boys at both schools construed emotional outbursts as a sign of weakness and femininity, and peers mercilessly teased the few boys who cried when hurt or confronted. At Woodrow Wilson, for example, I observed an interaction between Ross (whom I mentioned in chapter 4) and a boy named Kendrick in Mr. Blandford's math class. Kendrick, a rail-thin boy wearing the generic sneakers and pants that most Woodrow Wilson students considered to be lame, was picked on by other boys. At one point during the class, Ross simply turned around and slugged Kendrick on the arm. Trading punches was common practice at the school, but Kendrick did not hit back, instead ignoring Ross. Soon Mr. Blandford was asking Kendrick if he had ever gotten his cell phone back, which had been stolen. Kendrick responded that he had not, which, after Mr. Blandford moved across the room, prompted Ross and another boy, Shammond, to make fun of Kendrick. Ross said, "Yeah, he was beat up, then he got his phone robbed, then he cried!"

Shammond laughed: "Yeah, he was all trying to fight under the bleachers with those bony knuckles!" Kendrick chose to ignore the boys' taunts and seemed to be eager for the class to end.

Because he had apparently failed to fight his assailant well, the boys may have still made fun of him, even if he had not cried. But Ross broached the taunting specifically because Kendrick *had* cried. Even in situations involving an egregious assault, peers discouraged boys from displaying any emotional vulnerability. This stolid mastery over physical and emotional distress infused various play-fighting games at both schools. Such games were common when I was growing up in Appalachian North Carolina: we called them *trade licks* or *bust knuckles*—play fights in which boys were supposed to hurt each other while demonstrating an unflappable disregard for pain. At Clayton, boys played a game called *don't flinch:* they would begin to hit someone but stop just before making contact. If the person reacted to protect himself, or flinched, then he would get hit twice. If he did not flinch, he could hit the other person. Boys at Woodrow Wilson played similar fighting games.

According to Ferguson (2000) fantasized fighting initiates boys into "the protocol of enduring physical pain and mental anguish," which is seen as foundational for masculinity (187). Indeed, I observed virtually no girls at either school who ritually play fought in this way. Girls certainly fought back in a playful manner if provoked, sometimes even punching the other person; but they did not actively and regularly involve each other in ritualized games of physical aggression and pain management.

Boys used play fighting as an ongoing way to demonstrate masculinity that did not result in the more severe repercussions of real fighting. However, the line between play and reality was thin. Play fighting could quickly escalate, and sometimes it influenced teachers' views of boys as overly aggressive, as in this example from my field notes at Woodrow Wilson.

> Ms. Williams, tenth-grade English: Ms. Williams finishes the lesson early and lets the kids have free time. Several boys race toward the computers on the side of the room and a couple of them start wrestling each other to get to a computer first. Ms. Williams yells, "Hey!" and comes over to break up the dispute.
>
> Later, while working on the computers, a stocky boy named Danny and a boy with long hair named Kalin start to push and hit each other. Several students around them are laughing. Soon things heat up a little—the boys are laughing, but Danny gets up, assumes a boxer's stance, and hits Kalin hard on the shoulder. The blow makes a loud smack that catches Ms. Williams's attention. She comes over to separate the boys and warns Danny, who threw the punch. Danny protests, "But he hit me first!"
>
> After class, I talk to Ms. Williams. I mention that the class is large. She says that it is her largest and probably rowdiest class.
>
> I say that I also noticed there are several more boys than girls in the class. Ms. Williams says that that makes the class harder to manage: "The boys are definitely more physical. Like that fight at the end that I had to stop. They said they were just playing, but I'm like, one—you're not supposed to play around like that, and two—those things almost always turn into a real fight if you don't stop them."

My school observations reinforced Ms. Williams's assertions about play fighting: these altercations often escalated until stopped by a school official.

Other students typically exacerbated the situation by laughing and cheering on the potential combatants. These ritualized but increasingly tense physical interchanges reinforced the view that "boys are definitely more physical," which was exactly the perception that boys sought to cultivate. But the line between masculinity and hypermasculinity, like the line between play fighting and real fighting, remained tenuously thin. In both cases, the threat of the later ensured the symbolic dominance of the former. Hegemonic masculinity at both schools was established, at its core, through power and dominance. The potential threat of physical aggression and the potential to endure physical pain both signaled masculine dominance through the body. Because males, either through biology or the life process of gendered physical conditioning (Martin 1998), often possess bodily resources for achieving physical superiority, this reinforced a general link between masculinity and power (Messner 1992).

Girl Fights

Although boys at both schools fought more often than girls did, girls sometimes did fight with alacrity. So if fighting symbolically displays dominant masculinity, what does it mean when girls fight? In one of the few sociological studies of girls and fighting, Nikki Jones (2010) explains that urban girls are ensconced in contexts "shaped profoundly by entrenched poverty, the threat of violence in everyday life, and by the code of the street" (78). Under such circumstances survival becomes paramount, and girls, like boys, must do whatever is necessary to protect their safety (Jones 2010). Jones documents how some girls in her study scuttled traditional gendered expectations by embracing the street identity of a girl fighter. I found that girls at Clayton and Woodrow Wilson frequently made similar decisions. Those who fought appeared to disrupt associations of masculinity with physical aggression and toughness, and stretched school boundaries of masculinity and femininity. However, how teachers and students—especially boys—interpreted these fights served to re-center gendered norms and the power of masculinity.

"WE GOTTA LOTTA ROUGH GIRLS"

Most girls at Woodrow Wilson and Clayton did not physically harm others. However, for both sets of girls, fighting and being a girl were not necessarily incompatible. This observation differs somewhat from research among girls in higher-income schools, where aggression more often takes relational or verbal forms (Simmons 2002). One day I was observing a group of school counselors at Woodrow Wilson as they led a classroom guidance lesson on bullying (also mentioned in chapter 6). The counselors, a white woman and an African American woman (who was the lead teacher), explained the definition and forms of bullying to the ninth-grade class. The information they conveyed made distinctions in bullying according to gender. They stated that with boys "bullying is more physical" and with girls "bullying is more relational." After making these statements, the lead counselor asked the class, "How do girls bully?"

A girl named Taniqua, who was sitting near the back of the class, shouted, "By hitting!"

This was obviously not the answer the counselor was looking for. She ignored Taniqua's comment and prompted the class: "Now, are girls more likely to be physical, or to use their words?"

"Use their words!" an eager boy named Tayshaun called out. The counselor agreed with Tayshaun and then read information about how bullying can be verbal as well as physical. Meanwhile, Taniqua looked puzzled.

I agree with the counselors' assertions that bullying can be verbal as well as physical, but neat divisions by gender were not evident at either Woodrow Wilson or Clayton. Girls certainly used words aggressively; but as Taniqua stated, they also used fists aggressively. In my interviews, fewer girls than boys emphasized the importance of physically standing up for oneself if threatened. However, many did claim that physical self-defense was often necessary in their environments. When I asked Chelsie at Clayton how fighting affected perceptions of girls' femininity, she explained that girls, like boys, had to fight to protect themselves.

> CHELSIE: Around here if you can't fend for yourself, you won't make it.
>   You gotta be tough around here—you can't back down.
> E. M.: And that's true regardless of gender?
> CHELSIE: Yeah.

Girls at both schools described their contexts as potentially hostile and emphasized that girls as well as boys could present themselves as physically tough. I asked Rebecca at Clayton if girls' fights differed from boys' fights. She laughed and said, "Well, we gotta lotta rough girls! I have actually not seen a slap out of a girl. I seen punches—they punch, they don't slap! . . . A lotta our girls aren't afraid to punch. They get in fights over at the [local gas station] parking lot, which is crazy." At Woodrow Wilson, students also stated that girls could be rough like boys, and Kenda explained that girls could use fighting to establish status and a name: "They want to feel like, okay, I'm the baddest female, so they need to fight everyone around them just so they can feel like they're on top." Although girls at both schools still fought less than boys did, physical intimidation and confrontations pervaded their everyday lives. For some, fighting even became a way of life.

"SOMETIMES I FIGHT JUST TO BE FIGHTIN'!"

Some girls converted their willingness to fight into a fight-based career or identity. Jones (2010) documents several girls in her study who crafted seemingly masculine identities as violent fighters. I did not interview any girls who thought of *fighter* as their primary identity; but some certainly had extensive experience with fighting (including against boys), and some even sought out fights. One example was Courtney at Woodrow Wilson, whom I mentioned in chapter 7. Courtney claimed that she had been in countless fights since early childhood. As you may recall, she struggled in ninth grade and was retained, partly because she spent considerable time out of school on suspensions for fighting. During our interview, she discussed several altercations that had provoked her to fight with both girls and boys. When I asked if she fought primarily to protect herself and other people, she responded, "Um-hmm—and sometimes I fight just to be fightin'!"

> E. M.: So sometimes you're just like one of these people that just likes to fight! Now why is that, do you think? Just get in a bad mood?
> COURTNEY: Somebody say somethin' wrong to me, and I just . . . hit 'em.
> E. M.: And is that because you're in a bad mood in the first place, or is that because you feel like they're putting you down or—?
> COURTNEY: Like if I'm in a bad mood and I don't like you and you say somethin' wrong to me, I'm a fight you. But if I'm in a bad mood and I like you and you say somethin' wrong to me, I'm a fight you still!

As Courtney admitted, readiness and ability to fight were more common among boys: "Some girls they just pull hair and some girls they fight like dudes. Dudes, they just fight just to be fightin'." She explained that the men in her family had taught her to fight:

> Well I got an older brother that be tryin' to bully me, so I gotta let him know. 'Cause I got uncles when I used to be little that instead of whoopin' me, they'd punch me in my chest and tell me not to cry or you'll get another punch. Like if I get in a fight when I was little, and I don't want to fight 'em, I come back and my father be like "You better go fight her, if you don't fight her I'm gonna whoop you! So you go out there and fight, if you don't want a whoopin', you better fight!"

At Clayton, Janna demonstrated a similar fighting mentality and conditioning. Like Courtney, she often fought boys and claimed to fight as well as many of them did. Janna told me several fight stories, replete with graphic accounts of her physical aggression. In one she highlighted physical injury, a tendency that was more common among boys: "My freshman year me and Sam got into a fight, a fist fight, and I hauled off and punched him. And as they was takin' us to the office, I hauled off and punched my locker. I broke my finger. It was fun!"

Janna expressed a boylike aggression and interest in the physical pain of fighting. She professed to love fights and said that she was rewarded for them at home:

> My dad says if somebody is runnin' their mouth about somebody that you know, and if they're going to run their mouth about you, haul off and punch 'em. If they don't stop, haul off and punch 'em. . . . In sixth grade when I got in a fight I got like fifty dollars, plus I got to go to eat with my dad. I loved it!

Clearly, young women can develop an extensive capacity for physical violence, not just relational aggression. Nonetheless, I noted that girls' fighting stretched and eventually reinforced fighting as a vehicle for masculinity. My findings parallel Miller's (2001) analysis of female gang members, many of whom framed themselves as "one of the guys," a claim to superiority implying that they were stronger and more street savvy than most girls were (197). Both Courtney and Janna mentioned that men had taught them how to fight, and both claimed that they possessed the ability to fight like boys. Thus, even when female bodies wrestled, punched, and broke bones, such actions retained auras of masculinity and superiority.

"CAT FIGHTS"

Students also preserved the inherent masculinity of fighting by drawing distinctions between the reasons and form of girl fights and boy fights. For most students at both schools, boy fights were perceived to be "real fights," while girl fights were belittled as "cat fights." Boys made this distinction most forcefully: all the boys I interviewed claimed that girl fights were crazier than boy fights. Donte at Woodrow Wilson explained, "Girls go nuts!" Brent at Clayton described "cat fights" as chaotic:

> Oh, they get messy! [He laughs]. . . . Slingin' 'em around by their hair and slammin' their heads on the ground and ever'thing. Shooo. [He laughs] The guys, the only thing they do is swing a couple punches, a couple of kicks, and that's about it. I mean, [girls] grab each other by the hair of the head, slam 'em on the ground. They get violent! [He laughs.]

Several boys characterized girl fights as shockingly frenzied. LaMarcus at Woodrow Wilson said, "Girls are violent!" But boys' descriptions often referred to such violence as uncontrolled emotional outbursts involving devalued fighting techniques, such as pulling hair, scratching, slapping, and kicking. These descriptions painted girls' fights as inferior to boys', which, according to the boys, typically followed more rational rules. Corie at Woodrow Wilson explained:

> Boys, we have more of a—like a code to fighting. Like one on one and we can keep it civilized to the point where, okay, I'll meet you after school, or meet me over here, you know. But girls, when they fight it's like anybody can jump in at any time—do whatever you gotta do to win—claw, scratch, and pick up something—bricks [he laughs], hair. I've seen a lot of stuff, they have tactics and stuff where before they fight they'll put [on] like Vaseline or lip gloss so that your face doesn't get scratched up. Or like when you're fightin', make sure to grab her hair and pull out the weave or somethin'. [He laughs.] It just gets crazy with the girls, but guys to a certain degree have an unspoken code to—where, when, how we fight. . . . Like you'll rarely see a dude kick in a fight unless it's his only option. But girls, they'll kick, scream, punch, scratch. You'll rarely see a guy do that, it's mostly . . . forms of boxing. Like just fists and that's all you have to work with.

Boys at both schools emphasized that boys more commonly followed a code of fighting, a characterization that denigrated girl fights and gave boy fights greater prestige and toughness. According to Shawn at Woodrow Wilson, "Guys, they just punch 'em in the face. They don't try to pull hair, they don't try to fight dirty, they just punch 'em in the face." Further, even though boys admitted girl fights could get violent, they tended to see these fights as less significant. I observed a ninth-grade English class at Woodrow Wilson in which a group of two boys and one girl were talking about fighting. The girl started to describe a fight she had just seen between two girls. One of the boys quickly stifled her, saying dismissively, "Girl fights don't count!" All the boys I interviewed laughed when describing the madness of girl fights. Moreover, girls such as Courtney and Janna, who described themselves as assuming masculine fighting postures, joined boys in derogating most girl fights. Janna described a recent one as "just a little slap fight. I mean, what's the point of fighting if you're just gonna slap?"

Boys also sexualized girl fights, describing most of them as stemming from disputes over access to boys. Thus, the boys echoed key features of emphasized femininity by constructing femininity as receptive to men (Connell 1987). Travis at Clayton said, "We like watching girls fight! Everybody's standing around when they're fighting, like 'Rip her shirt off' or something like that!"

Many of my interviewees—primarily boys but some girls too—stated that girls fought primarily over boys but that boys did not fight over girls. Kevin at Clayton said, "Like me being a guy, I wouldn't really fight over a girl, but girls fight over guys all the time." Teachers also supported this explanation of girl fights. Discussing fighting in his tenth-grade social studies class, Mr. Sampson at Woodrow Wilson insisted that "99 percent of the time" girls fought because of boys, although some girls in the class disagreed with him. After class he reiterated this rationale to me, saying that one of his male students had told him, "We don't fight over girls—we just share them!" Four of the girls I interviewed (two at each school) agreed that girls fought primarily over boys. However, they also emphasized that girls also fought for other, more independent reasons, such as to gain respect.

Drawing such distinctions in fighting technique and rationale positioned boy fights as not only superior but also more manly, thus maintaining the general masculine conclusion that real fighting conforms to certain rules and techniques. David at Woodrow Wilson explained this clearly:

> It's like anything goes in a girl fight. But a boy—like if a girl scratches, it's no problem, it's just a girl fight. But if a boy scratches, then he's like a punk, or like he ain't no man. He's all scratchin' and stuff! . . . You have to use your fists and that's all. You can't, like even if you kick, if you kick they just, they "Ah, what are you doing?" And they talk about you. So you gotta be man enough to use nothin' but your fists.

As I have mentioned, a boy who used so-called feminine techniques could be branded a pussy, even when he did fight. Acknowledgment of such techniques helped reestablish boundaries of masculinity and femininity and the presumed superiority of masculinity. Even when girls did punch—and punch well—many boys refused to acknowledge their actions as a serious threat. Boys at both schools, for example, said they would not punch a girl even if attacked. Roger at Clayton recalled how he had ignored one girl (whom he described as "pretty manly") after she punched him.

> ROGER: She stepped back a couple feet, came at me and came down
> right there [he points to his eye] pretty hard. I said, 'If that's all as
> hard as you can hit, you better go get some practice or something.'
> But I didn't want her to hit me again.
> E. M.: So you said that, but it actually did hurt?
> ROGER: Yeah.

In a thoughtful analysis of multiple forms of femininity and relations to hegemonic masculinity, Mimi Schippers (2007) asserts that masculine characteristics, "when embodied by women, constitute a refusal to complement hegemonic masculinity in relation to subordination and therefore are threatening to male dominance. For this reason, they must be contained" (95). At Clayton and Woodrow Wilson, students "contained" girls' fighting and reinforced hegemonic masculinity by framing girl fights as less serious and less rational and by claiming that they were usually over access to boys.

"BEAUTIFUL, BUT TOUGH"

Still, girls' fighting was not completely co-opted to reinforce masculine dominance and feminine subordination. At both schools, fighting allowed girls to craft a tough image that other girls respected and boys even admired. Instead of seeing girl fighters as manly and therefore undesirable, some boys approved of girls who could fight well. This view intersected with local constructions of place. In both environments, the fact that girls could fight like boys reinforced the perceived roughness of the areas. Travis, for example, said, "Girls around here are pretty tough." Many boys described local tough girls with pride, possibly because living in an area where even girls used physical forms of aggression and protection made the boys themselves feel tougher.

At Woodrow Wilson especially, boys said that fighting did not necessarily compromise a girl's femininity. In fact, boys such as LaMarcus said that fighting ability could enhance a girl's allure.

> E. M.: For girls, when they get in a fight, is it kinda like people think
> they're less feminine or something like that?
> LAMARCUS: No.
> E. M.: I mean, because you know, if you think about fighting, it's kinda
> like—
> LAMARCUS: Male-ish.
> E. M.: Yeah, so—
> LAMARCUS: No, people don't think like that. If anything, they'll like the
> girl who won more. 'Cause if it's like a girl fight and they win, then
> more boys are gonna wanna talk to that girl. . . . 'Cause people like
> the toughest girl. That's how it is, so—like last year when that fight
> broke out, the girl that won, a lot of people wanted to be with her.

This ability to conflate toughness with femininity represents a shift in traditional notions of feminine passivity. In referring to the fighting ability of girls at Woodrow Wilson, Donte explained, "They so beautiful, but tough. So beautiful, but tough."

Interestingly, girls expressed more ambivalence about fighting. Except for Courtney and Janna, the girls I spoke with distanced themselves from fighting, although five of the sixteen girls I interviewed said that they themselves had been in a fight. Chelsie, for example, said she did not want to talk about a fight she had recently been in and seemed embarrassed by it. Other girls proudly and fervently proclaimed that they had never been in a fight. When I asked Alicia at Woodrow Wilson if she had ever been in a fight, she replied, "Never. I'm a good girl." The boys I interviewed, on the other hand, all said they had been in a fight, and many excitedly told me their fight stories in explicit detail. This indicates a key difference in fighting as gender performance: the idiom of fighting remained eminently masculine and virtually compulsory in order for boys to achieve masculinity. For girls, fighting was more of a last-ditch method of conflict resolution, not a representation of gender. Fighting might not necessarily compromise femininity, but it did not allow girls to achieve it either. Girls might be "tough," but they still needed to be "beautiful." As a result, fighting continued to broadcast masculinity, serving as both conflict resolution and a masculine end in itself. According to Jamie at Clayton, "Most of the girls have a purpose to fight, like the other girl makes them mad for a pretty good reason or something. And guys, they just—'You wanna fight?' 'Yeah, okay.' [She mock-punches.]" Girls could participate in the "sport" of fighting; but like so many other sports, it remained a vehicle and beacon of masculinity.

Fight Club

Fighting at both schools functioned as an underground sport that resisted rather than supported official school norms and values. It swelled in the undercurrents of school life, produced and cheered on by students who felt bored, marginalized, or spurned by the schools. Although only a minority of students actually fought, the majority supported fights as a welcome diversion. Fights at both schools drew interested crowds who tended to encourage rather than thwart the fight or impending fight. Students at Woodrow Wilson made videos of fights with their cell phones and posted them on the Internet. This "spectator sport" behavior stemmed from students' boredom with plodding school routines, which fights obviously shattered. In referring to school social life, Darius at Woodrow Wilson said, "There's not really much to talk about unless there's a fight!" Preston at Clayton said that students enjoyed watching fights, adding, "It livens up the day, I suppose would be the best way to put it!" Although more ambivalent than boys, girls also saw fighting as a welcome diversion. Lyndsie described it as a show rather than something that reflected deep divisions among students: "It's not like 'Oh, you fought him, you can't be friends with us'—it's not anything like that. It's just something we like to watch, I guess!"

Some boys fully embraced the identity and mentality of the fighter. For students without resources such as money, academic performance, or athletic ability, fighting was a way to achieve notoriety and self-efficacy. At Clayton, a group of boys adopted fighting as an ongoing practice and identity. These boys, mentioned in chapter 5, were called the "fighters"; they included Travis, Roger, Robert, Brent, and a few others. The fighters espoused a deep commitment to and almost joy about fighting. All came from low-income backgrounds with bad family names or negative community reputations that compromised respectability. For them, fighting was a "compensatory manhood act" that challenged and alleviated disadvantages by allowing them to assert a powerful masculinity (Schrock and Schwalbe 2009, 287). In particular, these boys derided the toughness of elite preps, but they also appeared to fight against the stigma of rutter. For instance, the first time I heard the term *rutter* was when Roger said that he intended to fight another boy for calling him that despised word.

At school the fighters, like some of the bad boys in Ferguson's work (2000), appeared to embrace the *troublemaker* label. Roger, for example, explained how he and a friend had gotten into fights regularly during middle school:

> ROGER: We used to go up 'ere and we'd get in fights ever' day. If we
>   couldn't find no one else to fight we'd fight each other. [He laughs.]
> E. M.: Was it because you guys didn't like each other, or was it for fun?
> ROGER: I don't know—we was troublemakers, I guess!

At the time of our interview, Roger was trying to distance himself from that label because he wanted to graduate from high school and enter the military. Brent, on the other hand, appeared to be too deeply enamored with the craft of fighting to abandon it. In our interview, his eyes shone with excitement when he described fighting.

> E. M.: Where do [fights] happen usually: it just depends, like "meet me
>   here" or whatever?
> BRENT [excited]: Yeah. See there's this one destination I like. It's one of
>   my favorite fighting places. [He laughs.] And it's like right out of
>   town, it's like right out 'ere by the woods where nobody can get
>   caught by the cops, and if anyone calls the cops you can get away
>   from 'em, like ever'body scatter through the woods and everything.
>   That's the place I prefer.

Brent waxed philosophical, describing the fight as a free space for expression and conflict resolution. This contrasted with his views of school, which he perceived as constricting and unfair. He claimed that economically privileged preps "try to run the school" and that the school favored the preps over "middle-class" students like himself.

> E. M: Do you think that preps get away with a little bit more?
> BRENT: Oh, yeah! I know that's true! . . . A couple of years ago, I think
> it was down in middle school, I got in a fight with this kid, right?
> And, well, only thing he got was, I think he got like an hour after
> school. And I got put in, I think at the time they called it ISS over
> at the alternative school. I got put over there for like ten days for it.
> And all they got was an hour after school for it!

School restrictions and what he perceived as unfair treatment prompted Brent to move most of his fights off school grounds to the area "by the woods." In addition, he said that fights during school, although humorous, "sucked." He explained why:

> Not enough action. They get broke up too soon so you really don't—
> see, you fight in school you get broke up too soon, you don't really get
> to express your actions, you know? 'Cause the reason you fight is
> 'cause of anger. Well, that's the reason I fight, is 'cause of anger. And
> after you hit 'im four or five times, your anger gets released. But if it
> happens in school and you get pulled off of 'em before you can hit 'em
> then you end up getting into another fight with 'em.

Viewing a fight as a space for the expression of anger and unfettered actions, Brent claimed that fighting had its own manly code and did not need institutional interference:

> It's an agreement, you know, whoever wins, wins, and whoever loses,
> loses, you know. It's like, say, this dude's on top of this other guy
> beatin' 'im, you know. Somebody around the circle will pull the guy
> off the other guy when he got a good enough beatin' and they shake
> hands and go about their way. And it'd be over with then.

During our conversation, Brent suddenly showed me the knuckles on his hands. They were gnarled and scarred, pockmarked with deep red wounds. He told me proudly, "See them two scars right 'ere? See, 'em are just healing. And my pinky knuckle's broken 'cause I just got into a fight the other day!" Perhaps because they felt marginalized in other ways, fighting gave the fighters a sense of empowerment, freedom, and clarity that was lacking in other areas of their lives. But as with Brent, such expressions of freedom and masculinity did not come without serious physical and academic costs.

"The Other Top Ten"

Fighting produced a tough, defiant masculinity, but it also led to suspensions and negative judgments from teachers and school administrators. According to their teachers, all the Clayton boys in the fighters group were problem students. When the principal and guidance counselor learned that I planned to interview Travis, for example, they informed me that he was "on watch" and that I would have to escort him to and from class for the interview. When I asked Mr. Wolf if I could take Travis out of his class for an interview, he laughed: "Yeah, he's one of the ones in Mr. Thomas's [the principal] top ten with a file about that thick. [He spreads his fingers.] This is not the good top ten—it's the other top ten." Roger was the only fighter who seemed able to override such perceptions. According to several teachers, he had been a major problem in ninth grade; but after repeating several classes, he improved both his behavior and his grades in tenth grade. Roger attributed this turnaround to his desire to enter the military as well as a better relationship with his new teachers—for instance, his tenth-grade English teacher Mr. Tanner, whom he described as "a way better teacher" than his ninth-grade instructor.

The behavior of the black boys at Woodrow Wilson was subject to intense scrutiny (see chapter 6). As Ferguson (2000) finds, even those who worked hard to present a schoolboy image hovered one misstep away from being known as a troublemaker. Fighting could be this misstep; and as Corie's experience (recounted in chapter 6) showed, it could move them closer to the criminal justice system. At both schools, fighting obstructed boys' attachment to school and ultimately their achievement. As other research corroborates, fighting is certainly detrimental to academic success (Staff and Kreager 2008); but so many boys at Clayton and Wilson identified it with the physical toughness and risk taking associated with masculinity that its school-related costs became insignificant. Travis explained, "[Fighters] don't care. They'll just get in trouble. They'd rather have people say this person beat up this person 'cause he's tryin' to act hard." For many boys in my study, proving toughness, achieving respect, and behaving like a man trumped the disciplinary consequences that interrupted academic achievement and progress.

Conclusion

Fighting and sports are two of the most evocative signals of masculine meaning and dominance. Both constitute masculinity through physical strength and power, and both feature prominently in schools, although fighting is against the rules. In my analysis, fighting and sports (especially male contact sports such as football) are similar in that they link masculinity to physical forms of aggression and toughness and remind everyone that male bodies possess a greater capacity for such qualities. They thereby become irrefutable spectacles of masculine power. Even when girls do fight or play sports, both of which now happen with greater frequency, others tend to perceive their efforts as less significant than the "real" forms practiced by boys.

Some girls, such as Janna and Courtney, pursued fighting in an understandable attempt to claim power and self-protection in harsh environments. Yet for these girls, as well as for a vast number of boys, this fleeting sense of power could not outweigh the enduring physical and academic repercussions of fighting. Although they performed well in school at the time I interviewed them, Janna and Courtney both repeated ninth grade largely because of suspensions. Their experience, while atypical for girls, is unfortunately far too common for boys. All the boys I interviewed claimed they had been in a fight, and most had received suspensions for fighting. This not only literally distanced them from school but also had potential to create a recursive relationship involving aggressive behavior, negative perceptions from school officials, and academic disengagement. For some boys, this inflamed an already combustible distrust of school authority.

Boys choose to fight not only because such behavior is part of their masculine tool kit but also because it confirms masculinity. Indeed, for boys in my study, fight avoidance impugned the very foundation of manhood. Although schools vehemently (and rightly) punish fighting, such punishment seems to contradict the currents of masculinity in society. With football and fighting, form and institutionalization might differ, but the message of masculinity remains the same. Was the hit stick so lauded at Clayton really any different from Brent's self-expression through fighting? Simply, one set of behaviors operated under institutional endorsement and was practiced primarily by boys celebrated in the school and community, whereas the other was outlawed by the institution and practiced primarily by boys stigmatized in the school and community. The fact that one practice of masculinity became hegemonic and the other marginalized stemmed more from perceptions of social class (and, at Woodrow Wilson, race) and morality than from the actual behavior. The real problem originated from broad cultural messages of what it means to be a man, not from the particular acts of aggression that further handcuffed these already disadvantaged boys.

Chapter 9   Conclusion

SCHOOLS ARE IMPORTANT SITES for the construction of gender, forging meanings of masculinity and femininity that guide academic behaviors and outcomes. The idea that doing gender influences educational processes and helps explain why boys and girls perform differently from one another in school was solidified for me during one routine day at Clayton when I was observing Mr. Clark's math class. He began class by opening a container of vibrantly colored blocks. The blocks, he explained animatedly, would help students understand math concepts by "exercising your math brains!" The students were less enthusiastic. They moped and brooded; their mood seemed to reflect the dim, lugubrious winter weather outside. At Mr. Clark's eager behest, the first few marched, as if to death, to the container of blocks. As instructed, each grabbed a handful of blocks and plodded back to his or her seat. While a second set of funereal students approached the container, Mr. Clark explained that class members were to count their blocks (total and by type) and then write their answers on the board. The goal of the activity was to calculate various statistics and probabilities.

But once students began writing their totals on the blindingly white dry-erase board, the activity quickly unraveled. Students began erasing their original totals and returning for more blocks as they competed to obtain certain amounts. Not all students competed for the same goal, however. Boys stretched out their hands in muscular determination, grabbing as many blocks as their hands possibly could. Other students cheered on the boys who were competing for the highest single total. Girls, by contrast, cupped their hands delicately around minute numbers of blocks. Some who had originally had high numbers actually erased their total and went back for fewer blocks, while boys did the opposite. One boy wrote on the board, next to the low total of a boy named Chase, "Chase sissy girl." Janna turned around to me and dryly observed, "The boys are trying to be bigger and the girls want to be smaller."

As this example has illustrated, gender performance infuses the everyday process of education. In many areas, such as football and cheerleading, schools are overtly gendered. In other areas, gender is more hidden but nevertheless present. Whether overt or covert, the accomplishment of gender in school can have profound consequences. As I have emphasized throughout this book, boys tend to approach school in ways consistent with masculinity and may use simple behaviors (such as picking up blocks) or more serious behaviors (such as fighting) as means to represent manliness, while girls tend to employ different school-relevant behaviors as means to demonstrate femininity. In other words, gender does not exist internally; the students' behaviors actually form gender. Boys and girls picked up the blocks differently, not because they were hardwired to do so but because the activity allowed them to show others the strength associated with masculinity and the gracefulness associated with femininity. Although the example may seem innocuous, it demonstrates that, when funneled through intersecting constraints of race, class, and place, gender enactments can have serious effects on achievement.

Back to the Gender Gap

My perspective on the gender gap differs from the arguments of most popular commentary, such as Gurian and Stevens's (2005) *The Minds of Boys* and Tyre's (2008) *The Trouble with Boys*, which have great influence on educators and parents. Although these books are well intentioned, they rest on a simplistic notion of gender. (For reviews, see McCready 2010 and Weaver-Hightower 2009.) They rely on two claims I challenge: (1) inherent, especially biological, differences between boys and girls primarily explain boys' lower achievement; and (2) the crisis surrounding boys' underachievement can be traced to gender alone, without substantial modifications of race, class, and local context. Yet boys in the schools I examined every week for a year and a half failed to achieve not because of inescapable biological urges but because their social contexts framed school-focused behavior as inconsistent with masculinity. Few local scripts for educationally successful manhood existed at Woodrow Wilson and Clayton, where hegemonic masculinity was defined primarily through physical attributes such as pragmatic manual skills or explosive athletic ability. Nonetheless, even within these pockets of disadvantage, diverse strategies of masculinity (some of which were educationally focused) emerged within and across the schools, underscoring personal agency in managing multiple, intersecting demands of gender, race, class, and place.

Place is an often-overlooked category in educational gender research; but as my fieldwork showed, it denotes both a geographical location and a complex social location embedded with meanings that guide behaviors and perceptions (Cresswell 2004). The communities of Woodrow Wilson and Clayton comprised unique histories, social identities, economic structures, social dynamics, and peer cultures, among other factors. Each place contended with different (although largely negative) outsider perceptions. Because the high schools were couched within these particular place-based webs of meanings and relations, each had unique resources and guidelines for doing masculinity and femininity. However, place also leveled challenges to masculinity, and boys at both schools often responded similarly by asserting the power and superiority of masculinity in educationally costly ways, such as by fighting or evoking contrived carelessness.

Masculinity, as contemporary theory and my findings emphasize, is a situated accomplishment shaped by local context, racialized experience, economic inequality, and other factors. Nonetheless, the accomplishment of masculinity, especially in its most exalted forms, tends to be geared toward strength, power, and control. When suggesting solutions for boys' underachievement in school, popular commentaries do not always take into account the intricacy, contradictions, and power embedded in masculinity; and some of these authors promote misguided and even dangerous policy recommendations. Gurian and Stevens (2005), for example, advocate entirely separate educational experiences for boys and girls. Although these authors claim to be attentive to supposed biological differences, their conclusions are really based on tired stereotypes, such as the idea that one should encourage "aggression nurturance" among boys (Gurian and Stevens 2005, 93). Other solutions, such as keeping boys' classrooms brightly lit, are just strange. Yet many schools follow these and other nostrums of the Gurian Institute (http://www .gurianinstitute.com), which promulgates the idea that boys and girls have completely different brains and learn in completely different ways.

Other popular approaches, although less radical, also rely on gender essentialism and promote a "boys will be boys" attitude. Tyre (2008), for example, encourages teachers to either tolerate boys' "naturally" obstreperous behavior or get out of teaching (284). So boys should be subject to a less restrictive set of rules than girls are? Many schools have begun implementing gender-separate educational environments to boost boys' achievement, under the assumption that girls (especially in secondary school) pose a distraction for boys, who try to show off for them. Such recommendations indirectly blame girls for boys' lack of performance. Moreover, there is no conclusive evidence that single-sex education improves boys' achievement if one controls for factors such as economics and school quality (Riordan 1990).

Such gender-distinctive educational approaches are mired in a static girls-versus-boys framework. By contrast, I wish to move toward a firm emphasis on gender as an ongoing social product. What this means for school policy is that dividing schools or classes by gender or enlisting specific programs only for boys are not the right approaches. Instead, schools must promote policies on a schoolwide basis to change definitions of masculinity and bring boys and girls together to resist the struggle for dominance that many boys fall prey to.

Understanding gender as an ongoing accomplishment illuminates the contradictions and misunderstandings freighted in boys' underachievement. This perspective reveals how boys and girls produce thoughts and actions as a means of representing gender and how this production can have important educational consequences. Further, masculinity studies, especially those guided by the work of Raewyn Connell (1987; 1995), emphasize how hegemonic, or preeminent, practices of masculinity strive for dominance over femininity and alternative expressions of masculinity. I saw such hegemonic masculinity at Woodrow Wilson and Clayton primarily through expressions of physical power and toughness, exemplified by the prominence of boys' athletics. Hegemony, as the concept's originator Antonio Gramsci (1971) made clear, is a continuous struggle. Thus, boys in the schools I studied marshaled different resources to sculpt strong projections of manhood. Although many of these resources—notably, fighting and contrived carelessness—led them away from school, boys used them precisely because they believed these tactics helped them demonstrate superiority over girls and boys whom they perceived to be effeminate .

Although I emphasize boys' and girls' agency in making decisions about school, I do not want my depictions to fuel stereotypes or function as individualistic explanations for boys' underperformance. African American boys, in particular, are subject to stereotypes that depict them as not caring about education or hard work; yet even boys such as Wesley and Donte were more than fun-loving clowns. My interview with Donte revealed his deep insights on a number of important topics, as evidenced by his lucid description of his brush with gang life. Although Wesley joked his way through many classes, he would ask to do his work out in the hall (perhaps out of sight of other boys) if he sensed he were falling behind. According to Ms. Williams, when Wesley made this decision, he completed his work exceptionally well. In other words, Donte, Wesley, and others were able to shrewdly navigate their way through the minefield of stereotypes and pressures that African American males face daily.

SUPPORTING DIVERSE MASCULINITIES

Boys at Woodrow Wilson and Clayton made their choices from the severely limited hand that society had dealt to them. We cannot continue to simply blame these boys for poor individual decisions. Instead, we need to ask our-selves, in light of persistent economic disadvantage and unemployment, con-tinuing racism, ballooning incarceration rates, and rigid ideals of manhood, what do we really provide to help these boys succeed? Here I suggest some ways in which schools can support both boys and girls by helping redefine masculinity so that it better aligns with school and achievement.

Iconic jocks and cheerleaders may be well-worn clichés, but they con-tinue to set the hegemonic standards for masculinity and femininity in most U.S. schools. This was true at both schools in my research, although Woodrow Wilson provided more space for alternative masculinities. Some researchers have argued that male-only contact sports such as football promote a damag-ing paragon of masculinity based on combat, dominance, and stoicism (Eder, Evans, and Parker 1997). Further, especially for African American boys, athletics represent a highly unlikely career path that they nonetheless concentrate on as a realistic possibility (Brooks 2009; May 2008).

Such evidence of the dark side of athletics has prompted suggestions to eliminate sports, especially violent contact sports, from schools (Eder et al. 1997). On the surface, my findings appear to support such a view. I noted that boys blocked from athletics because of physical challenges, lack of interest, or other factors often attempted to achieve masculinity through clownin', fighting, or other behaviors that could get them into trouble and deter them academically. Moreover, the physicality, power, and centrality of male sports emphatically convey the dominance of masculinity in schools. Nevertheless, I do not advocate eliminating football or other contact sports from school. Not only is this suggestion unfeasible, but it also overlooks many of the posi-tive benefits of athletics, such as the community ritual so visible at Clayton. Solutions must consider more than gender; they must also take into account the inequalities and attachments of place. Autocratically eliminating such rituals would only promote community alienation and resentment in already marginalized rural and urban areas such as those in my study.

Instead, I suggest that schools add other rituals to promote educational communities that do not relentlessly extol aggressive masculinity. Schools could begin by giving more serious support to female and co-gender sports as well as to other extracurricular activities. Such activities can provide alterna-tive models and outlets for a version of masculinity that is not based on dom-inance and physicality, allowing different boys (and girls) a greater chance to gain recognition and respect among peers. The visual and performing arts, for example, offer positive, school-attached outlets for recognition, belonging, and self-esteem in many schools. Yet such activities typically work on shoe-string budgets and are not well supported by educational and community resources. At both schools in my research, performing arts had nowhere near the support and prominence of athletics, especially football and boys' basket-ball. Woodrow Wilson was able to produce one small-cast play during my time there. Clayton had a very limited drama program and failed for years to hold any dramatic student production. This severely hindered non-athletic outlets for boys—something that has been shown to be very important to boys who do not fit the normative masculine mold (see McCready 2010; Pascoe 2007).

I envision much stronger performing and visual arts programs in disad-vantaged schools so that they can support larger and more regular community events. Unfortunately, in many school districts, such programs are balkanized into exclusive magnet academies at limited school sites and are limited to small numbers of students. Worse, many schools facing budget crises are cutting or eliminating arts programs altogether. Such programs should be widely available so that more schools, students, and neighborhoods can capitalize on the poten-tial community building and diverse gender expressions the arts can offer.

Schools can also "make space for diverse masculinities" (McCready 2010) by facilitating gay, lesbian, bisexual, and transgender (GLBT) or Gay/Straight Alliance (GSA) student groups. (Neither school in my research had these groups.) Such organizations provide outlets and social support for non-gender–conforming youth as well as employ straight youth as allies. Sam at Clayton, for example, would undoubtedly have benefited enormously from such a group, which might have changed the homophobic views of the straight students who made Sam's school life so difficult. This is the ultimate boon of allowing opportunities for diverse expressions of gender to flourish in schools: they not only ease the lives of students who are not gender normative but also encourage school community members to question and transgress rigid gender norms themselves. Such flexibility can produce open-mindedness among students, which can subvert ideals of gender dominance and hierarchy. As I have shown, such ideals form the roots of boys' underachievement.

Programs do not need to specifically target boys in order to improve boys' achievement. For example, many boys (and fewer girls) at both schools got into trouble for physically aggressive behavior such as fighting, which seriously impeded their academic progress. Creating a climate of trust and well-being among all students could reduce fighting in schools, especially improving the academic progress of boys but ultimately helping all students. I have shown that students who were prone to fight revealed a sense of alienation from for-mal sources of social control, including schools and law enforcement (see also

Morris 2010). Enacting harsh discipline measures such as extended suspensions, expulsions, or referrals to the juvenile justice system did not solve this problem; punishment simply magnified students' sense of distance from school. Although I am not suggesting that student fights should go unpunished, I believe that such punishment must be balanced with an equal attention to why fighting occurs and viable options for students to resolve disputes verbally rather than physically. School-supported peer mediation programs are excellent solutions. These programs do not use the power of external school authority to punish or arbitrate disagreements but provide students with a nonviolent forum of equals who work together toward conflict resolution.

INTERPRETING DIVERSE MASCULINITIES

Sociologists such as Dance (2002) and educational researchers such as Delpit ([1996] 2006) demonstrate that the interactional styles of urban minority students are often misinterpreted in schools. Boys in urban environments craft tough fronts to survive on the streets but find that schools demand a different presentation of self (Dance 2002; Goffman 1959). This phenomenon is influenced by definitions of masculinity as well as race, class, and place. Although tough posturing is detrimental to boys' school success, it becomes critical for the achievement of masculinity. Yet in many cases such posturing is really just a masculine strategy to navigate gender accountability while masking admissions of vulnerability.

Some of the most moving moments in my research came when I interviewed Kevin at Clayton and Darius at Woodrow Wilson. On the surface, Kevin was all bluster and bravado, eschewing seemingly pointless school rules and bragging about his boxing and fighting ability. Inside, however—and in a way he would probably never admit—Kevin secreted feelings of shame and vulnerability arising from his modest family background and lack of popularity. Yet teachers did not view Kevin in this complicated way: one described him as someone who would be "trouble down the line."

Unlike Kevin, Darius was a quiet, reserved student. But like Kevin, he had to overcome difficult situations in his personal life (his father's death), which contributed to his difficulty in school, especially in learning math. Also like Kevin, Darius crafted a stalwart, masculine solution to this problem by disengaging from math class. His math teacher took this as a sign of indifference and, as is often the case when teachers have many students, did not go out of her way to help him. Darius, in fact, did not appear to welcome such help because it would have revealed his inner vulnerability about learning. Instead, he devised the unwise strategy of sleeping in class and later trying to understand the material on his own.

Educators should not merely accept the recalcitrant behavior of boys such as Kevin and Darius, as researchers such as Tyre (2008) suggest, but should seek to interpret what purpose such behavior serves and help boys to seek alternative means of expression that do not further distance them from school. To do this, the educational system needs to increase the number of teachers and school counselors available to students. Many of the school personnel I observed were simply too overworked and were dealing with too many students to devote the time and energy needed for them to see past some boys' brusque or indifferent exteriors. Instead of being punished or ignored, disengaged boys should be given the encouragement and resources to discuss their feelings with qualified guidance counselors. Allowing boys to better understand the origins of their own detachment from school can help break down the walls between disadvantaged boys and achievement. At the same time, teachers and other school personnel need to be trained to see past these walls.

Many schools struggling with the severely flagging achievement of boys implement programs or interventions targeted especially at male students. My findings indicate that such approaches should be implemented with caution or not at all. Gender differentiation is often the first step in gender inequality (Schrock and Schwalbe 2009). In teaching boys to be men, educators must not emphasize manhood as one-dimensional or dominant. As I have shown, it is the association of masculinity with superiority that ironically draws boys away from academics. Even when well meaning, educators should avoid promoting a view of masculinity as different from and superior to femininity. In my research, such notions of masculine superiority encouraged a carefree approach to schoolwork for boys, while girls exerted greater effort and achieved greater results.

SMART THINKING

Boys' strategies to conceal the difficulty they had in learning material or the effort they needed to put into studying were strangely reinforced by widespread assumptions that these boys were truly smart. At both schools, girls were virtually never described as highly intelligent, but teachers and peers described even low-performing boys this way.[1] Psychologist Carol Dweck (2007) argues that praising students for possessing innate intellectual ability can be surprisingly counterproductive. She finds that students who believe that their intelligence is internally fixed may not strive to demonstrate their intellectual ability through academic effort. In other words, students who are continually told they are smart often become academically lazy. Dweck's (2007) research suggests that students who perceive learning as a process of intellectual growth requiring hard work tend to better meet academic challenges and maximize their abilities. She recommends that instead of praising students for their innate talent, teachers should praise students for how they apply themselves in the learning process and demonstrate intellectual growth. Thus, by focusing on effort and process, teachers can encourage all students to make the most of their varying abilities.

My findings from Woodrow Wilson and Clayton suggest that perceptions of inherent intelligence are strongly gendered. This echoes research by Sadker and Sadker (1994) and Luttrell (1997). The working-class women in Luttrell's (1997) study almost all named men when asked for examples of people who possessed "real intelligence" (28–29). Similarly, Sadker and Sadker (1994) find that teachers tend to praise boys for their intelligence and girls for their efforts (96). These studies align with my findings that teachers tended to describe boys as "smart, but lazy" and girls as students who "work hard." Drawing from Dweck (2007), I assert that such perceptions actually hinder boys. The almost unconscious association between masculinity and real intelligence fuels contrived carelessness; and in extreme cases, laziness virtually serves as an indicator of intelligence. Following this logic, I believe that one of the most powerful ways in which teachers can improve boys' achievement is to praise and reward students' academic efforts while lessening the concentration on students' inherent talents. Here again, such an alteration for educational practice does not require a specific or separate program for boys. Instead, students of both genders can benefit from academic environments focused on demonstrated work and achievement instead of murky presumptions about who is really smart.

From Boys to Gender

The best way to understand gender differences in achievement is to understand gender as an emerging product of ongoing interaction. Boys and girls arrange their behaviors in ways that create, reproduce, and sometimes modify notions of masculinity and femininity. Such gender constructions are not neutral but tend to follow prevailing social patterns in which masculinity connotes and occupies positions of superiority. These patterns are deeply sculpted by intersections with race, social class, and place. By situating gender differences in this more textured framework, we can better understand how overriding notions of manly strength produce hidden and enduring costs. Yet we continue to send many of our boys down pathways of masculinity that lead only to dead ends, forcing them to learn the hard way that academic effort is important. Education can be a beacon for new, inclusive, healthy masculinities, but schools must think beyond haggard stereotypes and divisions. Boys and girls both benefit when we fully comprehend and address the problems of gender, not simply the problems of boys.

Appendix   Research Methods

Process and Representation

"Let me know when you figure everyone around here out, because I've lived here my whole life and I still can't explain it!" said Mr. Kerr as he spotted me in the hallway at Clayton. Such playful chiding became a running joke between Mr. Kerr and me throughout my fieldwork. Other teachers and students were less vocal but still showed awareness of (and some trepidation about) my presence at the school as a researcher. At Woodrow Wilson, the same sentiment emerged: students and teachers assumed I had selected the school because something was wrong with them. For instance, one day when I sat in a math class, Javon asked me what I was doing there. I answered with my standard line: "Writing a book about what life is like for high school kids."

Javon immediately said, without sarcasm, "Oh, like how bad a school this is—like how we're all ghetto and stuff." Such assumptions paralleled students' dour perceptions of their schools' reputations (see chapter 2). Despite my insistence that I was not there to recycle negative images of the schools, such views affected my access to participants and raised issues of representation in my research.

The Research Process

As a white, middle-class academic in his mid-thirties, I couldn't have been more different from most of my participants. On a number of occasions, this became palpably and painfully clear. For example, one day at Woodrow Wilson, I was talking to Ms. Williams while she let the students have some free time on the computers. Wesley and some of his friends started watching an Internet video that another student had posted of himself rapping. The boys laughed hysterically at the student's song. "He's tryin' to act like he all hard!" Wesley exclaimed. Then, to emphasize how little credibility the rapper had, Wesley pointed to me and said, "That's like him tryin' to rap!" The incident vividly underlined the way in which my whiteness, my age, and perhaps my general geekiness was creating social distance between myself and my participants at the school. Although my Clayton participants were white, other issues of distance emerged, especially age and occupational background (as well as geekiness). Although I attempted to narrow the distance, I do not believe I could have ever completely closed those gaps.

Because such differences had the potential to affect my access to research participants, I waited until the end of my fieldwork to recruit students for interviews. At that point, I had followed the students through ninth grade into the better part of tenth grade, so I had gotten to know them and they were familiar with me. Our interviews, which appeared to go very well, took place in a private location within each school and were digitally recorded. The shortest were forty-five minutes long; the longest lasted an hour and thirty minutes. Students opened up to me during these dialogues, sometimes in very personal ways. I often found their views and stories interesting, touching, and insightful. This approach highlights a key strength of ethnography: because I had multiple points of contact with my participants over time, my awareness of their worlds grew, as did our familiarity with each other, which allowed me to achieve a deeper view of their social reality.

Unfortunately, I had difficulty actually getting students in for the interviews. Following the instructions of my university's Institutional Review Board, I had to obtain written permission from parents before interviewing any students. I chose to solicit this permission by sending consent forms home with the students I had selected to interview, along with a letter to parents explaining the research and rationale for the interview. However, several students neglected to bring this form home. Only one student said that his parent had refused to sign; the others all lost the forms or just never followed through. In some instances, students may have not wanted to do the interview and were too timid to tell me. In many other cases, students openly asked if they could get out of class for an interview, but I had to explain that I could not do so without a signed parental consent form.

My purposive sampling design (see Lofland, Snow, Anderson, and Lofland 2006) necessitated the inclusion of both high- and low-achieving students. Not surprisingly, the low-achieving students were more likely to neglect their forms. Thus, throughout the process of recruitment I had to make sure I did not overselect for higher-achieving students. Similarly, I tried to not overselect popular students, many of whom came from more privileged backgrounds—something Barrie Thorne (1993) calls avoiding "big man" bias (97). This approach was easier to implement at Clayton than it was at Woodrow

Table A.1
Clayton Student Respondents

Pseudonym	Mother's Occupation and Education	Father's Occupation and Education
Brent	Homemaker, tenth grade	Custodian, unknown
Zack	Cashier, high school diploma	Unknown, eleventh grade*
Rebecca	Office assistant, associate's degree	Machinist, high school diploma
Travis	Foster parent, GED	Disabled, eleventh grade
Emily	Unknown, high school diploma*	Machinist, high school diploma
Kaycee	Food service, high school diploma	Unemployed and odd jobs, tenth grade*
Lyndsie	Special needs coordinator, master's degree*	Coal miner, high school diploma
Roger	Unemployed, unknown*	Tree trimmer, ninth grade
Janna	Unemployed, tenth grade*	Disabled, high school diploma
Kevin	Office assistant, associate's degree	Disabled, eleventh grade
Preston	Nurse, associate's degree	Unemployed and odd jobs, high school diploma*
Jamie	Homemaker, associate's degree	Police officer, high school diploma
Harry	Dental assistant, bachelor's degree	Entrepreneur, associate's degree
Chelsie	Cashier, high school diploma	Oil-rig worker, high school diploma*
Robert	Nurse's aide, high school diploma	Mechanic, high school diploma

*Student did not live with this parent at the time of the interview.

Wilson. As tables A.1 and A.2 show, my sample from Woodrow Wilson was slightly higher than the Clayton sample in terms of parents' education and occupational status. At Woodrow Wilson more respondents' parents held a high school degree, and fewer were unemployed. Although this may slightly skew comparisons between the schools, the majority of samples from both school are working class in both educational and occupational background.

In addition to interviews, field notes were my primary source of data. I observed in classrooms, hallways, lunchrooms, outside school, sporting events, school ceremonies, and school functions. I also observed within each community, eating in local establishments, browsing in stores, and walking down the streets. Because of my interest in academic achievement, the bulk of my observations took place in classrooms. High school classrooms are convenient locations for observation because one can take notes (as I did) directly in a field notebook relatively unobtrusively, which enhances fidelity. Of course, students noticed my presence, often asking what I was doing there and what types of things I was writing down. But being in a classroom setting in which the majority of students were writing in notebooks or on worksheets meant that my note taking was usually not awkward. When a class did not lend itself readily to note taking (such as vocational classes at Clayton), I attempted to recall my observations as soon as possible after the class was over.

Table A.2
Woodrow Wilson Student Respondents

Pseudonym	Mother's Occupation and Education	Father's Occupation and Education
Kalvin	Home day care worker, high school diploma	Warehouse worker, high school diploma
Darius	Secretary, associate's degree	Deceased, high school diploma
Ivory	Surveyor, bachelor's degree	Computer technician, associate's degree*
David	Secretary, high school diploma	Machinist, associate's degree
Vanessa	Secretary, high school diploma	Machinist, high school diploma
Shontae	Clerical worker, high school diploma	Technician, high school diploma*
Kenda	Clerical worker, high school diploma	Truck driver, high school diploma*
LaMarcus	Unknown, unknown**	Fast food manager, high school diploma**
Corie	Clerical worker, enrolled in four-year college	Bus driver, high school diploma*
Donte	Home day care worker, high school diploma	Mechanic, eleventh grade
Quentin	Teacher's aide, associate's degree	Chef, high school diploma
Courtney	Nurse's aide, tenth grade*	Lawn care worker, tenth grade
Candace	Nurse's aide, high school diploma	Carpenter, high school diploma*
Alicia	Retail store manager, bachelor's degree	Retired firefighter, associate's degree
Brittany	Warehouse worker, high school diploma	Mechanic, high school diploma
Shawn	Clerical worker, high school diploma	Clerical worker, bachelor's degree

*Student did not live with this parent at the time of the interview.

**Both biological parents (listed) were deceased. Student lived with foster parents.

NOTE: Vanessa, Shontae, and Kenda were interviewed together.

Among other observations, I jotted down details of what people said and wore, facial expressions, class dynamics, and subject matter. Despite the many miles I drove between the two schools (sometimes visiting both on the same day), I forced myself to write expanded versions of my field notes into a computer file every night after leaving the field. Similarly, I transcribed interviews with all thirty-one students as soon as possible after conducting them. This quick data logging not only improved accuracy but allowed me to begin the initial process of identifying emerging research themes.

As I progressed through my fieldwork, I tracked emerging themes as they developed by using brief theoretical memos (Lofland et al. 2006; Maxwell 2005). As I will explain, I treated such emerging themes delicately so that they did not distort subsequent data collection. Keeping track of such possibilities, however, allowed me to check these emergent assumptions through other data sources in the field, thereby increasing validity (see Lewis 2003, 207). Upon leaving the field, I analyzed data more systematically. To code more than 1,000 pages of field notes and interview transcripts, I first used an open coding scheme (Emerson, Fretz, and Shaw 1995), reading through the data line by line and interpreting each example in a basic way—for example, "student does not have homework." Open coding encompassed the entire corpus of data; I did not ignore or minimize any information. After open coding, I read through the data once again, coding in a more focused way. In this process, I developed broader and more theoretically relevant codes, such as "lack of preparation for class—boys" and "lack of preparation for class—girls." From this, I connected codes into relevant themes, analyzing various data sources, including field notes, interviews, and school records both within and across the two schools. Throughout the analysis I made sure to check assumptions to minimize bias. For example, I included disconfirming evidence, such as girls who were not prepared for class, in addition to evidence supporting primary themes, such as boys' lack of class preparation. This ensured that, although the majority of evidence supported the theme, I did not solely consider the supportive examples.

My social background almost certainly influenced the data I collected. At both schools, students and teachers were initially somewhat hesitant around me. At Woodrow Wilson in particular, my whiteness highlighted my outsider status, which may have affected what students and, to a lesser extent, teachers revealed to me. For example, I found that few of the African American students I interviewed discussed racism and discrimination directly in interviews. However, they did intimate these topics more indirectly, through discussions of school funding and resources as well as school discipline. It is plausible that these students were reluctant to discuss such issues with a white man, anticipating that such conversations could be construed as playing the race card or making unfounded excuses and complaints. Nevertheless, as I have asserted elsewhere (Morris 2006), the influence of social background did not render these data invalid. Instead, as I will discuss, I remained aware of sources of social distance between me and my participants and took specific measures to recognize and reduce them.

Representing the Schools

Both schools suffered from place-based stereotypes. Clayton endured the reputation of being a backwards hillbilly school in rural Appalachia. Grotesque stereotypes of ignorance, moral depravity, and laziness continue to haunt people from the region (Billings, Norman, and Ledford 1999), while different but equally damaging stereotypes of crime and immorality have distorted perceptions of urban African Americans. Such negative images can be perpetuated through scholarly writing (Billings et al. 1999; Dance 2002). While I did not want my research to reinforce such stereotypes, my outsider status heightened the risk of misinterpretation and unwitting perpetuation of untoward views of my participants (Hosokawa [2009] 2010).

Moreover, I collected information that, according to some interpretations, might resonate with stereotypical assumptions. My analysis of fighting at both schools, for example, threatened to cast these schools and students as brutish and violent. More particularly, as I mentioned in chapter 6, I struggled with how to handle my use of the n word at Woodrow Wilson. Yet because, in both instances, I found inclusion of such material to be important to the analysis, I did not want to make the opposite mistake of producing a superficial story of gender that avoided complex and controversial issues.

I found myself constantly questioning whether or not my analysis reflected hidden biases of race, class, gender, sexual orientation, and age along with a host of other social categories in which I differed from my respondents. To balance these tensions, I enlisted two strategies in my research process. First, although some participants at both schools expressed initial skepticism of me, I worked to build trust throughout my fieldwork (Hosokawa [2009] 2010). One way was through my consistent presence in the schools. Because of the comparative design of the ethnography, this was more difficult than it would have been if I had focused on one school. Still, I worked to ensure that I visited each school for one to four days every week. I also focused on particular classes and teachers so that participants could become more familiar with me. In addition, I helped out around the schools as much as possible. This had two benefits: it increased my presence and, perhaps more importantly, allowed me to give something back to the schools in return for all the support they had provided. Although neither school accepted my offers to tutor, I was able to help the librarians organize materials and undertake smaller tasks within classrooms.

Second, throughout the research process I worked to keep an open mind and regularly check my assumptions. Paul Rock (2001) cleverly terms this a "naïve by design" mindset (32). I entered the schools with broad research interests and a design of how I wanted to conduct the study but without a rigid set of hypotheses or the myopic intention of looking for something in particular. In fact, I intended to broadly study intersections of class, gender, race, and place, especially in terms of the "acting white" debate (see Downey 2008). However, within my first month of fieldwork, I quickly learned about the gender gap at the schools and concentrated my analysis on that topic.

I believe that the primary goal of ethnography is to learn from your participants. Such learning is a holistic process and cannot happen if thinking is too compartmentalized or researchers are concerned only with what they think they already know or want to prove. In several cases, as I have noted, my findings surprised me. In other instances, my initial assumptions or intuitions proved to be false as I continued my research. I maintained openness with my emerging themes, checking them as I continued to collect data rather than using them as the primary framework for subsequent data collection. For example, I did not expect the majority of my male interviewees at Woodrow Wilson to emphasize the importance of book smarts, especially because in my early interviews at Clayton boys had expressed far more criticism of book smarts. Although I had initially assumed these responses would be similar, the variation became a key area of difference for boys across the two schools.

Similarly, some of my early assumptions required modification. For example, early on, boys at both schools discussed fighting with me, which aligned with my previous knowledge of masculinity—that fighting is an important mode of masculine expression. Of course, as chapter 8 attests, I retained this focus on fighting as a representation of masculinity. However, the story became complicated as I began to learn that girls at both schools also used physical violence. Ignoring these emerging findings about girls and fighting may have yielded a tighter analysis but not a more accurate one. I remained unsure of how exactly to incorporate this inconvenient issue until I analyzed the data after leaving the field. As I coded data and worked to triangulate from different data sources (interviews with students, conversations with teachers, field notes, and school records), I began to see that girl fights challenged many tenets of masculinity, showing girls as active agents in gender construction, but that interpretations of these fights tended to diminish and feminize them. Thus, my consideration of seemingly incongruous information honed and deepened the analysis.

Issues of representation go beyond the mere mechanics of research design and analysis. They reflect deeply imbedded asymmetries between the various worlds we live in—white-black, rural-urban, academic-blue collar, masculine-feminine. The stories I tell here are produced from such asymmetrical worlds and bear the inevitable stamp of my particular location within them. I have attempted as much as possible to empathize with, but not to romanticize, my participants. I have also attempted to show diversity and agency within the groups that I studied, something often lacking from accounts of inner-city or rural areas. (See Dance [2002], Gray [2009], and Jones [2010] for critiques.) I hope this book provides a vivid, complex, and sensitive account of masculinity in schools. Readers are open to their own interpretations, which I have little control over. However, in light of the sometimes negative world of critical educational studies, I wish to underscore that much of what I observed at Woodrow Wilson and Clayton consisted of hardworking, dedicated, and amiable teaching and learning. Several of the teachers and students I had the pleasure to meet at both schools were nothing short of inspiring. Clayton and Woodrow Wilson were not bad schools. Their students were not bad kids. These were simply schools, communities, and individuals trying to do their best under difficult circumstances.

Notes

Chapter 1 Introduction

1. Woodrow Wilson is a pseudonym, as are all personal and place names in this book. In addition, I do not cite information drawn from publicly available sources such as the U.S. Census and newspapers in explicit form. Both conventions are necessary to protect participant confidentiality.
2. There is an important and vast literature on intersectionality, or the integrated study of race, class, and gender. Foundational works in this vein include Collins (1990), Crenshaw (1991), and Spelman (1988). More recent scholarship includes Glenn (2002), Pascale (2007), Pyke and Johnson (2003), and Zinn and Dill (1996), among countless others. For applications of intersectionality to education, see Bettie (2003) and Morris (2007). I should note that I focus here on the social construction of gender but that race and class should also be understood as ongoing social processes rather than static demographic variables (see Bettie 2003, 37). Thus, race and class shape gender, but gender also shapes race and class.

Chapter 2 Respect and Respectability

1. For example, the percentage of residents in this tract reporting that they had obtained a bachelor's degree or higher (35.9) was more than twice as high as the tract with the next largest percentage of those obtaining a bachelor's degree or higher (15.5). Excluding this tract, 12.3 percent of residents in the remaining tracts had no high school diploma, and just 12.1 percent had attained a bachelor's degree or higher.
2. Following the No Child Left Behind education law, the state of Ohio rated schools in the following categories (from lowest to highest) based on academic indicators such as proficiency test scores and attendance rates: Academic Emergency, Academic Watch, Continuous Improvement, Effective, Excellent.
3. I can think of two possible explanations for this discrepancy. First, some research indicates that rural residents are reluctant to accept forms of government economic assistance, even when they qualify (Duncan 1999; Sherman 2006). Second, the Woodrow Wilson community may have become more low income between the time of the U.S. Census Bureau's 2000 data collection and the time I performed my fieldwork (2005–2007).
4. Although I draw out the peer cultures of respect and respectability, I want to emphasize that this distinction was subtle. As numerous authors such as Anderson (1999) and Duneier (1992) find, moral decency and hard work have strong value

in inner-city communities and can be sources of respect. Similarly, some students at Clayton emphasized the importance of respect as achieved through physical toughness and intimidation. The difference refers primarily to social dynamics and structures of place: at urban Woodrow Wilson students worked to be known, whereas in rural Clayton they were already known and worked instead to manage their preexisting reputations.

Chapter 4   Too Cool for School: Masculinity and the Contradictions of Achievement

1. Donte had eleven siblings in total.
2. This perspective is often attributed to Fordham and Ogbu (1986). However, as both authors have argued (Ogbu 2004; Fordham 2008), this characterization over-simplifies their theory and findings. The view that African American students equate high achievement with whiteness and therefore resist it stems more from popular-culture representations of the phenomenon than scholarly research on it. For reviews of research on acting white, see Fordham (2008) and Downey (2008).

Chapter 5   Rednecks and Rutters: Rural Masculinity and Class Anxiety

1. I want to emphasize that women, both currently and historically, perform much hidden labor in rural communities, work that can be as physically demanding as men's but may not get either public praise and remuneration (Dunaway 2008).
2. The two slight diversions from this viewpoint were Janna, who said that book smarts were "kind of" important, and Lyndsie, who believed that success required an "interaction" between book smarts and common sense.
3. This distinction also reflected boundaries between concepts of purity and contamination, which differentiated class status and whiteness (Morris 2009; see also Douglas 1966).
4. A few women and girls embraced the term, too, following a currently popular country song titled "Redneck Woman." One car in town had a bumper sticker that read, "Hell yeah, I'm a redneck woman!" But the very fact that the word *redneck* had to be coupled with the word *woman* indicated the inherent masculinity of *redneck*. Other bumper stickers, for example, simply read, "redneck," not "redneck man."
5. Sam declined to interview with me, so I do not know how this student self-identified by gender. I will therefore refer to Sam simply by first name or with the mixed pronouns *s/he* and *he/r*.

Chapter 6   Clownin' and Riffin': Urban Masculinity and the Complexity of Race

1. According to the U.S. Census (2000), in the four census tracts that roughly comprised the attendance zone for Woodrow Wilson, an average of 68 percent of women worked in the paid labor force, and an average of 46 percent of families with children under eighteen years of age were headed by single women. In contrast, in the census tract comprising Clayton's attendance zone, the figures were 45 percent and 24 percent, respectively.
2. May (2008, 159) cites a study by Leonard (2007), which finds that, based on the current number of boys playing high school basketball across the United States, there is a 0.03 probability that they will play in college and a 0.001 probability that they will play professionally.

3. This practice, also called "playing the dozens" and many other names, has an extensive history in many black communities (Majors and Billson 1992).

4. Of course, it is difficult to precisely define white speech. However, the exaggeratedly formal tone that some Woodrow Wilson boys used paralleled students' answers when I asked what came to mind when they thought about white people and white behaviors. In my interviews, students used words such as *proper*, *nerdy*, and *uptight* to describe white mannerisms and added that white people did not often use slang.

Chapter 7   *"Girls Just Care about It More"*: *Femininity and Achievement as Resistance*

1. I realize that the question "should the man be the main provider for the family" reflects a heteronormative bias. However, I purposely intended the question to ascertain students' perceptions of traditional family gender roles.

Chapter 9   **Conclusion**

1. This finding runs somewhat counter to research on stereotypical perceptions of Appalachian and African American students as unintelligent. Research with African American students in particular has uncovered damaging academic effects of such stereotypes (Noguera 2003; Steele 1997). It is possible that, in efforts to openly resist race and place prejudice, teachers in my research emphasized that lower-performing students in the schools were actually intelligent, even if they did not show high performance. Nevertheless, such descriptions still varied by gender. Ultimately this type of feedback, even if well intentioned, only papers over the problem and can contribute to contrived carelessness among boys.

References

American Association of University Women (AAUW). 1992. *How Schools Shortchange Girls*. Report. Washington, D.C.: AAUW Educational Foundation and National Educational Association.

American Sociological Association. 2007. *Race, Ethnicity, and the Criminal Justice System*. Washington, D.C.: American Sociological Association. Accessed September 26, 2007, from http://asanet.org.

Anderson, Elijah. 1990. *Streetwise: Race, Class, and Change in an Urban Community*. Chicago: University of Chicago Press.

———. 1999. *Code of the Street: Decency, Violence, and Moral Life of the Inner City*. New York: Norton.

Anderson, Leon, and David A. Snow. 2001. "Inequality and the Self: Exploring Connections from an Interactionist Perspective." *Symbolic Interaction* 24, no. 4: 395–406.

Avishai, Orit. 2008. "'Doing Religion' in a Secular World: Women in Conservative Religions and the Question of Agency." *Gender and Society* 22, no. 4: 409–33.

Bartkowski, John P., and Jen'nan Ghazal Read. 2003. "Veiled Submission: Gender, Power, and Identity among Evangelical and Muslim Women in the United States." *Qualitative Sociology* 26, no. 1: 71–92.

Batteau, Allen. 1982. "Mosbys and Broomsedge: The Semantics of Class in an Appalachian Kinship System." *American Ethnologist* 9, no. 3: 445–66.

Bettie, Julie. 2003. *Women without Class: Girls, Race, and Identity*. Berkeley: University of California Press.

Billings, Dwight B., Gurney Norman, and Katherine Ledford. 1999. *Confronting Appalachian Stereotypes: Back Talk from an American Region*. Lexington: University Press of Kentucky Press.

Black, Timothy. 2009. *When a Heart Turns Rock Solid: The Lives of Three Puerto Rican Brothers on and off the Streets*. New York: Pantheon.

Bobbitt-Zeher, Donna. 2007. "The Gender Income Gap and the Role of Education." *Sociology of Education* 80: 1–22.

Bourdieu, Pierre. 1984. *Distinction: A Social Critique of the Judgement of Taste*. New York: Routledge and Kegan Paul.

———. 1986. "The Forms of Capital." In *Handbook of Theory and Research for the Sociology*, edited by J. G. Richardson, 241–58. New York: Greenwood.

———. 2001. *Masculine Domination*. Stanford, Calif.: Stanford University Press.

Bourdieu, Pierre, and Jean-Claude Passeron. 1977. *Reproduction in Education, Society and Culture*. London: Sage.

Bourgois, Phillippe. 1996. *In Search of Respect: Selling Crack in El Barrio*. New York: Cambridge University Press.

Bowles, Samuel, and Herbert Gintis. 1976. *Schooling in Capitalist America*. New York: Basic Books.

Brooks, Scott. 2009. *Black Men Can't Shoot*. Chicago: University of Chicago Press.

Buchmann, Claudia, and Thomas A. DiPrete. 2006. "The Growing Female Advantage in College Completion: The Role of Family Background and Academic Achievement." *American Sociological Review* 71: 515–41.

Buchmann, Claudia, Thomas A. DiPrete, and Anne McDaniel. 2008. "Gender Inequalities in Education." *Annual Review of Sociology* 34: 319–37.

Butler, Judith. 1999. *Gender Trouble: Feminism and the Subversion of Identity*. New York: Routledge.

Bye, Linda Marie. 2009. "'How to Be a Rural Man': Young Men's Performances and Negotiations of Rural Masculinities." *Journal of Rural Studies* 25, no. 3: 278–88.

Campbell, Hugh, Michael Mayerfield Bell, and Margaret Finney. 2006. *Country Boys: Masculinity and Rural Life*. University Park: Pennsylvania State University Press.

Carter, Prudence L. 2005. *Keepin' It Real: School Success beyond Black and White*. New York: Oxford University Press.

Chudowsky, Naomi, and Victor Chudowsky. 2010. *State Test Score Trends through 2007–2008, Part 5: Are There Differences in Achievement between Boys and Girls?* Washington, D.C.: Center on Education Policy. Accessed May 23, 2011, from http://www.cep-dc.org.

Cohen, Albert K. 1955. *Delinquent Boys: The Culture of the Gang*. New York: Free Press.

Collins, Patricia Hill. 1990. *Black Feminist Thought: Knowledge, Consciousness and the Politics of Empowerment*. New York: Routledge.

Connell, Raewyn W. 1987. *Gender and Power*. Stanford, Calif.: Stanford University Press.

———. 1995. *Masculinities*. Berkeley: University of California Press.

———. 1996. "Teaching the Boys: New Research on Masculinity, and Gender Strategies for Schools." *Teachers College Record* 98: 206–35.

Connell, Raewyn W., and James W. Messerschmidt. 2005. "Hegemonic Masculinity: Rethinking the Concept." *Gender and Society* 19, no. 6: 829–59.

Corbett, Michael. 2007. *Learning to Leave: The Irony of Schooling in a Coastal Community*. Halifax, Canada: Fernwood.

Courtenay, Will H. 2006. "Men's Health: Situating Risk in the Negotiation of Masculinity." In *Country Boys: Masculinity and Rural Life*, edited by Hugh Campbell, Michael Mayerfield Bell, and Margaret Finney, 139–58. University Park: Pennsylvania State University Press.

Crenshaw, Kimberle. W. 1991. "A Black Feminist Critique of Antidiscrimination Law and Politics." In *The Politics of Law: A Progressive Critique*, 2d ed., edited by David Kairys, 195–218. New York: Pantheon.

Cresswell, Tim. 2004. *Place: A Short Introduction*. Oxford: Blackwell.

Daly, Mary. 1973. *Beyond God the Father: Toward a Philosophy of Women's Liberation*. Boston: Beacon.

Dance, Lory Janelle. 2002. *Tough Fronts: The Impact of Street Culture on Schooling*. London: Routledge.

Davidman, Lynn. 1991. *Tradition in a Rootless World: Women Turn to Orthodox Judaism*. Berkeley: University of California Press.

Delpit, Lisa. [1996] 2006. *Other People's Children: Cultural Conflict in the Classroom*. New York: New Press.

de Vaus, David, and Ian McAllister. 1987. "Gender Differences in Religion: A Test of the Structural Location Theory." *American Sociological Review* 52, no. 4: 472–81.

Devine, John. 1996. *Maximum Security: The Culture of Violence in Inner-City Schools*. Chicago: University of Chicago Press.

DeYoung, A. 1995. *The Life and Death of a Rural American High School: Farewell, Little Kanawha*. New York: Garland.

Dickar, Maryann. 2008. *Corridor Cultures: Mapping Student Resistance at an Urban High School*. New York: New York University Press.

Douglas, Mary. 1966. *Purity and Danger: An Analysis of the Concepts of Pollution and Taboo*. New York: Routledge.

Downey, Douglas B. 2008. "Black/White Differences in School Performance: The Oppositional Culture Explanation." *Annual Review of Sociology* 34: 107–26.

Downey, Douglas B., and Anastasia S. Vogt Yuan. 2005. "Sex Differences in School Performance during High School: Puzzling Patterns and Possible Explanations." *Sociological Quarterly* 46: 299–321.

Dumais, Susan A. 2002. "Cultural Capital, Gender, and School Success: The Role of Habitus." *Sociology of Education* 75: 44–68.

Dunaway, Wilma A. 2008. *Women, Work, and Family in the Antebellum Mountain South*. New York: Cambridge University Press.

Duncan, Cynthia M. 1999. *Worlds Apart: Why Rural Poverty Persists in Rural America*. New Haven: Yale University Press.

Duneier, M. 1992. *Slim's Table: Race, Respectability and Masculinity*. Chicago: University of Chicago Press.

Dweck, Carol S. 2007. "The Perils and Promises of Praise." *Educational Leadership* 65: 34–39.

Eder, Donna, Catherine Colleen Evans, and Stephen Parker. 1997. *School Talk: Gender and Adolescent Culture*. New Brunswick, N.J.: Rutgers University Press.

Edwards, H. 1973. *Sociology of Sport*. Homewood, Ill.: Dorsey.

Ehrmann, Nicholas, and Douglas S. Massey. 2008. "Gender-Specific Effects of Ecological Conditions on College Achievement." *Social Science Research* 37: 220–38.

Emerson, Robert M., Rachel I. Fretz, and Linda L. Shaw. 1995. *Writing Ethnographic Fieldnotes*. Chicago Guide to Writing, Editing, and Publishing. Chicago: University of Chicago Press.

Entwisle, Doris R., Karl L. Alexander, and Linda S. Olson. 1994. "The Gender Gap in Math: Its Possible Origins in Neighborhood Effects." *American Sociological Review* 59: 822–38.

———. 2007. "Early Schooling: The Handicap of Being Poor and Male." *Sociology of Education* 80, no. 2: 114–38.

Ezzell, Matthew B. 2009. "'Barbie Dolls' on the Pitch: Identity Work, Defensive Othering, and Inequality in Women's Rugby." *Social Problems* 56, no. 1: 111–31.

Farley, Reynolds, Charlotte Steeh, Maria Krysan, Tara Jackson, and Keith Reeves. 1994. "Stereotypes and Segregation: Neighborhoods in the Detroit Area." *American Journal of Sociology* 100, no. 3: 750–80.

Feliciano, Cynthia, and Ruben G. Rumbaut. 2005. "Gendered Paths: Educational and Occupational Expectations and Outcomes among Adult Children of Immigrants." *Ethnic and Racial Studies* 28:1087–1118.

Fellows, Will. 1996. *Farm Boys: Lives of Gay Men from the Rural Midwest*. Madison: University of Wisconsin Press.

Fenstermaker, Sarah, Candace West, and Don H. Zimmerman. 2002. "Gender Inequality: New Conceptual Terrain." In *Doing Gender, Doing Difference: Inequality, Power, and Institutional Change*, edited by Sarah Fenstermaker and Candace West, 25–40. New York: Routledge.

Ferguson, Ann Arnett. 2000. *Bad Boys: Public Schools in the Making of Black Masculinity*. Ann Arbor: University of Michigan Press.

Flores-Gonzalez, Nilda. 2002. *School Kids/Street Kids: Identity Development in Latino Students*. New York: Teachers College Press.

Foley, Douglas E. 1990. *Learning Capitalist Culture: Deep in the Heart of Tejas*. Philadelphia: University of Pennsylvania Press.

Fordham, Signithia. 1993. "'Those Loud Black Girls': (Black) Women, Silence, and Gender 'Passing' in the Academy." *Anthropology and Education Quarterly* 24, no. 1: 3–32.

———. 2008. "Beyond Capital High: On Dual Citizenship and the Strange Career of 'Acting White.'" *Anthropology and Education Quarterly* 39, no. 3: 227–46.

Fordham, Signithia, and John U. Ogbu. 1986. "Black Students' School Success: Coping with the "Burden of 'Acting White.'" *Urban Review* 18, no. 3: 176–206.

Geertz, Clifford. 1973. *The Interpretation of Cultures*. New York: Basic Books.

Gilligan, Carol. 1982. *In a Different Voice: Psychological Theory and Women's Development*. Cambridge, Mass.: Harvard University Press.

Glenn, Evelyn Nakano. 2002. *Unequal Freedom: How Race and Gender Shaped American Citizenship and Labor*. Cambridge, Mass.: Harvard University Press.

Goffman, Erving. 1959. *The Presentation of Self in Everyday Life*. New York: Doubleday.

———. 1963. *Stigma: Notes on the Management of Spoiled Identity*. Englewood Cliffs, N.J.: Prentice Hall.

———. 1971. *Relations in Public: Microstudies of the Public Order*. New York: Basic Books.

Gramsci, Antonio. 1971. *Selections from the Prison Notebooks*. London: Lawrence and Wishart.

Gray, Mary L. 2009. *Out in the Country: Youth, Media, and Queer Visibility in Rural America*. New York: New York University Press.

Grindstaff, Laura, and Emily West. 2006. "Cheerleading and the Gendered Politics of Sport." *Social Problems* 53, no. 4: 500–518.

Gurian, Michael, and Kathy Stevens. 2005. *The Minds of Boys: Saving Our Sons from Falling Behind in School and Life*. San Francisco: Jossey-Bass.

Hammond, Cathy, Dan Linton, Jay Smink, and Sam Drew. 2007. *Dropout Risk Factors and Exemplary Programs: A Technical Report*. Clemson, S.C.: National Dropout Prevention Center. Accessed May 23, 2011, from http://www.dropoutprevention.org/resource/major_reports/communities_in_schools.htm.

Hardie, Jessica Halliday. 2011. "Unpacking Aspirations: Class and Race Differences in Girls' Future Plans." Unpublished manuscript. Cited with permission of author.

Harrell, W. Andrew. 1986. "Masculinity and Farming Related Accidents." *Sex Roles* 15: 467–78.

Hartigan, John, Jr. 2003. "Who Are These White People?: 'Rednecks,' 'Hillbillies,' and 'White Trash' As Marked Racial Subjects." In *White Out: The Continuing Significance of Racism*, edited by Ashley W. Doane and Eduardo Bonilla-Silva, 95–112. New York: Routledge.

Hirschfield, Paul J. 2008. "Preparing for Prison?: The Criminalization of School Discipline in the USA." *Theoretical Criminology* 12, no. 1: 79–101.

Hosokawa, Fumiko. [2009] 2010. *Building Trust: Doing Research to Understand Ethnic Communities*. Lanham, Md.: Rowman and Littlefield.

Jackson, Carolyn, and Steven Dempster. 2009. "'I Sat Back on My Computer . . . with a Bottle of Whisky Next to Me': Constructing 'Cool' Masculinity through 'Effortless' Achievement in Secondary and Higher Education." *Journal of Gender Studies* 18, no. 4: 341–56.

Jarosz, Lucy, and Victoria Lawson. 2002. "'Sophisticated People versus Rednecks: Economic Restructuring and Class Difference in America's West." *Antipode* 34, no. 1: 8–27.

Jones, Nikki. 2009. "'I Was Aggressive for the Streets, Pretty for the Pictures': Gender, Difference, and the Inner-City Girl." *Gender and Society* 23: 89–93.

———. 2010. *Between Good and Ghetto: African American Girls and Inner-City Violence.* New Brunswick, N.J.: Rutgers University Press.

Keddie, Amanda. 2007. "Games of Subversion and Sabotage: Issues of Power, Masculinity, Class, Rurality, and Schooling." *British Journal of Sociology of Education* 28, no. 2: 181–94.

Kelley, Robin D. G. [1994] 1996. *Race Rebels: Culture, Politics, and the Black Working Class.* New York: Free Press.

Kennedy, Randall. 2003. *Nigger: The Strange Career of a Troublesome Word.* New York: Vintage.

Kimmel, Michael S. 1996. *Manhood in America: A Cultural History.* New York: Free Press.

———. 2000. "What about the Boys?" *WEEA Digest*, pp. 1–2, 7–8.

———. 2005. *The History of Men: Essays on the History of American and British Masculinities.* Albany: State University of New York Press.

King, Jacqueline E. 2000. *Gender Equity in Higher Education: Are Male Students at a Disadvantage?* Washington, D.C.: American Council on Education.

Kreager, Derek A. 2007. "Unnecessary Roughness?: School Sports, Peer Networks, and Male Adolescent Violence." *American Sociological Review* 72, no. 5: 705–24.

Kupchik, Aaron, and Nicholas Ellis. 2008. "School Discipline and Security: Fair for All Students?" *Youth and Society* 39, no. 4: 549–74.

Kupchik, Aaron, and Torin Monahan. 2006. "The New American School: Preparation for Post-Industrial Discipline." *British Journal of Sociology of Education* 27: 617–31.

Lacy, Karyn. 2007. *Blue-Chip Black: Race, Class, and Status in the New Black Middle Class.* Berkeley: University of California Press.

Lamont, Michèle. 2000. *The Dignity of Working Men: Morality and the Boundary of Race, Class, and Immigration.* Boston: Harvard Education Press.

Langenkamp, Amy G. 2010. "Academic Vulnerability and Resilience during the Transition to High School: The Role of Social Relationships and District Context." *Sociology of Education* 83, no. 1: 1–19.

Lareau, Annette. 2000. *Home Advantage: Social Class and Parental Intervention in Elementary Education.* Lanham, Md.: Rowman and Littlefield.

Leonard, Wilbert. 2007. *A Sociological Perspective of Sport.* 6th ed. Boston: Allyn and Bacon.

Lewis, Amanda E. 2003. *Race in the Schoolyard: Reproducing the Color Line in School.* New Brunswick, N.J.: Rutgers University Press.

Lobao, Linda M., Gregory Hooks, and Ann R. Tickamyer, eds. 2007. *The Sociology of Spatial Inequality.* Albany: State University of New York Press.

Lofland, John, David Snow, Leon Anderson, and Lyn Lofland. 2006. *Analyzing Social Settings: A Guide to Qualitative Observation and Analysis.* 4th ed. Belmont, Calif.: Wadsworth.

Lopez, Nancy. 2003. *Hopeful Girls, Troubled Boys.* New York: Routledge.

Luttrell, Wendy. 1997. *School-Smart and Mother-Wise: Working-Class Women's Identity and Schooling.* New York: Routledge.

Mac an Ghaill, Mairtin. 1996. "What about the Boys?: Schooling, Class and Crisis Masculinity." *Sociological Review* 44: 381–97.

MacLeod, Jay. 1995. *Ain't No Makin' It: Aspirations and Attainment in a Low Income Neighborhood.* 2d ed. Boulder, Colo.: Westview.

Majors, Richard, and Janet Mancini Billson. 1992. *Cool Pose: The Dilemmas of Black Manhood in America*. Lexington, Ky.: Lexington Books.

Martin, Karin A. 1998. "Becoming a Gendered Body: Practices of Preschools." *American Sociological Review* 63: 494–511.

Martino, Wayne, Michael Kehler, and Marcus B. Weaver-Hightower. 2009. *The Problem with Boys' Education: Beyond the Backlash*. New York: Routledge.

Maxwell, Joseph A. 2005. *Qualitative Research Design: An Interactive Approach*. 2d ed. Thousand Oaks, Calif.: Sage.

May, Reuben A. Buford. 2008. *Living through the Hoop: High School Basketball, Race, and the American Dream*. New York: New York University Press.

McCready, Lance T. 2010. *Making Space for Diverse Masculinities*. New York: Peter Lang.

Mead, Sara. 2006. *The Evidence Suggests Otherwise: The Truth about Boys and Girls*. Washington, D.C.: Education Sector.

Messerschmidt, James W. 1997. *Crime As Structured Action: Gender, Race, Class, and Crime in the Making*. Thousand Oaks, Calif.: Sage.

———. 2000. *Nine Lives: Adolescent Masculinities, the Body, and Violence*. Boulder, Colo.: Westview.

———. 2004. *Flesh and Blood: Adolescent Gender Diversity and Violence*. Lanham, Md.: Rowman and Littlefield.

Messner, Michael A. 1992. *Power at Play: Sports and the Problem of Masculinity*. Boston: Beacon.

———. 2000. "Barbie Girls versus Sea Monsters." *Gender and Society* 14, no. 6: 765–84.

———. 2002. *Taking the Field: Women, Men, and Sports*. Minneapolis: University of Minnesota Press.

———. 2009. *It's All for the Kids: Gender, Family, and Youth Sports*. Berkeley: University of California Press.

Mickelson, Roslyn Arlin. 1989. "Why Does Jane Read and Write So Well?: The Anomaly of Women's Achievement." *Sociology of Education* 62: 47–63.

———. 1990. "The Attitude-Achievement Paradox among Black Adolescents." *Sociology of Education* 63: 44–61.

———. 2003. "Gender, Bourdieu, and the Anomaly of Women's Achievement Redux." *Sociology of Education* 76, no. 4: 373–75.

Miller, Jody. 2001. *One of the Guys: Girls, Gangs, and Gender*. New York: Oxford University Press.

———. 2008. *Getting Played: African American Girls, Urban Inequality, and Gendered Violence*. New York: New York University Press.

Morris, Edward W. 2005. "'Tuck in That Shirt!': Race, Class, Gender, and Discipline in an Urban School." *Sociological Perspectives* 48, no. 1: 25–48.

———. 2006. *An Unexpected Minority: White Kids in an Urban School*. New Brunswick, N.J.: Rutgers University Press.

———. 2007. "'Ladies' or 'Loudies'?: Perceptions and Experiences of Black Girls in Classrooms." *Youth Society* 38, no. 4: 490–515.

———. 2008. "'Rednecks,' 'Rutters,' and 'Rithmetic: Social Class Masculinity and Schooling in a Rural Context." *Gender and Society* 22: 728–51.

———. 2009. "Rural Teenagers' Constructions of Class and Race." Paper presented at the annual meeting of the American Sociological Association, San Francisco, August 8.

———. 2010. "'Snitches End Up in Ditches' and Other Cautionary Tales." *Journal of Contemporary Criminal Justice* 26, no. 3: 254–72.

National Center for Education Statistics (NCES). 2007. "School Survey on Crime and Safety, 2005, Table 9." Accessed September 24, 2010, from http://nces.ed.gov.

———. 2010. "National Assessment of Educational Progress Long-Term Trend Assessments." Accessed January 11, 2010, from http://nces.ed.gov/nationsreportcard.

Noguera, Pedro. 2003. "The Trouble with Black Boys: The Role and Influence of Environmental and Cultural Factors on the Academic Performance of African American Males." *Urban Education* 38, no. 4: 431–59.

Ogbu, John U. 2004. "Collective Identity and the Burden of 'Acting White' in Black History, Community, and Education." *Urban Review* 36, no. 1: 1–35.

Orenstein, Peggy. 1994. *Schoolgirls: Young Women, Self-Esteem, and the Confidence Gap*. New York: Doubleday.

Pascale, Celine-Marie. 2007. *Making Sense of Race, Class and Gender: Commonsense, Power and Privilege in the United States*. New York: Routledge.

Pascoe, C. J. 2007. *Dude, You're a Fag: Masculinity and Sexuality in High School*. Berkeley: University of California Press.

Patillo-McCoy, Mary. 1999. *Black Picket Fences: Privilege and Peril among the Black Middle Class*. Chicago: University of Chicago Press.

Peter, Katharin, Laura Horn, and C. Dennis Carroll. 2005. *Gender Differences in Participation and Completion of Undergraduate Education and How They Have Changed Over Time*. Washington, D.C.: National Center for Educational Statistics. Accessed November 18, 2008, from http://nces.ed.gov/pubs2005/2005169.pdf.

Pevey, Carolyn, Christine L. Williams, and Christopher G. Ellison. 1996. "Male God Imagery and Female Submission: Lessons from a Southern Baptist Ladies' Bible Class." *Qualitative Sociology* 19, no. 2: 173–93.

Pini, Barbara, Robin Price, and Paula McDonald. 2010. "Teachers and the Emotional Dimensions of Class in Resource Affected Rural Australia." *British Journal of Sociology of Education* 31:17–30.

Powell, Mary Ann, and Toby L. Parcel. 1997. "Effects of Family Structure on the Earnings Attainment Process: Differences by Gender." *Journal of Marriage and the Family* 59: 419–33.

Pyke, Karen D. 1996. "Class-Based Masculinities: The Interdependence of Gender, Class, and Interpersonal Power." *Gender and Society* 10: 527–49.

Pyke, Karen D., and Denise L. Johnson. 2003. "Asian American Women and Racialized Femininities: "Doing" Gender across Cultural Worlds." *Gender and Society* 17, no. 1: 33–53.

Quillian, Lincoln, and Devah Pager. 2001. "Black Neighbors, Higher Crime?: The Role of Racial Stereotypes in Evaluations of Neighborhood Crime." *American Journal of Sociology* 107, no. 3: 717–67.

Riordan, Cornelius H. 1990. *Girls and Boys in School: Together or Separate?* New York: Teachers College Press.

Risman, Barbara J. 2004. "Gender As a Social Structure: Theory Wrestling with Activism." *Gender and Society* 18, no. 4: 429–50.

Rock, Paul. 2001. "Symbolic Interactionism and Ethnography." In *Handbook of Ethnography*, edited by Paul Atkinson, Amanda Coffey, Sara Delamont, John Lofland, and Lyn Lofland, 26–38. Thousand Oaks, Calif.: Sage.

Sadker, Myra, and David M. Sadker. 1994. *Failing at Fairness: How America's Schools Cheat Girls*. New York: Simon and Schuster.

Schippers, Mimi. 2007. "Recovering the Feminine Other: Masculinity, Femininity, and Gender Hegemony." *Theory and Society* 36, no. 1: 85–102.

Schrock, Douglas, and Michael Schwalbe. 2009. "Men, Masculinity, and Manhood Acts." *Annual Review of Sociology* 35: 277–95.

Schwalbe, Michael, Sandra Godwin, Daphne Holden, Douglas Schrock, Shealy Thompson, and Michele Wolkomir. 2000. "Generic Processes in the Reproduction of Inequality: An Interactionist Analysis." *Social Forces* 79, no. 2: 419–52.

Scott, James C. 1990. *Domination and the Arts of Resistance: Hidden Transcripts*. New Haven: Yale University Press.

Sennett, Richard, and Jonathan Cobb. 1972. *The Hidden Injuries of Class*. New York: Norton.

Sewell, Tony. [1997] 2000. *Black Masculinities and Schooling: How Black Boys Survive Modern Schooling*. London: Trentham.

Sherman, Jennifer. 2006. "Coping with Rural Poverty: Economic Survival and Moral Capital in Rural America." *Social Forces* 85, no. 2: 891–913.

Shettle, Carolyn, Shep Roey, Joy Mordica, Robert Perkins, Christina Nord, and Jelena Teodorovic. 2007. *The Nation's Report Card: America's High School Graduates*. National Center for Education Statistics. Washington, D.C.: U.S. Government Printing Office.

Shirley, Carla D. 2003. "'Rednecks' and 'White Trash': The Gendering of Whiteness." Paper presented at the Southern Sociological Society Meetings, New Orleans, April.

Simmons, Rachel. 2002. *Odd girl Out: The Hidden Culture of Aggression in Girls*. New York: Harcourt.

Skelton, Christine. 2001. *Schooling the Boys: Masculinities and Primary Education*. Educating Boys, Learning Gender. Florence, Ky.: Taylor and Francis.

Skiba, Russell J., Robert S. Michael, Abra Carroll Nardo, and Reece L. Peterson. 2002. "The Color of Discipline: Sources of Racial and Gender Disproportionality in School Punishment." *Urban Review* 34: 317–42.

Skiba, Russell J., and Reece Peterson. 1999. "The Dark Side of Zero Tolerance: Can Punishment Lead to Safe Schools?" *Phi Delta Kappan* 80, no. 5: 372–82.

Sommers, Christina Hoff. 2000. *The War against Boys: How Misguided Feminism Is Harming Our Young Men*. New York: Simon and Schuster.

Spelman, Elizabeth V. 1988. *Inessential Woman: Problems of Exclusion in Feminist Thought*. Boston: Beacon.

Staff, Jeremy, and Derek A. Kreager. 2008. "Too Cool for School?: Violence, Peer Status, and High School Dropout." *Social Forces* 87: 445–71.

Steele, Claude, M. 1997. "A Threat in the Air: How Stereotypes Shape the Intellectual Identities and Performance of Women and African-Americans." *American Psychologist* 52, no. 6: 613–29.

Stewart, Kathleen. 1996. *A Space on the Side of the Road: Cultural Poetics in an "Other" America*. Princeton, N.J.: Princeton University Press.

Thorne, Barrie. 1993. *Gender Play: Girls and Boys in School*. New Brunswick, N.J.: Rutgers University Press.

Tyre, Peg. 2008. *The Trouble with Boys: A Surprising Report Card on Our Sons, Their Problems at School, and What Parents and Educators Must Do*. New York: Three Rivers Press.

Tyson, Karolyn, William Darity, Jr., and Domini R. Castellino. 2005. "It's Not 'a Black Thing': Understanding the Burden of Acting White and Other Dilemmas of High Achievement." *American Sociological Review* 70, no. 4: 582–605.

U.S. Bureau of Justice Statistics. 2007. *Crime Rate per 100,000 Population*. Accessed May 28, 2009, from http://bjsdata.ojp.usdoj.gov.

U.S. Census Bureau. 2000. *Summary File 1 (SF 1) and Summary File 3 (SF 3)*. Accessed May 5, 2008, from http://www.cenus.gov.

Weaver-Hightower, Marcus B. 2003. "The 'Boy Turn' in Research on Gender and Education." *Review of Educational Research* 73, no. 4: 471–98.

———. 2009. "Issues of Boys' Education in the United States." In *The Problem with Boys' Education: Beyond the Backlash*, edited by Wayne Martino, Michael Kehler, and Marcus B. Weaver-Hightower, 1–35. New York: Routledge.

West, Candace, and Sarah Fenstermaker. 1995. "Doing Difference." *Gender and Society* 9: 8–37.

West, Candace, and Don Zimmerman. 1987. "Doing Gender." *Gender and Society* 1: 125–51.

Western, Bruce. 2006. *Punishment and Inequality in America*. New York: Russell Sage Foundation.

Williams, Christine L. 1995. *Still a Man's World: Men Who Do "Women's Work."* Berkeley: University of California Press.

Willis, Paul. 1977. *Learning to Labor: How Working Class Kids Get Working Class Jobs*. New York: Columbia University Press.

Wilson, William. J. 1996. *When Work Disappears: The World of the New Urban Poor*. New York: Knopf.

Yancey Martin, Patricia. 2003. "'Said and Done' versus 'Saying and Doing': Gendering Practices, Practicing Gender at Work." *Gender and Society* 17, no. 3: 342–66.

Yarrow, Michael. 1985. "Capitalism, Patriarchy and 'Men's Work': The System of Control of Production of Coal Mining." *Proceedings of the Eighth Annual Appalachian Studies Conference*, 29–47.

Zinn, Maxine Baca, and Bonnie Thornton Dill. 1996. "Theorizing Difference from Multiracial Feminism." *Feminist Studies* 22, no. 2: 321–31.

Index

Abdi (student, Wilson), 72, 73, 74
Abel, Mr. (principal, Clayton), 51, 52, 86
Adkins, Mr. (teacher, Wilson), 68, 133
Alicia (student, Wilson), 29, 67, 68, 115, 116, 120, 146
Amanda (student, Clayton), 140
Anderson, Elijah, 13, 29, 64, 99, 108, 113, 152
Angela (student, Wilson), 103
Ashlee (student, Clayton), 91, 141
authority: confronting, 67; defying, 30; distrust of, 109; hegemonic masculinity and, 74; institutional, 109; masculinity as liability during encounters with, 109; noncompliance with, 68; resistance to, 74
Avishai, Orit, 130

ballers, 104, 115–118
Bartkowski, John, 130
Batteau, Allen, 32
behavior: academic, 60, 70, 73, 84–85; for accomplishment of masculinity, 68; according to gender, 10; aggressive, 39, 41, 42, 48; anti-academic, 50, 69; boys' tendency to break/bend school rules, 17; carelessness, 14; classroom, 137–142; consistent with masculinity, 9; constraints on, 9; defiance, 14; educationally relevant, 53; effeminate, 13; gender differences in, 59; gendered, 131; indifferent, 48;

monitored by boys, 73; presentation of self through, 54; redneck, 94; school-oriented, 51, 75; self-image portrayal and, 54; superiority of masculine over feminine, 85; uncouth, 94; unmasculine, 70; verbally/physically combative, 41
Beth (student, Clayton), 141
Billings, Dwight, 26, 33
Black, Timothy, 64
Blake (student, Wilson), 66
Blandford, Mr. (teacher, Wilson), 119, 138, 155
Bobbit-Zeher, Donna, 3
boundaries: of appropriate masculinity, 74, 98; defining, 103; of gender-appropriate practice, 69; inscribed racial, 103; status, 69
Bourdieu, Pierre, 7, 75, 129
Bourgois, Philippe, 29
boys: anxieties over grasp of class subjects, 139, 140; association of school disengagement with masculinity by, 5, 53; avoidance of vulnerability, 138; biological differences in education and, 5–6; capacity for impulsive behavior, 5; casual approach to school, 15, 49, 53; claim for superior memories by, 58, 59, 60, 136; claim for lack of need to study, 124; comfort with minimal effort, 58; contrived carelessness of, 9, 14, 15, 49, 52–57, 62, 101, 124, 134; covering up academic efforts, 126;

Shontae (student, Wilson), 134
Shultz, Mr. (teacher, Wilson), 50, 51, 108
Simmons, Rachel, 157
Skelton, Christine, 8
Skiba, Russell, 63, 108, 110
social: achievement, 29; action, 28;
affinity, 29; capital, 29; categories of
difference, 9; challenges, 36; class, 29,
51, 92, 95, 100; criticism, 153;
differentiation, 9, 31; disadvantage,
15; disorganization, 33; distancing,
122; environments, 77; identity, 17,
28, 79; institutions, 9; interaction,
10; masculinity, 10, 67–69, 69;
mobility, 48; norms, 58, 153; power,
60; reality, 129; recognition, 28;
rewards, 67, 68, 74; sanctions, 74;
situations, 9; status, 41
socialization: alternative paths to
masculinity and, 99, 100; differing
modes of behavior and, 74; gender,
6–8; maintenance of differences by, 7;
role of power and inequality in gender
and, 7; sex-role, 74, 130–131, 135;
theory, 131
Sommers, Christina, 3, 7
sports, 115–118; academically-oriented
behavior and, 71; avoidance of "lame"
status and, 29; deep community
meaning of, 88; elite status from
participation in, 116; favoritism
stemming from, 117; girls' criticism
of school focus on, 147; hit stick,
89–91; inability to achieve true
toughness through, 96;
individualization in, 116; injuries
amassing respect in, 154, 155;
masculinity and, 87–91; participation
in, 31; as pathway to masculinity, 117,
118; positive benefits of, 173; as
potential career, 116, 117, 126;
recognition reserved for boys, 145; as
school-sanctioned path to
demonstration of masculinity, 88;
sense of pride and, 88; as stress relief,
41; as vehicle to masculinity, 116
Stevens, Kathy, 5

Stewart, Kathleen, 26
students: aggressive responses from, 40;
anxieties over planned careers, 38;
economically disadvantaged, 21,
22, 22*tab*; elite status for athletes,
116; external stigmas and, 28;
feelings about family background,
43; gendered responses to life
challenges, 35; hidden injuries, 15,
35–48; joking with teachers, 67;
management of challenges by
following masculine/feminine scripts,
36–48; motivation/constraint by quest
for respect, 32; overcoming family
reputation through school
achievement, 42–47; seeking
connections with others to mitigate
problems, 45; threats to dignity of, 36;
transgender, 97, 98

Taniqua (student, Wilson), 158
Tanner, Mr. (teacher, Clayton), 92,
137, 138
Tareek (student, Wilson), 55
Tayshaun (student, Wilson), 121, 158
teachers: acceptance of nonchalant
attitude from boys, 61; attention
monopolized by boys, 145;
confrontations with male students, 65;
defiance of by boys, 64–67;
descriptions of boys as unmotivated,
61; disciplining boys more than girls,
63; joking with students, 67; making
out games and, 67; perceptions of girls,
131–137; reinforcement of boys'
perceptions of masculinity by, 61;
responses to clowning, 118–123;
singling out boys as problem students,
64; views of fighting, 156
Teesha (student, Wilson), 146, 147
Terry, Mr. (teacher, Wilson), 61, 132
Thomas, Mr. (principal, Clayton), 2, 25,
64, 167
Thorne, Barrie, 7, 86
Tim (student, Clayton), 77, 78, 85
Tom (student, Clayton), 70, 74, 100
Tracey (student, Clayton), 61

About the Author

Edward W. Morris is an assistant professor of sociology at the University of Kentucky. He is the author of the award-winning book *An Unexpected Minority: White Kids in an Urban School* (Rutgers University Press, 2006).

CPSIA information can be obtained at www.ICGtesting.com
Printed in the USA
LVOW10s1918010715

444622LV00001B/107/P